On the Cutting Edge

Textile Collectors, Collections, and Traditions

Jeannette Lasansky
with
Celia Oliver
Nancy Gibson Tuckhorn
Julie Powell
Richard and Rosemarie Machmer
Alan G. Keyser
Eve Wheatcroft Granick
Gloria Seaman Allen
Rita Erickson
Barbara Schaffer
Merikay Waldvogel
Pat Nickols
Dorothy R. Zopf

An
Oral Traditions
Project

Cover: Detail of Henry Clay feathered star quilt, 91"l. × 89"w., made of indigo blue print and plain white cotton, hand pieced and quilted. Small portraits of Theodore Roosevelt and Charles Fairbanks, his 1904 running mate, flank a colorful Miss Liberty on the 2⅛" celluloid button and ribbon once worn by a delegate to the Des Moines convention; a 2" oval brooch of Teddy Roosevelt with an ornate metal frame, and a 1¼" Roosevelt Rough Rider celluloid button. Republican stitchers could try to "sew up" the election for Teddy with the spools of Roosevelt silk gimp thread, while recipients of the 1928 needlebook are asked by candidates Herbert Hoover and Meyers Cooper, Ohio governor hopeful, to "Stick to the Republican Party." Also, a Hoover/Curtis 1928 metal thimble, ¼"h. and a heavy early plastic one with a red top is for 1940 candidate Wendell Willkie. Woodrow Wilson positioned himself on "the cutting edge" of the 1912 campaign with a pair of portrait scissors. Collection of Julie and Robin Powell.

Inside cover: Roosevelt Teddy Bear cotton fabric. Teddy Roosevelt was an enthusiastic and active political figure. Clifford Berryman's cartoons about his hunting encounter with a small bear inspired the creation of many teddy bear toys and books. This yardage pictures a bear in a Rough Rider hat and hunting attire treeing a tired opossum. William Howard Taft, Roosevelt's 1912 presidential opponent, was nicknamed "Billy Possum." Collection of Julie and Robin Powell.

Title Page: Sawtooth cradle quilt with star corner blocks in prints and chambrays, 41½" sq. with applied print binding, muslin back, and 4-5 stitches per inch. Collection of Richard and Rosemarie Machmer.

Library of Congress Cataloging-in-Publication Data

On the cutting edge : textile collectors, collections, and traditions / Jeannette Lasansky, with Celia Oliver . . . [et al.]. p. cm.
Includes bibliographical references and index.
ISBN 0-917127-08-0 : $24.95
1. Quilts — United States — History. I. Lasansky, Jeannette.
II. Oral Traditions Project (Union County Historical Society)
NK9112.05 1994
746.9'7'073 — dc20 93-46431
CIP

Published by the Oral Traditions Project of the Union County Historical Society, County Courthouse, Lewisburg, Pennsylvania, 17837.

Production and finances: Jeannette Lasansky
Design: Karelis and Timm
Photography: Terry Wild Studio
Editing: Joseph G. Foster
Typography: SpectraComp, Inc.
Printing: Paulhamus Litho, Inc.

Acknowledgments

On the Cutting Edge/Textile Collectors, Collections, and Traditions is the fourth in a series of textile symposia volumes and the 15th book to appear in the Oral Traditions series on material culture since *Made of Mud/Stoneware Potteries of Central Pennsylvania 1834-1911* was printed in 1977.

The Bicentennial celebration in the United States set in motion plans for parades, re-enactments, reprints of 19th-century local histories as well as projects involving original research. While many of these activities were short-lived, others have continued to exist and sometimes thrive. The Oral Traditions Project is one of the survivors.

We hope that our enthusiasm for the people and the objects they have crafted, has been passed on through our work. We welcome you to join us at next symposia at Franklin & Marshall in June 1996, "Painted for a Purpose: the Ordinary and the Extraordinary." There, more than at any other time, one can grasp the complexities of this world we have sought to capture.

We wish to thank the following people for making the 1993 symposium at Franklin & Marshall College as wonderful as it was: the Special Events staff headed by Marilyn Davidson and her assistant, Gloria Schleicher; the Curator of Collections and head of the Rothman Gallery, Carol Faill; the Oral Traditions staff of Martha Root and Nancy Ruhl, and the Union County Historical Society's administrative assistant, Rita Barton.

Special thanks should also be extended to the hosts at the Historical Society of Berks County and Goschenhoppen Historians' quilt shows: Allison DuPont and Abe and Nancy Roan respectively, and the Lancaster Historical Society for their hosting the opening reception, presentation, and exhibition — some of which is featured on the book's cover and inside cover. Also, thanks to the Mainline Quilters for their financial gift which helped to underwrite the mailings to past and potential symposium registrants as well as to pay for cover photography costs. A special thank you is extended to the audience which included representatives from 25 different quilt documentation projects — thanks to the active enthusiasm of Shelly Zegart, and to the speakers and panelists: Julie Powell, Carol Faill, Celia Oliver, Nancy Gibson Tuckhorn, Richard and Rosemarie Machmer, Vernon Gunnion, Alan G. Keyser, Gloria Seaman Allen, Rita Erickson, Barbara Schaffer, Merikay Waldvogel, Pat Nickols, Dorothy Zopf, Eve Wheatcroft Granick, and Nancy Roan.

Jeannette Lasansky
May 1994

Contents

Mary Jane Carns

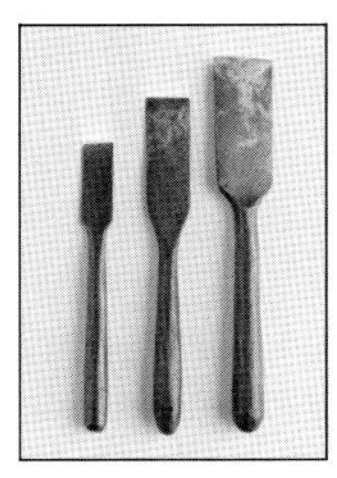

Electra Havemeyer Webb and Shelburne's Quilt Collection

Celia Oliver

Title blocks and essay headlines: forged button holers and seam rippers or thread pickers: 3¼-5⅛"h. Collection of Richard and Rosemarie Machmer.

Counterpane made and signed by Mary Jane Carr of Lancaster, Pennsylvania in 1854. (Shelburne Museum #10-327). Courtesy of the Shelburne Museum.

When the Shelburne Museum opened to the public in 1951, Electra Havemeyer Webb had been collecting American furniture, decorative arts, folk sculpture, and textiles since 1910. Her collections, which numbered over 9,000 objects, were exhibited in nine buildings. The public and media were intrigued. *Life* magazine published color photos of the exhibitions and an article which stated:

> Everyone knows that America was founded by bold and adventurous people, but the fact that they were also artistic and made many beautiful things was scarcely recognized until the past few decades. Not until the 1920s were the arts, crafts and products of early settlers systematically sought by collectors and museums. Now, to supplement Ford's Greenfield Village, Rockefeller's Williamsburg and du Pont's Winterthur, Mrs. J. Watson Webb has opened a new museum on 14 acres in Shelburne, Vermont. Here in nine buildings, almost all over a hundred years old, are the homey treasures of an earlier America which show, through the familiar things of everyday use, how America looked and lived before the machine age.[1]

Electra Webb is known today as the founder of a major American museum and a collector of American folk art, furniture, and decorative arts. But we have to wonder how she came to collect and build one of the country's most comprehensive collections of Americana. By studying Webb's family and its lifestyle, her life and the types of material she collected as well as the artistic and cultural environment of the late-19th and early 20th centuries, we can gain a better understanding of her as a collector. Our sources will include books, periodicals, contemporary accounts, and Shelburne Museum archives.

Electra Havemeyer Webb's life-long appreciation for art, culture, and design, as well as her motivation to collect great things and share them with the public, was undoubtedly developed from talking with her parents and peers, watching them amass their collections, studying those collections, and visiting great museums and art collections around the world. Her appreciation of American architecture as an art form was inspired by her husband's interest and his early preservation efforts. Her interest in American history, antiques; and art can be linked to the renewed emphasis and study of America's Colonial era which was popular in the early 1900s-1930s, a style of architecture and interior decoration now known as the Colonial Revival.

A careful examination of the variety and the type of material Electra Webb acquired reveals themes and interests which carry throughout her collections of what had been everyday objects in their time. She preferred pieces with highly decorated and embellished surfaces, depicting unusual figures and forms, designs based on graphic geometric forms and curvilinear patterns as well as genre scenes illustrating everyday life, historic events, and architecture. These preferences can be related to the art and architecture she lived with and experienced as a child and young adult; her parents' collections of European paintings and Asian pottery, metalwork and textiles; her husband's interest in American architecture, the Aesthetic style and Arts and Crafts Movement popular in the late-19th century, and the Art Nouveau and Colonial Revival styles of the early 20th century. These cultural movements, although diverse, share a dedication to outstanding craftsmanship in the creation of utilitarian objects.

Electra Havemeyer was born in 1888, the third and youngest child of Louisine Elder and Henry Osborne Havemeyer, the owner and president of the American Sugar Refining Company. She was raised with the advantages of great riches and learned at an early age to appreciate fine art. Her parents also taught their children to develop their own abilities, to be humble about the advantages they enjoyed, and to care for other people.

The Havemeyers took their children on numerous trips to the western United States,

Europe, and Egypt, seeking to cultivate their artistic understanding by exposing them to different parts of the world. The European trips invariably involved locating and acquiring objects and works of art for the Havemeyers' collections. Electra Webb later commented, "My mother took me out of school and told the teacher 'What she will lose scholastically, she will gain by seeing the countries and beautiful places and the different museums.' Well, I think I could have done with more teaching, but my trips were an inspiration to me."[2]

H.O. and Louisine Havemeyer were two of the most passionate and important collectors in America's gilded age, developing many diverse collections of great depth and range. They are best known as collectors of European Old Master, 19th-century and Impressionist paintings. However, they were also great collectors of Asian art: wood-block prints and hand-painted screens (many depicting Japanese textiles woven in patterns resembling 19th-century American quilts and coverlets); bronze sword fittings cast in geometric patterns; pottery and ceramics glazed and decorated with bold and often abstract patterns, and richly colored, woven and embroidered textiles and carpets.[3] From living with and studying these works of art, their daughter, Electra, learned how and why it was important to collect art. "I do not believe I have ever read or heard any reason . . . why certain people like to collect," she wrote. "However, I am sure I did inherit the desire and came by it through both parents."[4] "This early training, the living with and the looking at art of great beauty and variety gave me a true appreciation of quality — and the desire to collect for myself."[5]

She also learned the merits of exploring a genre and followed this more encyclopedic approach while she acquired American textiles, folk sculpture, dolls, and prints. Her father, who collected French impressionist and 19th-century Spanish art, when the general public considered it peculiar and unconventional,[6] often told her, "It takes nerve as well as taste to be a collector,"[7] a remark this young woman absorbed and later demonstrated.

In 1889, the Havemeyers built a house on the corner of New York's Fifth Avenue and East 66th Street. They commissioned Charles Colman and Louis Tiffany, proponents of the Aesthetic style, to decorate its interior. The Aesthetic style they worked in emphasized the use of varied surface treatments on walls, ceilings, and furnishings; a wide variety of materials; and designs inspired by objects produced in what they regarded as exotic cultures: Indian, Islamic, and Japanese. Following an essential rule of the style, Tiffany and Colman designed each room to house one of the family's collections. Paintings, ceramics, sculpture and textiles were integrated into the color, texture, and structure of each room's space. Walls and ceilings were painted, stenciled and covered with embroidered silk fabric or elaborately carved panels, organized in squares of pattern and design. The furniture was made to harmonize with the surface decoration and embroideries. Kimonos and carpets were displayed on walls, furniture, and floors.[8]

Although Electra Webb never collected textiles or decorative arts produced in the Aesthetic style, I propose that they inspired her interest in surface treatments and patterns. This is made evident by her collections of printed fabric, bandboxes, lithographed prints, ceramics, carved and paint-decorated furniture, and many quilts and textiles with appliqué, quilting, embroidery, paint, and other surface decoration.

After her father died in 1907, Electra Havemeyer accompanied her mother on numerous trips to Europe and began to form her own art collection. She described her feelings in a letter to her future husband, "I would like to be so rich that I could buy any works of Art I wanted . . . How can anyone like jewels when they can buy pictures.[9] Just think of the courage I have to expect to keep on in Father's footsteps in the way of collecting Art."[10] One month later she wrote, "I spent a very large sum for a fine picture by Goya (I don't know if you know the painter) and I dread to think what you would say. It is a portrait of a small girl of six, too cunning and sweet but really very fine. I am so pleased to feel that I am starting a collection as that is what I intend to do with Father's money."[11]

Electra Havemeyer married James Watson Webb in 1910 and they often visited his parents, William Seward Webb, the president of

Second floor painting gallery at the Havemeyer House, 1 East 66th Street, New York City, ca. 1892. The Havemeyer House, decorated by Louis Comfort Tiffany and Charles Colman, also served as a gallery for the family's extensive collections of European Old Master and Impressionist paintings and Asian prints, screeens, textiles, and ceramics. The paintings gallery illustrates the overall effect that was achieved through the use of decorative woodwork, metalwork, papers, and stenciling on walls and ceiling. Courtesy of the Metropolitan Museum of Art, New York.

the Wagner Palace Railroad Car Company, and Lila Vanderbilt Webb, at their elaborate 110-room estate on the shores of Lake Champlain, in Shelburne, Vermont.[12] Although Electra Webb found the grand Romanesque-style mansion overly formal, she was strongly attracted to the simplicity and functional beauty of the surrounding New England architecture and countryside. The young couple decided they would like their own country home, so they requested the use of a vacant brick farmhouse built in 1847 on the estate. When faced with decorating what came to be called the "Brick House," the young Mrs. Webb searched for a decorating style which related to her new-found interest in early American architecture, an alternative to the ornate Aesthetic and Romanesque decorating style used in her first house in Syosset, Long Island. She later regarded this attempt as a failure. "We foolishly built two houses at once; one on Long Island, there trying to use many things belonging to my family and many of the Webbs' from their New York home at 680 Fifth Avenue. This resulted in a house neither of us liked. Shelburne, the lovely little brick house, we added on to, . . . this was most successful."[13]

Popular periodicals of the early 20th century, such as *House Beautiful* and *The Designer*, featured articles on how to evoke the spirit of the colonial past by decorating with American antiques, furniture, wallpaper, and fabric.[14] Advocates rejected the late-19th-century decorating styles as ostentatious; they believed that art, architecture and furnishings made before 1840 — when America entered the industrial age — possessed "integrity of workmanship, thoughtful use of honest, sound materials, and accurate awareness of design principles."[15] Laura Shelby Lee, the author of "Fundamentals of Interior Decorating," *House Beautiful*, February, 1919, praised a Colonial Revival living room for having "simple, clean lines with great harmony and proportion of the furniture and accessories," and described a library furnished in the Aesthetic mode as "spoiled by over-ornamentation and overcrowding to such a degree that no harmony can be found in it."

The Colonial style was much in keeping with the informal and relaxed lifestyle Electra Webb wanted to achieve in their Vermont home. She began to acquire and fill the house with country style furniture and accessories. "I did look at books and pictures," she said, "but never seemed to have any time to study history and dates."[16] Articles in the magazine, *House Beautiful*, June 1917 and July 1918, from her personal library have dog-eared pages at photographs that bear a great similarity to interiors at the Brick House: dining rooms furnished with Windsor-style chairs gathered around a table, living rooms with slip-covered furniture, scenic wallpaper and prints on the walls, and hooked rugs on scrubbed wood floors.[17]

Over the next ten years, Electra Webb had little time to actively acquire a collection. She raised four children and, during World War I, lived in New York City and helped with the war effort by rolling bandages. In 1921, the young couple sold the Syosset house and bought "a very small old cottage" in Westbury, Long Island. "There I really began to love the old houses and antiques. . . As the children grew up, we added one room, then another. I truly did love doing it and all the time I was trying to find the old wallpapers, furniture, rugs and prints that would look well. I found plenty and more still . . . This is about the time I started to collect in earnest."[18] To a certain extent she was following the decorating trends of the era, but she added her own instincts and a connoisseurship developed from a life-long immersion in the art world.

Although collecting and decorating with American antiques was clearly popular at this time, it was not the norm to assemble such widely varied materials and objects en masse. Once again, Electra Webb was probably following her parents' precedent, collecting in great numbers to reach beyond the norm, seeking out rare and unusual forms as well as the most common. Not one, but many hooked rugs covered her wooden plank floors. Samplers, lithographed landscapes, seascapes, and hunting prints were hung on walls covered with handprinted and painted wallpaper. Transfer printed ceramics, pewter, and stoneware pottery filled cupboards, tables, and mantels. Quilts, bedcovers, and other textiles were used on beds, chairs, and even lamp-

A 1940 photograph of the Webb's Westbury, Long Island sitting room illustrates the collector's preference for the Colonial Revival style of interior decoration and her use of wallpaper, prints, ceramics, textiles, and surface-decorated furniture and accessories to create a strong overall pattern. Courtesy of the Shelburne Museum.

shades. Her son, James Watson Webb, Jr., later remarked that his mother liked the bright colors and patterns in quilts and coverlets, feeling that these textiles created a comfortable interior setting with the New England country furniture she enjoyed.[19] It was fortunate that Electra Webb had developed a strong belief in her own collecting instincts, because her efforts were not well received. Although her husband, James Watson, had a great appreciation for American architecture, he did not care for the furniture and folk art she collected. He preferred to shoot, hunt, fish and focus on his polo career. Even her children as they were growing up described her collections as "mother's junk,"[20] while her mother, Louisine, strongly disapproved of her daughter's hatboxes, quilts, hooked rugs, carved eagles, cigar store trade figures, and what she described as "kitchen furniture."[21] In fact, Louisine declared, "Well, it's hard for a mother to raise a child with Rembrandts and Manets and Corots, and see what taste she's fallen to."[22]

Over the next 20 years, Electra Webb trained her eye and broadened her tastes in American antiques. She visited galleries and museum exhibitions like the "Early American Art" exhibit of American folk art held by the Whitney Studio Club in 1924, and the period rooms at the Metropolitan Museum of Art, which opened in the same year. Popular periodicals and books on antiques and decorating in her library included *Colonial Homes and Their Furnishings*, *A House in Good Taste*, and *The Quest of the Colonial*.[23] In 1922, she subscribed to a newly published magazine, *Antiques*, undoubtedly attracted to the subtitle: "A Magazine *for Collectors and Others* who find an interest in *Times Past &* in the articles of daily use & Adornment devised by the Forefathers." The introduction describes "collectors [as] that tribe of people . . . who experience, in the search for the rare or the remote, a peculiar zest, like the zest of the hunter or fisherman."[24] Each monthly issue contained articles and photographs of furniture, quilts and hooked rugs, embroidery, and china. The "Museum and the Collector," a monthly feature, described how museums focus their collections to reach the public, while another, "Little-known Masterpieces," was illustrated with "An 18th century Patchwork Quilt."[25] Reviewing the early issues of this magazine now, one can imagine that Electra Webb might have felt that finally someone had published a magazine dedicated to her.

As she collected, her eye and sense of design became more refined; her collections grew at an astronomical rate. "Thank God there is no collector's anonymous," she later remarked to author Aline B. Saarinen.[26] "I've collected all my life. I filled . . . our homes with collections, and my attic, of course, was a wonderful place.[27] The rooms were over-furnished . . . The closets were filled. I just couldn't let good pieces go by . . . china, porcelain, pottery, pewter, glass, dolls, quilts, cigar store Indians, eagles, folk art. . . . They all seemed to appeal to me."[28] By 1945, she had completely furnished two houses and began to think about establishing a museum in Vermont.

During this time other major collectors had established museums: John D. Rockefeller's Williamsburg and Henry Ford's Greenfield Village opened in the late-1920s; Henry Francis du Pont's Winterthur in 1930; the Wells brothers' Sturbridge Village in 1938; Abby Aldrich Rockefeller's Folk Art Center in 1939; and Clarke's Farmer's Museum and Fennimore House in Cooperstown in 1942. These museums inspired Electra Webb to make her collections available to the public and to share her appreciation of the things that express, "the craftsmanship and ingenuity of our forefathers."[29]

Her opportunity came in 1947 when her husband's family announced that William Seward Webb's collection of 47 horsedrawn vehicles would be sold. It was a chance to realize a dream. Electra Webb later wrote, "I couldn't bear to have these carriages go, so I said 'would you consider giving them to me if I had a little piece of property and kept them in Shelburne where they could be seen by others and not go away from Shelburne?' They were all delighted. Now that was the spark that lit the fire, and I had my opening. And that was the start of the Shelburne Museum . . . Well, from then on there was no holding me."[30] She located a barn that suited her purpose, purchased eight acres along Route 7 in Shelburne, and the project was begun. One after another buildings were located, acquired, dismantled and moved to the museum, reconstructed, and each filled with Electra Webb's collections.

By 1957, 21 of the 27 major collections exhibited at the Museum were developed by Electra Webb; these included furniture, hatboxes, folk sculpture, dolls, quilts, rugs and textiles. She often acquired one piece at a time, but she was also known to add dozens of objects at once. Museum documents record her purchasing over two dozen lithograph prints on one day, and three quilts on another. Family members remember her reviewing a dealer's truckload of rugs, quickly selecting some and passing by others.

Electra Webb purchased her antiques through a variety of dealers and auction houses in New England, New York, and Philadelphia. While some dealers brought antiques to Vermont for her approval, she also visited others who lived nearby: Richard Gipson and Roger Wentworth in Arlington, Vermont;

Hillary Underwood in Woodstock, Vermont; and Henry Coger in Ashley Falls, Massachusetts.

Her enthusiastic and friendly nature helped Electra Webb form many connections and friendships with fellow collectors and antique dealers. When informed of her museum project, these people responded in kind, locating, researching and documenting artifacts for the collections. Florence Peto of New Jersey, the pioneering and well-known author, lecturer and quiltmaker, began working with Electra Webb to develop and document the Shelburne quilt collection. In 1950, Peto presented her with a copy of Peto's book, *American Quilts* (New York: The American Historical Company, 1939) and inscribed it, "To Electra Webb with all good wishes for success in the project dear to her, Sincerely, Florence Peto." Peto worked closely with the Museum until the founder's death in 1960, and over the years acquired many wonderful quilts for the collection. Katherine Prentis Murphy, a fellow collector, was so enthused with the Museum, she helped Electra Webb furnish a house with 17th- and 18th-century furniture and decorative arts, which now stands as a testament to the Colonial Revival style. John K. Byard, an antiques dealer from Connecticut who also worked with the Flints of Deerfield, helped Electra Webb locate the type of furniture and accessories she wanted for the houses. Correspondence includes discussions of the furniture and textiles he acquired including the well-known 1814 appliqué counterpane by Anne Robinson. In recognition of their long friendship and his dedication to the Museum, Electra Webb dedicated one of their joint projects, the Stencil House, to Byard.

As the Museum grew, individuals throughout Vermont and New England contacted the Museum seeking a permanent home for their cherished family heirlooms and their private collections. The family of Consuela Bailey, a Vermont Lieutenant Governor, donated over 100 artifacts from their ancestral family farm in Sheldon, Vermont. The gift included farm tools, clothing, spinning and weaving equipment, and bedcovers. In 1952, 35 quilts were acquired from Alice McLean, a White Plains, New York collector, and in 1953, a collection of over 3,000 woodworking tools were given by Frank Wildung of Washington, D.C. He even moved to Vermont to curate the collection.

As the Museum collections and exhibitions took shape, Electra Webb contacted experts to help her with various collections: Charles Montgomery from Winterthur for pewter; Edith Halpert, owner of the Downtown Gallery, New York, for folk sculpture; and Maxim Karolik of Boston for paintings. While Florence Peto focused on the quilt collection, Electra Webb worked with Elizabeth Spangler of Pennsylvania as well as Cora Ginsberg and Nancy McLelland of New York City to develop other aspects of the textile, bandbox, and wallpaper collections.

As buildings were acquired for the Museum, the founder worked carefully to place them in an appropriate setting, using a three-dimensional model of the buildings and grounds to help her, Museum staff, and New York landscape designer Umberto Innocenti visualize the 30-acre site. "I didn't want to create a village," she later explained . . . "I was anxious to create something in arrangement and conception that had not been tried."[31] Alice Winchester, author and editor of the *Magazine Antiques*, was the first to describe the Shelburne Museum as "a collection of collections" and Electra Webb agreed. "It's not a restoration," she said, "it's not a village; it's just a grouping of houses collected because of their beauty or their historical value and the same with my collections inside. It's things that I have loved and that I want preserved whether they are English, or whether they are American . . ."[32]

Although the interiors of the historic houses are reminiscent of those at other museums, she achieved a very different environment and mood. Stenciled walls, painted furniture, pottery, pewter, and decorative textiles help create interiors notable for their distinctive profusion of colorful pattern and texture. Electra Webb delighted in the unusual, and her sense of humor reveals itself in exhibits that juxtapose everyday objects with wonderfully out-of-scale objects. In one gallery rows of Toby

Electra H. Webb's interest in out-of-scale objects led her to acquire this 1846 rocking chair trade sign, which once stood on the roof of the Morrisville Chair Factory, Morrisville, Vermont. She is pictured here in front of the Stagecoach Inn at the Shelburne Museum with her long-time friend, Zasu Pitts. Courtesy of the Shelburne Museum.

Detail of whole cloth quilt made from English blue resist-printed and dyed fabric was owned by the Demarest family of Bergen County, New Jersey, ca. 1770-1780. (Shelburne Museum #10-58). Courtesy of the Shelburne Museum.

jugs are displayed with oversized Staffordshire pitchers and in another an eight-foot tall rocking chair trade sign and full-sized carved eagles are exhibited against walls covered with room-sized hooked rugs.

For the serious collector, she grouped tools, dolls, ceramics, and weathervanes in massive displays. Coverlets and quilts were exhibited in the Hat and Fragrance Textile Galleries, a renovated 1800 distillery building. It was the first time a major American textile collection of such exceptional depth, range, and quality had been made so immediately accessible to the viewer. Visitors walked through galleries filled with quilts, embroidered counterpanes, woven blankets, coverlets, furnishing fabrics, rugs, samplers, needlework, costumes, hatboxes, and other decorative accessories. Quilts were mounted on panels which turned like the pages of a book. Electra Webb later described this building as the one exhibit where she felt she could "go a little bit wild."[33]

This collection of quilts and bedcovers stands as one of the largest, broadest, and most diverse in the country. First collected as colorful and useful accessories to use in her home, Electra Webb had come to regard them as both works of art and documents of American history. She worked to build an exceptional collection which exhibited the depth and range of 18th- and 19th-century American bedcovers and the wide variety of fabrics, needlework, and printing techniques used on them. Under her direction the collection grew from 100 bedcovers in 1947, when the Museum opened, to almost 400 in 1960 at the time of her death. Of these 400 bedcovers, more than half were quilts (83 whole or plain cloth, 86 pieced, and 70 appliqué), the other half included 86 handwoven coverlets, 56 embroidered and five paint-decorated spreads — all of which relate closely in style and pattern to the quilts she collected.[34]

A careful examination of these textiles reveals the type of design format Electra Webb preferred. Like most collectors of her era, she preferred traditional quilts and textiles from the 18th and 19th century. Approximately one quarter or 100 bedcovers are made in the medallion style with central motifs. Another 100 are made in allover patterns with the entire surface of the bedcover filled with design motifs either quilted, appliquéd, pieced, embroidered, printed, or woven on a ground fabric. The remaining 200 bedcovers are designed in the block style, with individual pattern blocks set on a grid.

The Shelburne Museum bedcover collection also illustrates the same range of design and subjects reflected in Electra Webb's other collections. The curvilinear patterns found on appliqué quilts and in the elegant quilting patterns of whole cloth quilts she acquired — exemplified by serpentine vines and intertwined bird and floral forms — contrast sharply with her other textiles with strong geometric patterns: pieced quilts, handwoven coverlets, and checked linens. She also collected textiles illustrating narrative scenes of everyday life and historical events as well as bedcovers which depict unusual and imaginative combinations — often whimsical — of figures, flowers, and plants.

Floral patterns which combined Electra Webb's interest in elegant, curvilinear, and representational motifs grew to include more than one quarter of the bedcovers. The patterns range from medallion style quilts with tree of life and floral wreaths, to floral sprays and wreaths arranged in block style grids, and single flower motifs scattered in an all-over pattern. One of the most important aspects of the collection are the bedcovers decorated with variations of the tree of life pattern. Following the example set by her father, she was exploring a genre, collecting textiles made in different time periods, and illustrating a wide range of workmanship and fabric. Included are printed and embroidered bedcovers, and 18th- and 19th-century appliqué with flowering trees and bushes, birds and flowers, and wildlife motifs. The design motifs featured on the Anne Robinson appliqué counterpane, made in 1814, are very similar to the motifs which also appear on samplers, embroidered pictures, and stumpwork in the Webb collections.[35]

Her collection of whole cloth quilts made from floral printed fabric illustrate every type of 18th-and 19th-century printing technique: wood block, copperplate, and roller-printed textiles, and further demonstrate Electra Webb's love of pattern and design. Electra Webb's interest in printed fabrics also led her to acquire appliqué quilts with small floral design motifs scattered over a plain ground fabric imitating imported textiles. One 20th-century example, a pieced and appliquéd crib-size quilt called Calico Garden, was made by Florence Peto in the 1950s with 18th- and 19th-century fabrics and given to Electra Webb for the Shelburne collection.[36]

Electra Webb's large collection of floral appliqué and pieced quilts reflects not only her strong interest in representational figures, but also the popularity of floral quilt patterns in the mid-19th century. The collection includes almost 50 floral pieced and appliqué block style quilts with such patterns as roses, pomegranates, laurel leaves, and lilies. Two of the collection's "botanical album" quilts are virtual garden encyclopedias, each depicting over two dozen 19th-century varieties of fruit and flowers.

When decorating the bedrooms of the Mu-

Quilt, made in the late-18th century by a member of the Dumont family of Alabama, features the tree of life pattern in reverse appliqué. (Shelburne Museum #10-188). Courtesy of the Shelburne Museum.

seum's historic houses, the founder preferred to use late-18th- and early 19th-century whole cloth wool quilts, enjoying the bold contrast of the bright orange, red, pink, brown, and blue colors to the other furnishings. The elegant scrolling vines and flowers relate to the sinuous curves of 18th-century embroidery and resist printed textiles she collected. One of the most beautiful examples was made by Melinda Brown of Corinth, Vermont, ca.1800 in a deep green color, backed by a handwoven wool fabric dyed a rich brown.[37]

This love of quilted pattern also led her to acquire numerous mid-19th-century white-on-white whole cloth quilts for the museum's collection. Usually designed in a medallion format, the central patterns include floral wreaths and stars. While most of the examples are hand-quilted, she also collected several factory-woven Marseille quilts as well as a machine-sewn quilt made by M.J. Foster, marked "Singer Machine Work."[38]

Electra Webb's interest in bold, graphic design is reflected in her large collections of paint-decorated furniture and accessories as well as quilts and bedcovers arranged in balanced, symmetrical mosaic-like patterns. More than 60 mid-19th-century bedcovers depict floral, star, and abstract designs in mosaic, tile-like patterns. All bear a strong resemblance to the wallpaper and woven carpeting popular in the period. An example of this pattern type is a Mariner's Compass quilt located for Shelburne's collection by Florence Peto, which depicts nine intricately pieced 64-point medallions balanced with a delicate leaf and orange slice motif. A second mariner's compass quilt in the collection, made by Mary Canfield Benedict of Arlington, Vermont before her marriage in 1852, is pieced with 32-point star-like compasses, each set within a box, sashed with the same red and blue fabric.[39]

1840s pieced quilt with sawtooth bands and rainbow-colored ombré fabrics. (Shelburne Museum #10-338). Courtesy of the Shelburne Museum. Photo by Ken Burris

Electra Webb also collected geometric pieced quilts with three-dimensional patterns including Tumbling Blocks, Nine-Patch, log cabin and Irish Chain, all of which owe their optical illusionary quality to the use of fabrics with contrasting values. An unusual example of this technique is a pieced and appliqué medallion-style quilt, reportedly made by a wounded Civil War soldier during his recovery. Square frames of richly colored mosaic piecework alternate with bands of parading figures and lead the viewer's eye around the quilt creating a very dynamic design which appears to rise above the white background. [40]

Electra Webb's interest in history and everyday life led her to collect a wide variety of textiles printed with detailed scenes. The Webb collection included scenic copperplate toiles, block and roller-printed yardage, bedhangings, and over 20 whole cloth quilts. The fabrics used depict classical figures, farms and villages, historical figures and events, and architectural details. These bedcovers, when combined with her collection of wall paper panels and over 200 bandboxes also printed with narrative scenes, provide a fascinating glimpse of American history.

Electra Webb once declared that she "tried to find the art in folk art,"[41] and admired artists who chose to represent images of their everyday world in their work. She sought textiles which exemplified the ingenuity, creativity, and imagination of the maker, developing a collection of 38 quilts, embroidered blankets, jacquard coverlets, and textiles unique for their depiction of unusual figures and forms. All relate strongly to the collections of folk sculpture, weathervanes, and whirligigs for which she is also well known. An excellent illustration of this genre is a crazy-style quilt made of plain and patterned cotton fabrics made by Mrs. Samuel Glover Haskins of Granville, Vermont. Each of the 42 blocks features a man, woman, domestic, farm, wild or exotic animal appliquéd in the center of the randomly pieced background. She described the Haskins quilt as "rather amusing because [it is] so crude, and the maker wanted to make

Presentation style quilt has 49 squares signed by its maker; one is initialed "L.V." and dated "Feb.10th, 1865." One square features the debate between Abraham Lincoln and Stephen Douglas. (Shelburne Museum #10-203). Courtesy of the Shelburne Museum.

it more decorative [so she] put in the animals and heads."[42]

Figures and forms are also featured in many of the album quilts in the collection. Examples range from appliqué block style quilts with crude renditions of the family pet dog and a vase of flowers to elegant, formally rendered Baltimore-style examples such as the ca.1847 Major Samuel Ringgold quilt. This quilt contains floral wreaths and sprays, as well as Masonic motifs, a harp, heart, two eagles, and a patriotic monument dedicated to Ringgold, a hero of the Mexican American war.

An interest in surface design also led Electra Webb to collect bedcovers with a variety of surface treatments: painted, stenciled, embroidered, multi-layered appliqué, and heavily padded quilting. The green stenciled oak leaf and orange slice pattern on one quilt is so skillfully executed that the pattern appears to be made of cloth rather than paint. This effect is amplified by the quilting stitches worked along the edges of the stenciled design.[43] Many quilts in the collection use stuffed work to supplement a simple design. For example, a pieced trilobe flowers quilt includes quilted and padded designs of clipper ships, flower baskets, and medallions.[44]

When the Shelburne Museum founder died in 1960 it lost an intrepid leader. Electra Havemeyer Webb had set an amazing, and sometimes overwhelming, precedent. Over the years, Museum staff has sought quilts and other bedcovers which continue Electra Webb's collecting themes and focus when possible on textiles with a documented history of ownership. To supplement the collection of bedcovers with the tree of life motif, we acquired an appliqué quilt made in the early 1800s by Jeriesha Kelsey of Boston, Massachusetts which depicts a tree of life surrounded by serpentine floral vines. A pieced and appliquéd quilt made by Mrs. Ellen Fullard of Providence, Rhode Island, features a boldly-colored Bethlehem Star surrounded with birds and hearts was added to collection of star quilts, while an appliqué Presidential Wreath pattern quilt, made by a member of the Travers family in Sands Lake, New York, complements the numerous variations of floral quilts.

Electra Webb had a special interest in Vermont objects. We have made a special effort to find exceptional Vermont quilts for the collection. Recent acquisitions include a dramatic sunflower quilt made by Carrie Carpenter of Northfield, Vermont, in the 1870s, and two quilts made by different generations of the Brush family of Jericho, Vermont, an 1810s wool quilt pieced in boldly colored stripes, and an 1840s cotton quilt pieced in a flying geese medallion pattern.

Friends and family who supported the

founder as she built the Museum continue to donate important artifacts to the Museum's collection. Alice Winchester, a noted authority on American Folk Art and a great friend of Electra Webb, presented the Museum with a crazy quilt made by her grandmother, Mary Severance of Middlebury, Vermont in the 1880s. Severance, an accomplished artist, embellished the quilt with oil painted landscapes, figures, and a whimsical frog playing a fiddle.

The Museum has also identified several areas in the collection which needed to be strengthened in order to have a well-rounded collection. For example, in the mid-1980s, a number of Amish quilts were added to the collection where there had been none as well as 20th-century quilts of which Electra Webb had collected only two. These include a group of six floral appliqué quilts made by Anna Baker of Ohio, in patterns and colors very typical of the era, and an original white-on-white quilt, designed and made by Bertha Meckstroth of Glencoe, Illinois in 1931. The latter depicts an eagle feathering her nest with a verse worked in reverse appliqué, "He shall cover thee with his feathers and under his wings shall thou trust." Its acquisition complements the numerous 19th-century white-on-white quilts in the collection, as well as those incorporating reverse appliqué and heavily padded quilting.

Detail of quilt which features five pieced feathered stars offset by four eagles quilted and heavily padded in high relief. Under each eagle is quilted the words "A Star Spangled Banner" and a phrase from the song. Along the bottom edge is stitched "Alexander Cramndin Jr. made by his mother. 1840." (Shelburne Museum #10-169) Courtesy of the Shelburne Museum.

Today, the Museum includes 37 exhibit buildings filled with over 80,000 objects, including over 750 quilts and other bedcovers. More than 170,000 people annually visit special exhibitions, educational programs, and seminars. Curatorial staff works closely with conservators to preserve, treat and exhibit the Museum's textile collections and Shelburne has recently received a $600,000 grant from the National Endowment for the Humanities to retrofit and improve the environment in 33 exhibit buildings including the Hat and Fragrance Textile Gallery.

The textile exhibitions at the Shelburne Museum continue to offer an unparalleled opportunity to view the breadth and depth of creativity that went into making American quilts and other bedcovers. Museum visitors enjoy viewing the more than 150 quilts and bedcovers on exhibit during the summer season. Rotating exhibits in the Hat and Fragrance Textile Gallery present the full range of bedcovers in the collection, incorporating examples from Electra Webb's original collection with recent acquisitions. Each year appropriate quilts and bedcovers are selected for over 30 beds and cradles in the Museum's historic houses. Handwoven coverlets and pieced wool quilts decorate the French Canadian Sawyer's Cabin; bedcovers from Vermont families are used in the Dutton House from Cavendish, Vermont; and quilts and counterpanes with unusual decorative techniques are exhibited in the Stencil House where the hand-stenciled walls serve as a backdrop for paint-decorated furniture and accessories. Electra Havemeyer Webb received many tributes over the years for her work at the Shelburne Museum. She took great pride in the Museum and its collections, but continued to share the credit with everyone who had worked with her. In 1959, the *Magazine Antiques* published *The Antiques Treasury*, a book of articles on several American museums. In her introduction for the Shelburne Museum article, Electra Webb included this comment, "We have been called pioneers in the museum field, which is a fine tribute and gives us confidence. We have never thought of ourselves as pioneers. We have collected the things that seem to us, at least, to have beauty, and we have placed them in buildings that seem to us to have integrity and charm. We have all worked conscientiously and hard in an effort to preserve many worthwhile objects from our fine American heritage and we are most grateful for the recognition the Shelburne Museum has received."[45]

End Notes

[1]"A Visit to Our Past: New Vermont Museum Shows How Americans Used to Live," *Life* 35:1 (July 6, 1953): 46.

[2]Electra Havemeyer Webb, "The Shelburne Museum and How It Grew," unpublished speech delivered at Colonial Williamsburg Antiques Forum, Williamsburg, Virginia, January 30, 1958, transcribed tape recording in Shelburne Museum Archives.

[3]For a complete discussion on the Havemeyers and their collections, see *Splendid Legacy: The Havemeyer Collection* (New York: Metropolitan Museum of Art, 1993); also Frances Weitzenhoffer's *The Havemeyers: Impressionism Comes to America* (New York: Harry N. Abrams, 1986).

[4]Webb, Museum Notes, unpublished manuscript in

Shelburne Museum Archives, 1.

[5]Webb, "Americana at Shelburne," Exhibit Guide to the *East Side House Winter Antique Show*, 1957.

[6]Metropolitan Museum of Art, *Splendid Legacy: The Havemeyer Collection*, (New York: Metropolitan Museum of Art, 1993), 17.

[7]Aline B. Saarinen, *The Proud Possessors*, New York: Random House, 1958, 301.

[8]Metropolitan Museum of Art, *Splendid Legacy: The Havemeyer Collection*, 187. For a discussion of Aesthetic style in America, see *In Pursuit of Beauty: Americans and the Aesthetic Movement*, (New York: Rizzoli and the Metropolitan Museum of Art, 1986).

[9]Letter from Electra H. Webb to James Watson Webb, March 11, 1909, Frances Weitzenhoffer, "Louisine Havemeyer and Electra Havemeyer Webb," the *Magazine Antiques*, 133: 2, February 1988, 435.

[10]Letter from Electra H. Webb to James Watson Webb, March 13, 1909, ibid, 435.

[11]Letter from Electra H. Webb to James Watson Webb, April 27, 1909, ibid, 433-434.

[12]For an in depth discussion of the estate with photographs, see Joe Sherman, *The House at Shelburne Farms*, (Middlebury, Vermont: Paul Eriksson, 1986).

[13]Electra H. Webb, *Museum Notes*, unpublished manuscript, Shelburne Museum Archives, 5.

[14]The Colonial Revival style, popular in 1900-1930, inspired the design and use of architecture, art and furnishings adapted from America forms dating from early settlement to 1840. For additional information, see introduction by Kenneth Ames in *The Colonial Revival in America*, ed. Alan Axelrod (New York, W.W. Norton & Co., 1985); Bridget A. May, "Progressivism and the Colonial Revival: The Modern Colonial Home," 1900-1920, *Winterthur Portfolio*, 26: 2/3, Summer/Autumn, 1991. For a contemporary account of the movement's influence on interior decoration, see Joseph Downs' foreword, *Living With Antiques*, ed. by Alice Winchester, (New York: Robert M. McBride & Co., 1922).

[15]Winchester, *Living With Antiques*, 1.

[16]Webb, *Museum Notes*, 5.

[17]"Martin House," *House Beautiful*, June 1917, 9-11; Ralph Bergenen, "A House that was Born a Barn," *House Beautiful*, July 1918, 72-73.

[18]Webb, *Museum Notes*, 5-6.

[19]James Watson Webb, Jr., interview by author, Shelburne Museum, Shelburne, Vermont, May 1991.

[20]Webb, "The Shelburne Museum and How it Grew," 5.

[21]Weitzenhoffer, 435.

[22]Webb, "Shelburne Museum and How It Grew", 17.

[23]Mary H. Northend, *Colonial Homes and Their Furnishings* (Boston: Little Brown & Co, 1924); Elsie de Wolfe, *A House in Good Taste*, (New York: The Century Company, 1920), and Robert and Elizabeth Shakleton, *The Quest of the Colonial*, (New York: The Century Company, 1921) are just three of the decorating books published in this era which contained numerous photographs and advice on what, how, and where to buy American antiques.

[24]*Antiques* I:1, 1922, 8.

[25]*Antiques* I:2, February 1922, 67.

[26]Saarinen, 305.

[27]Webb, "Shelburne Museum and How It Grew", 5.

[28]Webb, *Museum Notes*, 6.

[29]letter dated Oct. 10, 1949, from Electra H. Webb to Louis C. Jones, Director, New York State, Historical Association at Cooperstown, Shelburne Museum Archives.

[30]Webb, "The Shelburne Museum and How It Grew," 6.

[31]Webb, "Americana at Shelburne," Guide to the *East Side House Winter Antique Show*, 1957.

[32]Webb, "The Shelburne Museum and How It Grew," 16.

[33]Ibid., 17.

[34]All the information regarding the bedcover categories can be found in the author's data base, July 1993.

[35]For an illustration, see *55 Famous Quilts from the Shelburne Museum*, ed. Celia Y. Oliver (New York: Dover, 1990), 22.

[36]Ibid., 43; for further discussion on Florence Peto see Joyce Gross, "Four Twentieth Century Quiltmakers," ed. Sally Garoutte, *Uncoverings 1980*, (Mill Valley, CA: American Quilt Study Group, 1981).

[37]For an illustration see *An American Sampler: Folk Art from the Shelburne Museum*, (Washington, D.C.: National Gallery of Art , 1987), 136.

[38]An illustration of this quilt is to be in *Quiltmaking in America: Beyond Mythology*, ed. Laurel Horton (San Francisco, CA: American Quilt Study Group, 1994).

[39]For an illustration see *An American Sampler: Folk Art from the Shelburne Museum*, 140, 159.

[40]For an illustration of this quilt, see *55 Famous Quilts From the Shelburne Museum*, 42.

[41]Saarinen, 297.

[42]Webb, "The Shelburne Museum and How It Grew," p. 22. This quilt is pictured in *An American Sampler: Folk Art from the Shelburne Museum*, 164-165.

[43]Ibid., 169.

[44]Ibid., 151.

[45]Electra H. Webb, "The Shelburne Museum at Shelburne, Vermont," *The Antiques Treasury*, (New York: E.P. Dutton, 1959), 279.

Celia Oliver has been at the Shelburne Museum in Vermont since 1979, first as registrar and in collections management — documenting a collection of over 80,000 objects, then as curator working primarily with the textiles. Over the past five years she has curated exhibitions with objects as seemingly disparate as the Colchester Lighthouse and disc and harrows. Her latest effort — an exhibition on the work of rug hooker extraordinary, Molly Nye Toby, opened in 1993. Celia received her degree in art history and museology from the University of Vermont and then became the curator at the Rokeby Museum. In 1991-1992 she served as director for the Vermont Historic Handwoven Textile Project and wrote All in a Day's Work/200 Years of Vermont Textiles, *also articles on the Shelburne collection appearing in the* Magazine Antiques, *in* 55 Quilts from the Shelburne Museum, *in* An American Sampler, *and in the Japanese catalog,* The Quilt.

The Evolution of the Quilt Collection at the DAR Museum

Nancy Gibson Tuckhorn

"Maze" quilt, ca. 1850, made of appliquéd solid-colored cottons, 79.5" × 83.5" by Margaret Cabell McClelland (1785-1863), Virginia. As a result of publicity generated for an exhibition of early Virginia quilts and the initiative of a very enthusiastic museum chapter chairman, this one-of-a-kind quilt was donated to the museum in 1987. Collection of the DAR Museum, # 87.87, gift of Margaret Gillespie Willis. Photo by Mark Gulezian.

Introduction: "A Century of Collecting"[1]

The Daughters of the American Revolution Museum is a decorative arts museum located in Washington, DC two blocks from the Washington Monument and in view of the White House. Its collection contains over 30,000 objects made or used in America in the 18th and 19th centuries. Part of the collection is on view in 33 period rooms that place the objects in a context that show regional preferences. An exhibition gallery highlights specific areas of the collection in a series of changing exhibitions. Quilts and coverlets from the collection are rotated two to three times a years on a bank of sliding racks, and two stable cases are backlit to highlight the white work bedcover collection.

Although the DAR Museum is not as well known as many other decorative arts museums founded in the late-19th century, its collecting policies almost always reflect contemporary collecting trends. It is true that each generation has to rewrite its history. This is not because the facts of history are no longer true, but because each generation asks different questions about the past. We are not necessarily interested in the same things our mothers were and we certainly are interested in some aspects of the past that our mothers ignored.

Using the official public record of the NSDAR, its annual report, plus 100 years of museum correspondence, I will show how the museum collection chronicles 100 years of changing interpretations of the history of American decorative arts.

Home and Country[2]

The foundation of the National Society Daughters of the American Revolution and its museum has its roots firmly planted in the Colonial Revival period. Evidence of this is everywhere in the society's early records. In its first annual report, the society gives these reasons for its founding: "Thoughtful American women noted with anxiety the prevailing ignorance of the country's institutions due to the great influx of foreign immigration . . . There was great danger that coming generations would utterly forget the purposes and ideals that gave strength and unity to the nation . . . , and the young must be taught a reverence for the past."[3]

A major icon of the Colonial Revival, the spinning wheel, was patented along with a flax-covered distaff, as the official insignia of the National Society Daughters of the American Revolution in 1891.[4] Since the mid-19th century, when many American towns were celebrating their bicentennial, the spinning wheel had been used to symbolize and romanticize the role of woman in colonial American life. The Colonial New England kitchen at the Brooklyn and Long Island Sanitary Fair of 1864 included several spinning wheels and spinners, as did the Centennial Exhibition in Philadelphia. The Pocumtuck Valley Memorial Association's Memorial Hall in Deerfield, Massachusetts, displayed spinning wheels in 1880, in what is considered to be the first permanent period room display in an American museum. Thus even before the wheel was adopted by the DAR as its insignia, it was permanently ingrained in the minds of most Americans as being associated with the women's role in colonial American life. Christopher Monkhouse states in his essay, "The Spinning Wheel as Artifact, Symbol, and Source of Design," that after the spinning wheel was formally adopted by the DAR as its symbol, it became mandatory to use the wheel in all patriotic displays.[5] Thus, not only did the DAR fully participate in the culture of the Colonial Revival but, in this case, it blazed the trail.

In September of 1890 300 application packets were sent to prospective DAR members. Included were printed slips of paper stating the objectives of the society: "To perpetuate the memory and spirit of the women and men of the Revolutionary period. To collect and preserve historical and biographical records, documents, and relics."[6] One month later 18 members were enrolled and the society made official its objectives, with the addition of one resolving to secure a fireproof building for the intended relics and papers.

There were those who were not in favor of this women's hereditary society and asked, "what was it for?" Others were disturbed by the social inequality, and some were opposed to women being in public work. One wrote that they feared "it would demoralize all who escaped the suffrage fever."[7] In spite of this, membership grew by the thousands. Records and relics were accumulating at such an alarming rate that by the end of 1891 the office of Historian General was formed to be custodian of the historical and biographical papers, and a Revolutionary Relics Committee was formed to handle the incoming objects. This committee formulated what could be called the museum's first collections management policy when they resolved to "secure as many such valuable mementos as possible."[8] The problem of finding a storage facility for these mementos was solved when the National Museum (Smithsonian Institution) agreed to house them until a permanent home could be built. During the first convention in 1892 (or congress as it is called), a building fund was set up using monies from life memberships and chapter charters. Six hundred and fifty dollars were raised that year and an official resolution was passed that called for the building to be made from "purely American materials, in honor of those who labored in the Revolution."[9] That building, Memorial Continental Hall, was finally built in 1910 and the relics housed at the Smithsonian Institution were returned to the society.

Bag, ca. 1840, England, of silk and glass beads. Family history states this bag was owned and used by Malatiah Younge, wife of Samuel Younge, a Revolutionary War soldier. Donated in 1890 by the great-granddaughter of Malatiah, it is noteworthy for having been the first object donated to the museum. Collection of the DAR Museum, # 1, gift of Miss Mary Letts. Photo by Mark Gulezian.

Most early objects given to the society in the first ten to twelve years were valued because of their patriotic or historic connection to the founders of our country. Textiles in particular were valued not as accumulated evidence of the social and cultural role of women in early America, as they would be today, but their value lay in their inherent relationship to the men of the colonial period.

The first object accessioned by the society was a beaded bag. Made in England around 1840, it has a family history of being owned and used by Malatiah Younge, the wife of Samuel Younge, a Revolutionary soldier. Other objects given in the first ten years include the spinning wheel that inspired the DAR insignia, candles and bullets made during the Revolutionary War, an infant's shirt, and a piece of wood from an elm tree known as the "Washington elm" because under it George Washington was said to have taken command of the American army on July 3, 1775. It is also clear from this list that the founders' definition of "revolutionary" was the same as their contemporary definition of "colonial." That is: anything made before 1840 seemed to suffice. In fact, the first quilt given to the collection was not given because it was an object of great beauty or because it was worked in a precise and exquisite manner. It was given because it had a family history of being made in the Revolutionary War period. In studying the fabrics in the quilt, it is evident that it was probably made in the first half of the 19th century. And I do not mean to be facetious, but the museum has quite a few quilts made during the Revolutionary War period out of 1840s fabrics!

The second quilt donated to the society was also given because of its historical importance. The pieced and appliquéd quilt has a family history of being made by the niece of Ethan Allen. Apparently this small bit of oral history was all that was necessary to justify the quilt being accepted into the collection. The donor did not even think it necessary to give us the maker's name. If I were given that quilt today, I would want to find out as much as possible about the maker. Where did she live? Was she educated? Was she affiliated with a church? Was she married? How many children did she have? What was her financial status? I would possibly even examine the quilting stitches to determine if she quilted it alone. I would search for evidence that would tell me as much as possible about her everyday life.

Detail of quilt, ca. 1810, pieced and appliquéd discharge-printed cottons, 90" × 86", with stuffed work. This medallion quilt was donated to the Museum in the 1890s with an unsubstantiated history of being made by the niece of Ethan Allen. It was given at a time when Colonial artifacts were the Museum's primary concern. Collection of the DAR Museum, #201. Courtesy of the DAR Museum.

Memorial Continental Hall was built by New York architect, Edward Pearce Casey in the Beaux-Arts style between 1904 and 1910. At its completion the Washington Evening Star *pronounced it to be "the costliest and most impressive monument of its kind ever built by women in this country or any other." It houses the DAR Museum which is located at 1776 "D" street, Washington, DC. Courtesy of the NSDAR*

The emphasis on collecting objects of historic importance not only pervaded the DAR Museum collection but was a factor in the collecting policies of other East Coast museums during this time. In the Introduction to Amelia Peck's book, *American Quilts and Coverlets in The Metropolitan Museum of Art*, Chairman of the Department of American Art, John K. Howat states, "Some quilts were purchased by the museum in the early decades of the 20th century; very often the overriding reason for their purchase was their history of ownership by a person or family known to have been prominent in colonial America."[10]

In 1914 the first curator was appointed to the museum. She was Catherine Barlow, a DAR member from the District of Columbia. This post, known as Curator General, came with a seat on the national board of management. Miss Barlow justified the need for a curator by stating: "We must bring the museum up to the standard of efficiency (obtained) among other institutions of a like character. The society has been greatly hampered in the past by the lack of a curator."[11] She also went on to acknowledge the need to classify the relics and to seek further contributions.

To accomplish her goal of raising the standards of the museum, she consulted with the Curator of Decorative Arts at the Metropolitan Museum of Art. There she became aware of the need to protect the collection from the environment. She had exhibition and storage cases made that were purportedly air, dust, and burglar proof. She set up a catalogue system that recorded accession number, location, donor, and the state from which the object was donated. And lastly she stated her guidelines for donations to the museum which were slightly more specific than had been previously given. She wrote, "... we want objects from as many pioneer women as we are able to reach."[12] This began a very short period of collecting in which the museum was being interpreted as a women's museum. A visitor wrote: "Your collecton is dainty and beautiful as it should be in a women's museum." Barlow replied, "You have a vision of what we hope the future to realize for us . . . A great measure of success in the museum today is forecast of what you can make it for the future."[13] She was not adopting totally new objectives for the museum, she was just adding the women's perspective. She stated the reason for this in her board report of 1918: "The gifts donated are improving in character as the requirements of a women's museum, in a women's organization, would naturally call for articles of the home, or the personal possessions of women."[14] The donations given to the museum in these years such as quilts, coverlets, linens, costumes, and many more small objects used or worn by women of the Revolutionary period, reflect her plea for articles relating to domestic life.

One of the most interesting objects in the

Catherine Britten Barlow (1852-1938), first Curator General of the DAR Museum, joined the National Society Daughters of the American Revolution in 1904 as a member from the District of Columbia. During her years as Curator General she put in place a catalogue system for the collection and succeeded in raising funds to store objects in secure, environmentally safe cases. It was also during her tenure that the first paid staff assistant was hired. Courtesy of the DAR Magazine.

collection given in this period was a bedrug. It is said to have been made by Molly Stark of Revolutionary War fame for her niece Molly Lothrop as a wedding present in 1773. For years this bedcover was erroneously referred to as a hooked rug in publications such as the *Magazine Antiques* and *Woman's Day*. It was not until the 1970s that an observant curator finally discovered that it was worked in a running stitch instead of being hooked, and was probably not made by Molly Stark. From its donation in 1922 to the 1980s it is mentioned in the NSDAR annual report on a regular basis. It was on permanent exhibition for at least 50 years, and in 1953 it was treated with a moth-destroying chemical. If that did not kill it, its exhibition site in 1960, a specially-built case located under a skylight, would. For the last ten years it has had a much-needed rest in a dark climate-controlled textile storage room.

A network of potential donors was developed through the DAR state societies and chapters. Each chapter was named for a historic person or event and its mission was to "educate each member about our country's past and to arouse the interest of the public at large about that past."[15] The National Board of Management encouraged state societies and chapters to incorporate as many events as possible that would highlight local history, into their yearly programs. Some of these early projects included: cabinet of relics donated by a Connecticut chapter to the New Haven Historical Society; a chapter in Atlanta gave a colonial tea to raise money to buy and restore "Meadow Gardens," the home of George Walton, a signer of the Declaration; and many chapters all over the country lent relics to the World's Columbian Exposition in 1893. These grass-roots efforts at highlighting and preserving local history helped to bring the Colonial Revival to the masses and was a factor in the Colonial Revival becoming a truly "national style."[16]

Beginning in 1917, each DAR chapter appointed a museum committee to uncover articles from the Revolutionary War period. The members of the committees were encouraged to be active in their pursuit of relics for the museum. The museum chairman of an Atlanta chapter sent a quilt to the museum and bemoaned the fact that she would probably never see the museum and wrote of how hard it was to find among the members, things that they were willing to part with that were interesting and had historical value. These women are the long-forgotten, unsung heroes of the DAR Museum, as almost 50% of objects in the collection had been ferreted out by them. The museum committees were then, and are still, the most important fundraising tool used by the museum to obtain objects and funds.

Important changes took place at the museum in the 1920s. The offices in Memorial Continental Hall were gradually being furnished with gifts to the museum. As more and more pieces of valuable antique furniture were accepted into the collection, the offices were relocated and the vacated rooms, furnished with these important antiques, became period rooms.

Period room settings were an extremely popular method of exhibiting objects in the 1920s and 1930s. Not only popular with museums, they were also used by department stores and expositions to show off valuable furnishings. It was no longer acceptable for museums to be just great storehouses for objects, such as dark wood cases filled with numerous examples of china, silver, or textiles. It was necessary for these objects along with furniture to be arranged in a way "that would make their aesthetic value clear and their social importance effective." It was thought that by arranging objects in room settings their true meaning would be obvious.[17]

One of the first state period rooms, the New Hampshire children's attic, was originally conceived in 1926, as a colonial nursery. Mrs. Lowell Hobart, Building and Grounds Chairman was keen on the idea of making this room a nursery. She wrote to say, ". . . put old-fashioned nursery wallpaper on the walls, rag rugs on the floor and have examples of cradles, nursery furniture, and toys of the colonial period . . ."[18] Today the room highlights the doll and toy collection. It is interesting to note that it was only two years prior to this room being conceived at the DAR Museum, that the American Wing opened at the Metropolitan Museum of Art, featuring period rooms. Henry Francis du Pont, founder of Winterthur, recalled this opening as the greatest decorative arts event of its time.

". . . the intangible responsibility that is ours . . ."[19]

As the role of museums changed from one of caretaker of large numbers of objects to one that sought to be an active educational and cultural force in the country, and arbiter of public taste, the DAR Museum broadened its scope to include these new changes.

Objects were coming into the collection in record numbers, with many being given to furnish the period rooms. As the numbers of rooms and objects multiplied, guidelines for donations had to be tightened and more strictly enforced. In her 1936 report to congress, the curator general, Mrs. Robert Reed, stated that the museum would only accept objects made or used in this country up to 1830. These objects had to have a verifiable date and be of historical importance. Duplicates would not be accepted; they were turning down spin-

ning wheels, but still accepting quilts. She also noted that the DAR Museum had been accepted for membership in the American Association of Museums. Membership in this prestigious organization meant the museum was executing its mission in an exemplary way, according to the standards of the day. Mrs. Reed wrote that the museum was an "accredited history museum . . . that was established to show the life and customs of our forefathers."[20] Gone was the concept of the museum being "a woman's museum." In spite of this, it was a time when large numbers of textiles, especially quilts were brought into the collection.

At the 1940 congress, Mrs. Reed gave a very detailed and long report spelling out the major responsibilities of the museum. These responsibilities mirrored contemporary trends that were evident in the museum world at the time. Mrs. Reed's report cited the museum's educational role as its most important mission. This role was carried out "by exhibiting objects in groups that tell a story of the customs and mode of living of the people and arts and crafts of our period, by holding special exhibits and gallery talks, by featuring historic and patriotic programs for school children and by comparing early methods with modern ones, old objects with the new, and illustrate progress in a concrete way."[21] Wanting to offer opportunities for research, the report also cited the need for a decorative arts research library that would be available to groups or individuals by appointment.[22]

She also cited the physical appearance of museum exhibitions as an important responsibility. She listed the careful selection of objects, authentic labeling, and an attractive arrangement, as requirements of an exhibition that would attract visitors and be a place for relaxation and entertainment. She said, "It should be restful and attractive, not tiring and (boring). It should instill lasting, rather than temporary interest and should develop a desire for more knowledge. It should be dynamic rather than static."[23] The focus on the aesthetic quality of exhibitions and the objects therein is one most museums were using to attract visitors and hold on to their position as arbiters of popular taste.

There was also a change in the type of ob-

The DAR Museum's "New Hampshire Children's Attic" was designed in the 1920s by Wallace Nutting, the distinguished antiquarian. He designed the room around an overmantel oil painting. Although the "daughters" disagreed on whether to call the room a nursery or a children's attic, they did agreed on the need to keep their museum current with contemporary museum practices. Courtesy of the DAR Museum.

Detail of Full Blown Poppy ca. 1870, of appliquéd and pieced roller-printed and solid-colored cottons, 98.5" × 93.5" was made by Lucy Howland Thatcher (1803-1894) in Lee, Massachusetts. A letter which accompanied this quilt when it was given in 1941 stated, ". . . quilts have been a serious research study in our family." It was given at a time when the Museum's interest in an objects aesthetics became more important. Collection of the DAR Museum, # 3825, gift of Miss Marion Thatcher and Mrs. Vera T. Schorer. Courtesy of the DAR Museum.

jects donated. Objects were no longer valued just for their historical importance, although for the DAR Museum that would always be an important factor. Emphasis was now being placed on objects with aesthetic value, such as textiles, miniatures, and furniture. Beautiful, well-crafted objects would highlight the sophisticated craftsmanship of American decorative arts and enhance the value of the collection.

How did the museum carry out these substantial responsibilities? Their first task was to hire a museum professional.[24] Helen S. Johnson came to the museum as secretary in 1939 with eleven years' experience at the Newark Museum and a certificate in Museum Training. She initiated a series of special exhibitions and gallery talks and published frequently in the DAR Magazine.

There were five exhibitions in two years, in spite of the fact that these were the years immediately preceding the United States entry in World War II. The first quilt exhibition at the museum was "Early American Bedcoverings," which opened in December of 1940 and stimulated an interest in the textile collection and attracted gifts.

With an increase in donations of textiles, a search for better storage space was instigated. In 1941 a room was found off the Continental Hall Library balcony and was fitted out with drawers to hold small to medium size textiles. This room was used for textile storage for the next 46 years.

The War Years

During World War II, the DAR Museum put most of the collection in storage. The building had been appropriated for use for the duration of the war by the American Red Cross and the Army and Navy Women's Auxiliary. A day nursery was set up in the basement to care for the children of some of the many women who were working in Washington during the war.

In spite of the upheaval experienced by the society during the war years, the museum went on about its business as usual. Small special exhibitions were still being held. A Steigel-like glass exhibition was the first loan exhibition ever held at the museum and it was touted as breaking all attendance records since the war cut off gas!

But working in Washington, in a building two blocks from the White House, did have its notable moments. On May 7, 1945, Rosalind Wright, museum director, ended a letter to a potential donor with this moving paragraph.

> I can't help noting this historic day — we have all been on the qui vive in Washington waiting for the President's announcement-sound trucks are set up in front of the White House and ever since 9 o'clock we have been on pins and needles for official confirmation of the long-awaited news from Eisenhower that the Germans have surrendered at last. But here is closing hour and we have not heard from the White House but certainly we can say grateful prayers tonight![25]

The Postwar Years

The years immediately following the war were ones of planning for the future. The Director of the American Association of Museums worked with the museum staff on a long-range plan, while the National Society drew up plans of its own consisting of construction of an addition to the administration building located between Memorial Continental Hall and Constitution Hall. It would consist of a gallery space for rotating exhibitions, along with administration offices. All objects in the collection would be stored, until the completion of this building, except 18 quilts and coverlets. These were exhibited on the balcony of the library. In fact, from 1949 until April of 1993, the library balcony was a common site for quilt exhibitions.

The museum collection grew at a steady pace during the 1950s, although the importance of the textile collection, as reflected in the number of times it is mentioned in the society's archival records, took a back seat to other parts of the museum collection. The Director of the museum from the early 1950s until 1964 was a former Smithsonian employee, Frank Klapthor. The types of objects collected in his day reflect his interest and area of expertise. Ceramics were brought into the collection in great numbers, along with glass and furniture. The fact that his wife, Margaret Klapthor was the curator of Political History and "First Ladies" collection at the Smithsonian Institution, may have been a factor in the DAR Museum's focus on collecting objects relating to the "First Ladies." During these years there was a very aggressive and somewhat successful campaign to uncover these objects. The most interesting of the objects given to the museum associated with the "First Ladies," was a white lace gown and black shawl identified as having been worn by Mary Todd Lincoln. It was loaned to the Smithsonian Institution in 1961 and officially given to them in 1963.

During Mr. Klapthor's time the museum was successful in adhering to the original collections management policy of accepting only those objects that date prior to 1830. New guidelines were also introduced, which reflected an interest in conservation. Only objects in good condition were wanted, and funds were solicited for conservation. The curator general stated in her report at the time, "Don't send it unless it's fabulous!" Duplicates of objects were still not accepted and it was suggested that the donor send as much family history as possible.

In the idealistic and turbulent times of the 1960s and early 1970s the relevance of the national society and its museum were questioned. They were seen as ivory towers outside the mainstream of society. The museum responded by committing itself to a more public role and opening itself up to the community. The museum proved it was serious about making these changes by seeking accreditation in the American Association of Museums. Although some considered the museum accredited in 1938, when asked to join the AAM, it was not until the early 1970s that the AAM put into place an official process of accreditation. In order to gain accreditation by this organization the museum had to expand its staff and programs and bring its collections management policy up to modern standards. A museum registrar was hired to set up strict guidelines for the handling and recording of objects, and the period rooms were opened to the public with tours being given by trained docents. Perishable items, such as textiles, were taken off permanent display and a new storage room was built for the quilt and coverlet collection with its own climate-control system. (It was not until 1987 that the entire museum was climate-controlled.) These changes allowed the museum to become accredited in 1973.

The "Women's Movement" of the 1960s and 1970s brought about a new-found interest in the role of women in the social and cultural life of this country. Colleges and universities legitimized this new area of study by funding Women's Studies programs. Curators of decorative arts collectons around the country realized their collections held a treasure trove of objects that could advance the knowledge and understanding of the social and cultural life of 18th- and 19th-century American women. The acceptance of women's history as a legitimate scholarly pursuit, and the realization that objects such as quilts, representing a lasting tradition, led to a softening of guidelines for donations to the DAR Museum textile collection. Ironically it was a man who accepted the first quilt into the collection with a known family history of being made after 1830. In 1969, curator of the museum, Jim Johnson, was willing to accept a quilt, in spite of the fact it was obviously made after 1830. The donor, the daughter of the maker, dated it around 1880. Material evidence corroborates this date. From this point on it was the policy of the museum to accept textiles that date to 1900, providing they had a family history, were made or used America, and were in good condition.

The last 20 years has seen the textile collection blossom in terms of the number and type of textiles donated and exhibited, and the quality of the scholarship devoted to their study. Since 1970, more than half of the quilt collection has been given to the museum and more than 20 exhibitions of quilts, coverlets, and needlework have been mounted. Two curators stand out as having advanced the field of study. Jean Federico, curator and director of the museum in the 1970s and early 1980s brought the textile collection out of storage and made it available through ambitious exhibition and educational programs, and by allowing outside scholars to use the collection for research. She published frequently, her article on white-work bedcoverings in the early 1980s for *Quilter's Journal* and the American Quilt Study Group's publication, *Uncoverings 1980*, is still a must-read for students and

Quilt, ca. 1810, of pieced and appliquéd block-printed cottons, 100" × 99", was owned by Tobias Watkins (1780-1855) of Baltimore, Maryland. The fabrics in this early bedcovering were produced at the Hewson Printworks outside Philadelphia and make this a most important quilt. Collection of the DAR Museum, # 74.290, gift of Mr. and Mrs. Kennedy C. Watkins. Photo by Mark Gulezian.

scholars interested in white-work bedcovers. Most importantly, she recognized the importance of an early 19th-century quilt made from cottons produced at the famed Hewson printworks and featured it in the exhibition, "America Sleeps," in 1976. It is the most important quilt in the collection, the fabric being the work of John Hewson, an English-born calico printer and Revolutionary War patriot who founded a calico printing business near Philadelphia from 1774 to his retirement in 1810. The maker is unidentifiable, but family history tells us it was owned by Marylander Dr. Tobias Watkins.

Gloria Seaman Allen, former curator and director of the DAR Museum, made a lasting contribution to the textile collection through her meticulously researched exhibitions and catalogues. Her exhibitions of Maryland and Virginia quilts broke new ground by introducing us to the social lives of quiltmakers in those two states through the use of probate records as evidence of their past. The results of these exhibitions were 40 quilts donated in a two-year period. Her articles in *Antiques* on New York and Pennsylvania coverlets resulted in over ten coverlets donated in a four-month period. All of these extremely popular exhibitions and articles resulted in a much-needed increase in the visibility of the museum and a heightened respect for its textile collection. The DAR Museum is no longer known as, "Washington's best kept secret!" She put it on the map!

Where is the DAR Museum today and what is its future? This spring the museum was reaccredited for the second time. It is one of only seven museums to be reaccredited twice. After 100 years the collection now numbers over 30,000 objects, 240 of which are quilts. Not surprisingly, these objects reflect the taste and status of the owners—largely middle-class, white, European Americans. In the last few years, the curators have attempted to broaden the collection to reflect the non-European presence in early America. Unfortunately, the DAR Museum does not have a large acquisitions fund that will enable it to compete in the marketplace against wealthier museums and collectors. It should be noted that the DAR has a long history of support of Native American schools. Many state societies own large Native American collections and some of these objects eventually make their way into the collection. The museum was recently given a peace pipe which belonged to Sitting Bull.

Museum Director and Chief Curator, Diane Dunkley stated in a lecture to a conference sponsored by the Virginia Association of Museums in 1993 that, "the DAR Museum is making a concerted effort to include in our exhibitions a broader cultural spectrum. The present exhibition, 'True Love and a Happy Home: Feminine Expectations and Cultural Experiences in Victorian America,' examines the cult and mythology of true womanhood. It is a woman's history exhibition encompassing women who for political leanings, life styles, economic/class status, race or religion would not ordinarily be members of the DAR. We are asking our visitors to think about cultural and sexual boundaries which imprisoned women in the past and to compare those gender roles with those of today."

The textile collection is at a crossroads. It can be said that it is a relatively complete collection of 18th- and 19th-century American textiles. Should we expand our cut-off date for donations to include textiles made in the 20th century or should we refine our existing colection by deaccessioning? The quilt and coverlet storage areas are full, and the majority of DAR members oppose deaccessioning. The fact of the matter is that very soon we will have to stop accepting donations unless a larger storage area is built. In the meantime I have moved back the cut-off date for donations to 1876 and even then will not accept anything that, to quote a former curator general, "isn't fabulous!"

End Notes

[1]"A Century of Collecting: The DAR Museum at 100 Years," exhibition dates: October 1, 1990 to April 22, 1991.

[2]"Home and Country" was established as the motto for the society in 1892.

[3]Report of the National Society Daughters of the American Revolution 1890-1897, 1st annual report, 1899, Government Printing Office, 35-36.

[4]Ibid., 30.

[5]Monkhouse, 169.

[6]1st annual report NSDAR, 5.

[7]Ibid., 9.

[8]Ibid., 48.

[9]Ibid., 38.

[10]Amelia Peck, *American Quilts and Coverlets In The Metropolitan Museum Of Art* (New York:The Metropolitan Museum of Art and Dutton Studio Books, 1990), 10.

[11]18th annual report NSDAR, 41.

[12]Ibid., 54-56.

[13]Ibid., 154-156.

[14]Ibid., 51-55.

[15]1st annual report, 49.

[16]Diane Dunkley, "The Colonial Revival," unpublished paper, 1989.

[17]For more information on the influence and relationship of museums, department stores and fairs in the 19th and 20th centuries see: Neil Harris, "Museums, Merchandising, and Popular Taste: The Struggle for Influence," *Material Culture and the Study of American Life* ed. Ian M.G. Quimby (Winterthur, Delaware, The Henry Francis DuPont Winterthur Museum, 1978), 140-174.

[18]Letter to Mrs. Edmund P. Moody from Mrs. Lowell Hobart, DAR Museum Archives, 1926.

[19]49th annual report, 89.

[20]45th annual report, 86.

[21]49th annual report, 89.

[22]The DAR Museum research library is located on the 3rd floor of the administration building and is open to the public by appointment only, Monday through Friday, 9:00 am to 4:00 pm.

[23]49th annual report, 89.

[24]The first non-DAR professional to work in the museum was Anna S. Walton, who was hired in 1918 and came with a diploma in Museum Work from the University of Chicago.

[25]Letter to Mrs. Haycock from Rosalind Wright, May 7, 1945.

Nancy Gibson Tuckhorn is associate curator of textiles at the DAR Museum in Washington, D. C. where she has been since 1985. In 1991 she mounted a major exhibition there on the work of Catherine Garnhardt, about whom she hopes to write further. She is on the boards of the Virginia Quilt Museum and the American Quilt Study Group where she has been in charge of fundraising. Nancy is also author of "A Profile of Quilts and Donors at the DAR Museum" (Uncoverings *1990) and is currently working on* Maryland Quilts *with co-author, Gloria Seaman Allen.*

FOR VICE PRESIDENT
CLEVELAND
AND
STEVENSON
THE
G. O. P.
GROVER CLEVELAND
DEMOCRATIC NOMINEE FOR PRESIDENT

Quilted Ballots

Political and Campaign Textiles

Julie Powell

Detail of a pieced quilt top, 88" × 77", features 11 red cotton Grover Cleveland bandannas from his 1888 and 1892 campaigns. In the center background is a McKinley/ Hobart 1896 campaign bandanna, 18" × 18", that touts the themes "Sound Money" and "Protection." The felt "beaver" top hat, 7" h. × 10¼" d., contains a large oval cardboard label proclaiming it "The 1892 G.O.P. Campaign Hat" and has pictures of Benjamin Harrison and Whitelaw Reid. A hand-carved wooden parade cane, 33"l., has a likeness of William Jennings Bryan as its head ornament and three separate carved letter messages down the shaft: "William J. Bryan President 1900," "Champion of the Democratic Rule," and "The Solon of the 19th Century." A hearty blast can be blown from the 1892 tin parade horn which has the candidates' names, Cleveland and Stevenson, stencilled on the side. Collection of the author.

Legend has it that George Washington fastened his first inaugural coat with a special set of brass or copper clothing buttons. Experts believe about 27 varieties of such clothing buttons were made dating from that inaugural ceremony and Washington's first term in office. These were in essence our first known political buttons. Other artifacts inspired by Washington's first inauguration and accession to the presidency in 1789 include Liverpool transferware tankards, bandannas, and tokens. The latter two traditions continue, though to a lesser degree, through present-day campaigns.

American political history reveals varied and vigorous approaches to a "run for the White House." The personalities and characteristics of the candidates and the ingenuity and financial resources available to the political parties were factors upon which the style and the attendant material culture of the campaigns depended. Today a lion's share of the money raised for campaigns is spent on television time, debates, and spot commercials where previously campaign funds were used to purchase and distibute buttons and lapel devices, ceramics, glassware, and textiles. Some political artifacts have changed in form and quality over time. Brass clothing buttons and tokens have evolved into celluloid and lithograph campaign buttons. China and glassware have continued to be produced but lack the beauty and elegance of their 19th-century ancestors. One constant remains among the ever evolving political artifacts — quilts. Talented and creative quilters continue today to express their patriotic and personal commitments with needle, thread, and fabric. This paper will itemize chronologically the range of political and campaign memorabilia with an emphasis on textiles, especially quilts.

George Washington and American independence were popular subjects for the English and Scottish textile printers. Designs were freely "borrowed" from historical paintings. These copper-plate printed furnishing fabrics were specifically intended for the American market. Quilts can be found at Winterthur, the Cooper-Hewitt Museum, and the Kentucky Historical Society constructed entirely of these fabrics, such as one entitled "The Apotheosis of Benjamin Franklin and George Washington." The design shows Washington driving the chariot of America; her shield reads, "American Independence, 1776."

The 1824 election had a crowded and diverse field of candidates: John Quincy Adams, Andrew Jackson, William Crawford, and Henry Clay. No candidate could get a majority of electoral votes. Therefore, the House of Representatives chose the new President from the three candidates with the highest number of votes. At the last minute, Clay shifted his votes to Adams, thereby assuring his victory. John Quincy Adams and Andrew Jackson were the first to distribute decidedly feminine campaign souvenirs nearly 100 years before women were granted the vote. These colorful cardboard thread boxes have velvet pincushion lids that read "Adams Forever" and "Jackson and No Corruption" and display the candidates portraits on the underside. Later, Lincoln is pictured on the cover of a small Mauchlineware box. The underside of its lid has a paper label which reads "Use Clark's O.N.T. Spool Cotton." The box may be simply a souvenir gift, but if it should happen to be a campaign piece, one wonders how many male voters were swayed by a container of cotton thread. Also, a pink Bristol glass boudoir oil lamp, decorated with hand-painted rosebuds bears the name Harrison, is dated 1892. Was it perhaps expected to shed a little Republican light on the female members of the household?

Jackson, who had lost in 1824, ran again and was victorious in 1828. One of the best historical patterned chintzes is blue and white yardage printed to commemorate Jackson's first inauguration of March 4, 1829. It pictures our first seven presidents, flanked by eagles and sailing ships. Jackson, in full military regalia, is set apart in an oval frame beneath which is the inscription, "Andrew Jackson Magnanimous in Peace Victorious in War."[1] Political tokens — coin-like disks bearing the faces and slogans of candidates — were popular and used generously by 19th-century campaigners. They were generally kept in pockets; some had holes at the top and were worn on watch chains or as lapel pins. One interesting example from 1840 has the bust of Major General W. H. Harrison on the front. An eagle on the back says, "Go it Tip, Come it Tyler."

1840 was a landmark year in the history of American politics; the hoopla-filled effort to elect William Henry Harrison marked the beginning of presidential campaigns as we know them today. The Whigs decided to present the educated, aristocratic general to the voters as a common man. The campaign unleashed an unsurpassed torrent of artifacts. Many of these embodied a log cabin, cider barrel theme. Mass rallies and torchlight parades attracted as many as 25,000-50,000 participants. And no wonder. They came to enjoy the music, speeches, sociability, and, last but not least, the hard cider. Log cabin campaign headquarters, with free-flowing cider barrels, were erected in most communities.

A Baltimore album-style quilt top, signed in ink by Rebecca Diggs and owned by the Smithsonian Institution has a block with the "Harrison" log cabin complete with all of the Whig Party attributes: front left, an inked inscription on the cider barrel; atop the roof is a raccoon, the Whig symbol of rural existence. Harrison proclaimed that his latchstring would always be out for veterans and other voters, an early version of today's "open door" policy. There appears to be a ink-lined latchstring on the right side of the cabin door.

Political yardage was plentiful in 1840. Some cotton chintz fabrics show Harrison, his log cabin, and its latchstring and cider barrel while a bandanna illustrates Harrison in an equestrian, military pose with sword drawn. Such textiles were joined by ceramic representations in the Harrison campaign. For example, John Ridgeway of Staffordshire, England, responded to the log cabin mania with his "Columbian Star" dinnerware which featured the central rural cabin scene.

One result of all this Whig hoopla was a record turnout of 80.2 percent of adult white male voters. As we exit the 1840 election, we can note that then, as now, sales of alcoholic beverages were probably prohibited on election day. There are rumors, however, of "election cakes," laced with whiskey, being served at the polls in Kentucky.

Henry Clay, "The Great Compromiser," was the Whigs next candidate in 1844. One of his tokens reads, "Henry Clay, the American System, United We Stand." Clay was an experienced statesman who sought the presidency three times without success. His campaigns left behind more than their fair share of political textiles. A Pennsylvania family named Young pieced and tied a quilt about the time of the 1844 Clay campaign. A great grandson donated it to the Barracks Museum in Trenton, New Jersey. The quilt's six campaign flags speak to its significant political value. Clay's portrait is seen in the star ground and his name and that of his running mate, Freylinghuysen, a New Jersey native, are printed in the white stripes.

Other Clay quilts include a feathered star quilt (see cover) and a silk quilt made by the candidate's wife Lucretia Hart Clay. Its central oval portrait of Clay and thirty other floral and scenic squares are worked in elaborate embroidery and broderie perse chintz appliqué. Mrs. Clay gave the quilt to the wife of Kentucky Governor John Crittenden in appreciation of their husbands' close personal and political friendship.[2]

Clay's 1844 opponent was Democrat James Knox Polk, who was not without similar memorabilia. A parade banner with Polk's portrait is the highlight of one quilt. The star to his right represents the State of Texas. George Dallas, Polk's vice-presidential partner, was mayor of Philadelphia early in his political career. Francis R. Shunk was the Pennsylvania gubernatorial candidate. Three of the parade flags used in the quilt bear the Polk-Dallas legend.[3]

Nancy and Donald Roan's study of textiles from the Goschenhoppen Folk Region, *Lest I Shall Be Forgotten, Anecdotes and Traditions of Quilts*, exhibited a second quilt containing

Quilt with Polk/Dallas/Shunk 1884 campaign parade flags, 80" × 73". Probably a utility bedcover, handmade of the brown prints and solid-colored cotton fabrics of the period. Collection of the Historical Society of Montgomery County, Norristown, Pennsylvania; gift of Miss Elizabeth Morgan. Courtesy of the Goschenhoppen Historians.

the Polk, Dallas, and Shunk names on two similar parade flags.[4] Francis Shunk lived in nearby Trappe, Montgomery County, Pennsylvania.

Miniature tintype and ferrotype photographs of presidential candidates began appearing in the late-1850s. These, like Washington's brass buttons, were precursors of contemporary campaign buttons. The ferrotypes were often mounted in circular brass frames that contained embossed names, slogans, or dates. One of the first, in 1860, was of Abraham Lincoln with Hannibal Hamlin, his running mate, on the reverse. In the early 1870s the first paper campaign photographs, albumin prints, also in brass embossed frames were introduced as lapel pins. The simple developing processes and lower material costs of albumin prints increased their use and popularity until ferrotypes were rarely found after the 1880s campaigns. Then, just before the turn of the century, a process to manufacture thin sheets of celluloid was adapted to the button industry. The campaign button became simply a metal disk covered by a colorful paper picture and a thin layer of celluloid, all held in place with a metal ring. The Whitehead and Hoag Company of Newark, New Jersey, patented the process in 1896. Campaigns ever after have enjoyed an ample supply of celluloid pinback buttons which replaced the earlier tokens, ferrotypes, and albumin photo lapel pieces. Lithographed pinback buttons came onto the scene in the 1916-1920 period; their designs are printed directly on a sheet of tin, cut out and bent back to form the rim. Both types of pins are still commonly used.[5]

All four 1860 presidential candidates: Abraham Lincoln, Stephen A. Douglas, John C. Breckenridge, and John Bell — are represented on one flag quilt made from campaign ribbons. Numerous ribbons have been cut and pieced into the remainder of the quilt. The ribbon that lies below the flag and between the numerals pictures the earlier 1852 Democratic slate of Franklin Pierce and William King. Still another ribbon, at the bottom, represents C. H. Strattan, who sought the county clerk's office. The Indiana State Museum in Indianapolis, owner of the quilt, indicates it was made by 13-year-old Maggie Frentz in 1876. It may represent a centennial endeavor which happens to contain a large number of earlier campaign ribbons.

Campaign ribbons were silk keepsakes with lithograph-printed candidates' names, pictures, and slogans. Relatively inexpensive to manufacture, they were used widely for nearly all campaigns. Later varieties called "portrait silks" were woven or embroidered by a few eastern seaboard companies and the British firm, Thomas Stevens. Ribbons often served as bookmarks and were, therefore, generally well-preserved.

The Republicans chose another war hero for their standard bearer in 1868. Brass campaign tokens are found which bear the image of General Ulysses S. Grant. Also, campaign yardage was printed specifically for the 1868 contest. Two different paisley-style striped fabrics were roller-printed for Grant's 1872 campaign. Their coloration of madder-style chocolate browns, reddish oranges, and light tans with black outlined figures is similar to dress yardage of the period but sports the slogan, "Let Us Have Peace."

Past president Lincoln, however, got top billing on a red, white and blue Grant campaign quilt emblazoned with Union stars which reads "Grant PR [president]/Colfax VI [vice-president]/Union Forever." Letters appliquéd across the two lower borders read, "This quilt was made by Elizabeth Holmes in her 68th year."

Another quilter, Susan Lowry, settled in California with her family in 1852. She made a pieced Birds-in-the-Air quilt about the time of the 1868 campaign. Susan used a recycled hand-painted parade banner that reads, "Thanks to God and Grant For Our Union Victories" for the back of her quilt.[6]

Red bandannas were perceived as a direct link to the common working man. The 1888 campaigns of both Harrison and Cleveland relied heavily on bandannas to deliver their messages to the voters. More than 50 varieties have been documented. Most campaigns from 1880-1900 were dominated by economic issues which were easily and inexpensively articulated on cloth. Daniell and Sons of New

A group of Lincoln 1860 and 1864 ferrotype images with embossed brass or metal frames, $\frac{7}{8}$"-1$\frac{1}{8}$"h; two suspended from decorative eagle-shaped lapel pins. Both rectangular pieces are albumin prints: one framed, the second in a book-shaped locket. Also, three pieces of roller printed yardage from both of U. S. Grant's campaigns. The piece on the left, from 1868, has oval framed portraits of Grant in uniform with a drum and bird design. Above the ovals is "Let Us Have Peace" and below, "US Grant" and its vertical stripes carry the legend, "US Grant/First In Peace/First In War." On the right is a repeating vertical design with eagle, flag and shield, from 1872, with "Grant" and "HW"(Henry Wilson, running mate) above the shield. The vertical stripes bear the repeating initials "USG." Below is a paisley-style print, also from 1872, that illustrates a musket, drum, bugle, and flag design. The horizontal stripes repeat "Grant and Wilson" and "Let Us Have Peace." Collection of the author.

Detail from an 1884 Cleveland/Hendricks crazy quilt showing a campaign ribbon, 3¼" × 4", with black printed portraits of the candidates and embroidered date on white satin. Above the ribbon is a large, 5" × 5", rooster, an early Democratic party symbol, embroidered in white thread on a black silk patch. Both pieces are framed with a decorative outline stitch. Collection of the author.

York City advertised red bandannas with white motifs at a cost of 9 cents each in the June 10, 1888 issue of *The New York Times*.[7] Some of these bandannas and handkerchiefs have been incorporated into period campaign quilts.

The following three quilts all utilize political bandannas as major elements in their designs. One, a bright yellow Lone Star quilt has black and white printed oval portraits, taken from a Cochrane's Turkey Red campaign bandanna and carefully placed in the center of each small corner star. "James A. Garfield, Republican Candidate for President," and "Chester A. Arthur, Republican Candidate for Vice-President," are printed below the portraits. A second quilt features a red bandanna as a well-placed central medallion. It is an unusual pieced quilt. Garfield, Arthur, and a pair of eagles peer out over a skillfully planned and constructed geometric design. The ribbon in the eagle's beak reads, "The Union and Constitution Forever."[8] The third quilt is a 1892 Harrison quilt which illustrates the abundant supply of bandanna yardage. Front and back are the same, lengths of seamed fabric proclaiming the pertinent issue of the campaign, "Protection To Home Industries." One can see printed dotted lines running through the fabric indicating where to cut and hem when making a single campaign handkerchief.

A persistent New Yorker, Grover Cleveland was both a successful and unsuccessful campaigner. He was the winning Democratic candidate in the 1884 election but lost in 1888 only to return victorious again in 1892. An ordinary crazy quilt becomes infinitely more interesting to a political collector when one notices a grumpy-looking Grover Cleveland and his running mate, Thomas Hendricks, in a 1884 campaign ribbon. Just above the ribbon is an embroidered rooster, the predecessor to the Democrats' donkey symbol. Cleveland's 1884 Republican opponents, James Blaine and John Logan, are pictured on a woven ribbon in another crazy quilt top. An unknown dedicated Democrat managed to procure 11 Cleveland red bandannas for her quilt top. One of the bandannas is from 1888; the others were used to support the 1892 Cleveland-Stevenson ticket.

In 1888, Grover Cleveland met his match in Benjamin Harrison. Harrison successfully deployed many of the tactics and symbolism that his grandfather, William Henry Harrison, had used in the landmark 1840 campaign — lots of political memorabilia.

"Tippecanoe and Morton Too" is one of three different kinds of campaign bandannas that were used in the construction of a quilt, components of which would have comfortably outfitted a whole contingent of bandanna-waving Harrison supporters in a torchlight parade.[9]

Harrison and Cleveland had a rematch in 1892. Historians ascribe Grover's success in this campaign not necessarily to Adlai Stevenson I, who is seen in a photograph with Cleveland on an ornate brass lapel pin, but to another powerful personal ally — his wife. Grover had courted and married the young and beautiful Frances Folsom. Frances and Grover were very much in the public eye, doing no damage at all to his image as a credible candidate. Advertising trade cards show Grover admiring Frances happily seated at a Household sewing machine and the couple blissfully entwined in a heart of Merrick thread.

The American woman's rights movement which began with the Seneca Falls, New York, convention in 1848 ushered in its own series of memorabilia to successfully promote passage of the 19th Amendment. Felt hat bands, Votes For Women lapel buttons, and Bissell carpet sweeper advertising fans are just a few of the many articles used to enhance the suffrage cause. Finally, American women could cast their first vote in a presidential election on November 2, 1920.

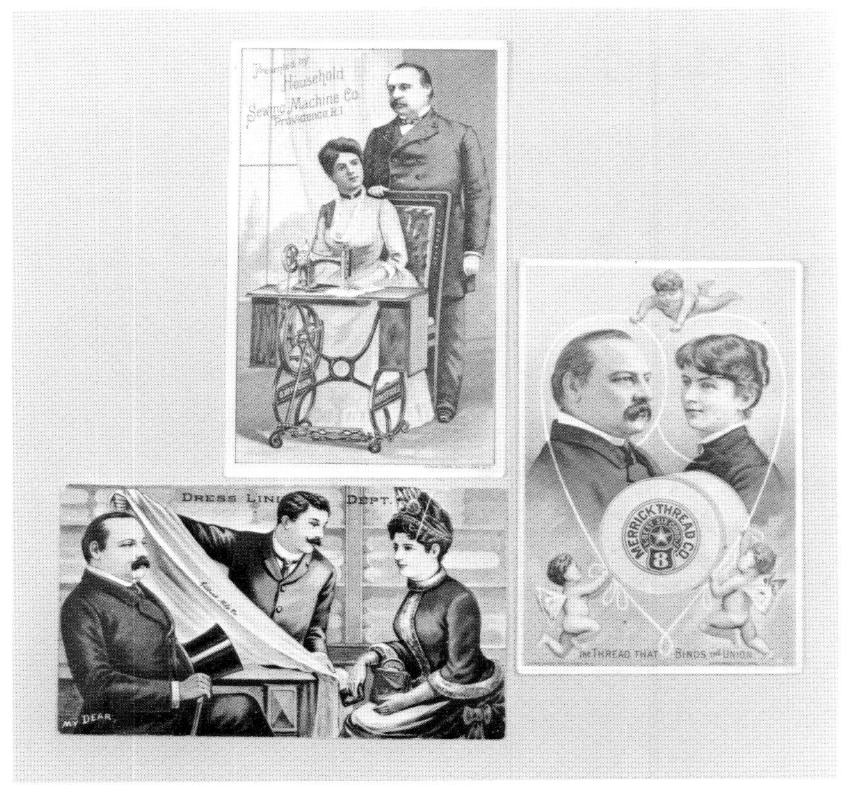

A group of advertising trade cards featuring Grover and Frances Cleveland, each 3" × 4½". Collection of the author.

Scenes from the book The Roosevelt Bears Their Travels and Adventures, *by Seymour Eaton, decorate all sides of this 8"h. × 4¼"w. pitcher made by the Buffalo Pottery Company, Buffalo, New York. Two early 1860s transfer printed children's plates, 5⅛"d., have raised embossed alphabet rims. They depict (left) President Abraham Lincoln and (right) General Winfield Scott. Collection of the author.*

The Ronald Reagan 1980 Inaugural Quilt is a brightly colored full-bed-sized piece designed by Ed Larson, Santa Fe, New Mexico, pieced and quilted by Fran Soika, Novelty, Ohio. Private collection. Courtesy of Ed Larson.

In the 20th century women and a few men who had made politically relevant quilts continued to do so. Fannie B. Shaw said she was inspired to make her quilt, *Prosperity Is Just Around the Corner*, by President Hoover's radio programs. She depicts many of the town's tradesmen and citizens in a wonderful three-dimensional setting. The center square shows her husband plowing his fields. The inscription reads, "The Backbone of the Nation Goes On." The Democrats' donkey, the Republicans' elephant, and Uncle Sam with a scroll promoting Farm Relief and Legal Beer can be seen in the lower row of blocks.[10]

Our most frequently elected President, Franklin Roosevelt, with his various campaigns and four terms of office, generated a plethora of campaign artifacts. Pinback buttons show him with his changing vice-presidential running mates: John Nance Garner in 1932 and 1936, Henry Wallace in 1940, and Harry Truman in 1944. An unknown FDR advocate from Texas embroidered "Roosevelt Third Term, 1941-1945" across the middle of her donkey quilt.[11]

One of Roosevelt's landslide victims in 1936 was Alf Landon from Kansas. On a Democratic Donkey quilt, each star was embroidered with the name of a state and the number of its electoral votes. The bottom center square noted "Landon and GOP." A single number eight is positioned below the GOP square in the border indicating both Mr. Lamdon's sole number of electoral votes and those of his home state.

The selection of World War II General Dwight Eisenhower by the Republicans in 1952 laid the foundation for a lively campaign. A very plain quilt top has a later version of the red bandanna for its center square. It features a smiling Eisenhower and urges the viewer to "Win With Ike."[12]

More recently, Jill Read, a Georgia quilter and member of Jimmy Carter's Peanut Brigade, who traveled with that group throughout the country campaigning in 1976, worked on a quilt between these trips. Her border contains embroidered peanut patches made exclusively for the New Hampshire primary. The quilt is titled *Jimmy Who?* because that was the question most frequently asked of campaign workers before Carter became nationally prominent.[13]

Ed Larson, a Santa Fe, New Mexico artist, designs quilts with strong political statements, draws them out full size on brown paper, and commissions selected quilters to construct and quilt them for him. Larson chose Ronald Reagan's 1980 inauguration as the subject of a remarkable quilt. It was made and quilted by Fran Soika of Novelty, Ohio. Pieced letters across the top read, "Hooray for Hollywood, our 40th Moral Majority President." Nancy, in red, stands at his side and Jimmy Carter exits off to the right side of the quilt. Earlier presidents he has depicted on quilts include Abraham Lincoln, Franklin D. Roosevelt, and Richard Nixon.

Finally, *Election '92* was made by Marion Mackey of West Chester, Pennsylvania while watching the campaign antics on television. She used photo transfer techniques to place the candidates into her pieced design featuring Clinton, Bush, and Perot.

Struggling for the right to vote and publicly express their political opinions, our quiltmaking ancestral soul sisters would probably rejoice at the 1992 victories achieved by female candidates for national, state, and local offices and the appointments of women to high level cabinet, administrative, and judiciary positions. Will we, the quiltmakers of the 1990s, join with Rebecca Diggs, Fannie Shaw, Fran Soika, Ed Larson, and Jill Read to celebrate, support, and protest in cloth the political endeavors we encounter in what remains of this, our 20th century and on into the 21st century?

End Notes

[1] A quilt made from this fabric is owned by the Museum of Political Life, West Hartford, Connecticut; gift of Diane and Fred Jorgensen.

[2] The quilt is at the Kentucky Museum, Bowling Green, Kentucky; Accession # 84.34.

[3] The quilt is in the White House Collection, Washington, D.C.

[4] Nancy and Donald Roan, *Lest I Shall Be Forgotten, Anecdotes and Traditions of Quilts* (Souderton, PA: Indian Valley Printing, Ltd., 1993), 80.

[5] Edmund B.; Sullivan, "Lapel Devices" *Collecting Political Americana* (Hanover, MA: The Christopher Publishing House, 1991), 23-38.

[6] Susan Lowry's quilt was documented by the California Heritage Quilt Project. See Jean Ray Laury, *Ho For California! Pioneer Women and Their Quilts* (New York: E.P. Dutton, 1990), 68-69.

[7] Otto Charles Thieme, "Wave High the Red Bandanna: Some Handkerchiefs of the 1888 Presidential Campaign," *American Material Culture: The Shape of Things Around Us*, ed. Edith Mayo. (Bowling Green, OH: Bowling Green State University Press, 1984), 92-111.

[8] The quilt is from the collection of Shelly Zegart, Louisville, Kentucky. See Katy Christopherson, *The Political and Campaign Quilt* (Frankfort,KY: 1984), 32-33.

[9] The quilt is owned by the Shelburne Museum in Vermont; Accession # 1964-238.

[10] Thomas K. Woodard and Blanche Greenstein, *Twentieth Century Quilts 1900-1950* (New York: E.P. Dutton, 1988), cover, iv-v.

[11] The Roosevelt donkey quilt is from the collection of Joyce Aufderheide.

[12] The Eisenhower quilt top is from the collection of the author.

[13] The Carter quilt is in the collection of its creator.

Julie Powell and her husband Robin have amassed a collection of political memorabilia including textiles which were featured in Ladies Circle of Patchwork Quilts, *October, 1992. Their collection formed the nucleus of the exhibition, "Patriotism, Politics, and Material Culture," shown at the Lancaster County Historical Society in the summer of 1993. Julie is in her second term on the board of directors of the national American Political Items Collectors. She is also co-owner of Vintage Textiles and Tools, a business selling historic quilts and related material. Julie is a quilter and member of both the Mainline and Heartstring Quilters guilds, a National Quilters Association certified judge, and a member of the American Quilt Study Group.*

Detail of block from 1840 Baltimore album style quilt top, signed in ink by Rebecca Diggs. The block explicitly details the William Henry Harrison Whig party campaign symbols, log cabin, cider barrel, raccoon and latchstring. Courtesy of Smithsonian Institution, Daisy Joseph Accession.

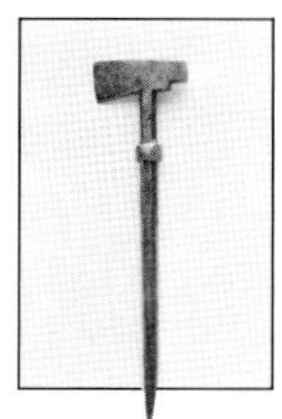

Rags Into Riches

The Collecting of Textiles and Needlework in Southeastern Pennsylvania

Richard and Rosemarie Machmer

We hope to bring you information based on our own experiences with 18th-, 19th-, and even 20th-century area textiles and to see how a general textile collection, such as ours, evolved from an original interest in other antiques. As we look at the textiles collected, we will talk about their functional uses; the sewing techniques used by the innovative seamstresses; textile arts relating to children; color as an interesting phenomenon; the differences in characteristics in the work of the Pennsylvania Germans, of the English-speaking Pennsylvanians such as the Quakers, and of the Moravians.

In the early 1960s, shopping for antique furniture in southeastern Pennsylvania was our primary venture. We were furnishing our home with quality Pennsylvania-German pieces from the immediate area. Of particular interest was the decorated dowry chest. At the same time we were also seeking out decorated cupboards, tables, sets of kitchen chairs, clocks, and slant front desks. Our main sources were local dealers, estate sales, flea markets, and shows. We were often "blind" to other quality items that were available.

We were advised at that time by the octogenarian antiques dealer Sallie Kegerise of Richland, Lebanon County, to buy quality blue and white as well as the rarer brown and white homespun linens. We also inspected piles of quilts, in every pattern and color imaginable, displayed on single beds in the Reinholds, Lancaster County, shop of folk artist/antiques dealer Hattie Brunner and the Alburtis, Lehigh County, home of Corra Lee Weller, who was primarily a show dealer. Although the linen bed ticks and the quilts were fairly priced at under $100 each, it was not until 1968 that quilts and textiles truly caught our fancy. So one can say that we became interested in quilts through our other collecting. Then this process evolved to the love of textiles of all sorts. In the end we purchased everything in the field but a loom. (Actually, we do own and display a tape loom.)

On April 27, 1968, at the Feeg family auction in Myerstown, Lebanon County, we acquired our first full-size quilt. It is a gorgeous one, with the appliqués fastened with fine buttonhole stitching. There is a lot of pink and rose in this design, the kiss of death then and now to decorators and quilt dealers. We feel they are wrong, since there are lovely examples where these colors work well with browns and other reds. The plain borders of the Feeg quilt demonstrate that great borders do not have to be elaborate. Its designs are all different, but of noticeable similarity, a feature of other typical Pennsylvania appliqués of the period. This quilt was first seen hanging from a clothesline strung diagonally across the dining room for all sale-goers to admire. One woman confided to her sister that she would buy this bedcover no matter what the cost and store it in her blanket chest forever. That seemed a pity for such a reigning beauty and so we had to outbid her to the sum of $77.50. We took our prize home, and since we are Pennsylvania Germans to whom cleanliness is second only to Godliness, we laundered it in our automatic washer and hung it on the line to dry. Many years later we learned from museum textile experts that on that day we had committed the most deadly of "quilt sins," but the result was fine, an example of beginner's luck.

Often single or groups of quilt patches were also available for sale. Quilting templates, too, were found repeatedly in cardboard form but were sometimes seen in tin. The Christ family of Strausstown, Berks County, was rather fortunate, since an ancestor, Samuel T. Christ (1876-1952), was a tinsmith who took the time to make their quilt patterns from zinc. The contours of these patterns show that a single person designed all of them. One also re-

Matching full-sized quilt of solid-colored and print cottons with muslin back and applied muslin binding, 69" × 83¼", and cradle quilt, 38¼" × 37¼", with applied print binding and print back, both 5-6 stitches per inch. Collection of Richard and Rosemarie Machmer.

Feeg quilt of solid-colored and print cottons in reverse appliqué and 1-4 layers of appliqué with buttonhole embroidery in various colored thread on appliqués' edge, 85¼" × 88". Muslin back with applied muslin binding and 6 stitches per inch. Collection of Richard and Rosemarie Machmer.

alizes that the women did not merely take out their scissors and materials and put them together. They planned ahead.

In the spring of 1970, we were amazed when in Fleetwood, Berks County, a small row home produced a cache of 14 matched pairs of very varied patchwork quilts. There were several variations of log cabin, an Irish Chain, a Drunkard's Path, a Tumbling Block, and a Nine Patch. At this sale two other couples and we acquired 13 pairs at prices under $55 each. The 14th pair was broken up by another bidder and we took home only one half of a pair. Later we photographed the quilts and the lucky bidders under the oak trees in our yard: Sue and Dave Cunningham of Denver, Lancaster County; Linda and Dick Levengood of Reading, Berks County[1]; and Rosemarie and Dick Machmer of Hamburg, Berks County. Incredibly, three weeks later, in the same town, another row home provided nine marvelous appliquéd charmers.

This was the period which heralded the great quilt explosion, driven somewhat by the popularity of the Shupp's Grove flea market in Adamstown, Lancaster County. Two New Yorkers, Tony Ellis and Bill Gallick, were the first active quilt buyers in this locale, followed by our long-time friend, Jolie Kelter.[2] It was not long before we saw Kate and Joel Kopp, and Tom Woodard and Blanche Greenstein in pursuit of quilts.[3] Each of the above had several contacts in the vicinity. Almost anyone with $1,000 capital could become a quilt dealer.[4]

For the next eight years, the New York dealers virtually dominated the market, at least doubling in their city shops the prices paid locally. There was continued upward spiral in prices due to demand and competition, not only among the pickers, but also among the top New York City dealers. Owing to the heavy supply of quality quilts, the low end of the line often was not as readily marketable in the city.

It was not until the mid-1970s that Michigan's Sandra Mitchell became active here also; and in 1976 Philadelphians Morris and Amy Finkel followed suit.[5]

The only time we ever questioned each other's judgment occurred in a home in West Chester, Chester County, when we considered the purchase of an 1830 Moravian wedding quilt for $1,900 — a prohibitive price for 1970. The quilter had used a combination of sewing techniques — both crewel embroidery and pieced patchwork. We took a day to consider whether we wanted to buy it, only to have it stored in a chest, since it was too costly to be displayed on a bed that was in use. We finally decided to purchase the quilt, only to swap-sell it a short time later. That was one of several that got away.[6]

As we recently sorted through and reminisced about our acquisitions, we came to a beautiful pair of appliqués in bright "Dutchy" colors, discovered in Oley, Berks County, in 1974 for the then unheard of price of $540. We also recalled how in 1976 we returned to Myerstown, the site of our initial success in 1968, and purchased a handsome red and yellow eagle appliqué for $125. The following year in downtown Easton, Northampton County, we came upon an early finely patched full-size quilt with a matching crib quilt — an unusual find.

Although we were accumulating a sizable group of quilts during this time period (1968-1978), it was not until the spring of 1980 that we secured an early multi-colored star with a pair of matching quilted pillow covers. In 1982, at an ever escalating price of $1,525, we finally added a Schoolhouse quilt to our supply. In fact, by this time, there were more and more dealers and collectors coming into southeastern Pennsylvania. This naturally drove prices upward. The top of the line and rarest quilts were avidly sought at prices previously unknown in the market.

Shupp's Grove still exists, but it has fierce competitors in the immediate vicinity, namely Renninger's Antique Market and Black Angus. On the weekends the astute must check out all three plus the numerous smaller outlets and co-ops.

Machmers, Levengoods, and Cunninghams on the day of the Fleetwood sale.

One of the stranger circumstances surrounding an addition to the collection occurred when an antiques dealer telephoned, saying that he had heard that we were collecting Indian artifacts, and he wondered if we would be interested in an Indian quilt. Much to our pleasure, it turned out to be appliquéd with four huge Indians in red on a white background, holding bows and arrows. One wonders if it was inspired by a love for the American Indian culture or by the weathervane on top of a neighboring barn.

Amish quilts in our immediate territory are very scarce, since few families of this sect settled in Berks County. However, at Jim Burk's York Antiques Show in 1978, we added an Ohio Amish quilt with a black background to our collection. This was augmented that same year by a Pennsylvania Amish with a rust background as a Christmas gift from our son Chris. Today we are delighted that these came our way.

Since collectors have a tendency to upgrade, through the years we were fortunate in having a ready market for any excess quilts at the Kutztown Folk Festival in Berks County. But in the mid-1980s, their policy changed, and they sold only new quilts. Without that outlet, we procured fewer and fewer quilts and became more and more selective.

We were also interested in what were commonly called "crib" quilts. This is perhaps a misnomer, since most of these are only three feet square and were used on antique cherry and walnut cradles, not on cribs. Many of

Indian quilt of solid-colored cottons, 96" × 90", with muslin back, front to back as edge treatment, and 7-9 stitches per inch. Collection of Richard and Rosemarie Machmer.

those we collected had designs not unlike our full-sized quilts: stars, log cabins, Nine Patch, and Irish Chain, to name a few. Cradle quilts are usually one-fourth the size of a large one. Some of them come in rare patterns, such as the Delectable Mountains and a wool challis log cabin.[7]

One of our cradle quilts — a star — contains all the classic forms we envision in a great quilt: corner blocks, good borders, a variety of compatible materials, multiple patterns, good sawtooth bordering, and heightened intensity seen on the five central blocks. Although cradle quilts are not rare, we feel they are probably found in a ratio of one to every 200 full-sized quilts. They may, therefore, be more expensive than the larger ones.

We rotate our large quilts by changing them on our beds monthly. This allows airing and modification in the folding. Our storage chests and shelves are lined with white cotton sheeting to eliminate any contact with wood. We also hang a cradle quilt in the hallway, where it receives no direct sun light. Underfoot are colorful rugs — some fashioned from small diamond-shaped patches of cotton fastened to a firm backing. We also find hooked rugs worked from strips of scrap wool. The thrifty women who worked them did not want to waste anything. Much more common are the massive braided rugs, in sizes as large as 15' x 20', skillfully blended in a wide range of colors and usually assembled from salvage — or good parts of previously worn clothing. Since quilts were generally kept in blanket chests, often when they came out at sale, they were as bright and cheerful in color as when they were assembled. Today when we use them as bedcovers or wall-hangings, these hues may fade from the ultraviolet rays of the sun.

Another segment of our collecting is the bolster covers and the pillow covers — often found in matching pairs. A bolster cover was used to encase the bed-wide double pillow found extensively in Pennsylvania German areas[8], especially Berks County. Pairs of matching single pillow covers are often found in the Oley Valley of this county. They were used when the family had company or "just for nice." They were never used day to day by family members. The colors are often similar to those painted on fraktur certificates, including yellows, reds, greens, and blues. Sometimes they are embroidered in counted cross stitch with the owners' initials and have needlework edges, a refinement and a delicacy.[9]

While putting together our quilt collection, we acquired other varieties of needlework. In the past, aging grandmothers usually spent their waning years in the homes of their sons and daughters. Some of their spare hours were spent sewing certain rare, splendid needlework objects, which, for want of a better name, we call "Granny Balls."[10] They were probably made for a favorite grandchild as a plaything, perhaps a ball to be rolled across the floor. These vary in size and color, as well as in construction method: crocheted, wrapped, or patchwork. In many cases, they contain a rattle to delight the child further.

Before modern times there were few stores selling finished clothing, dolls, and toys. These were all products of the home and are still available at auctions or shops in diverse degrees of preservation or wear. In these items, leftover fabrics were combined to make interesting combinations or make-dos. Here sewing arts are brought to the service of children. The toys, due to their scarcity, were far more cherished and cared for than the myriad of plastic ones available to the children of today.

Doll quilts have also become quite collectible, and although often machine sewn, are even scarcer than crib quilts. Finding a hand-done doll quilt with good borders and pattern is no easy task.

Sewing pockets, the catchall for women's thread, scissors, and needles, are also to be found. They are approximately 8" w. x 12" l., with a single slit running halfway down the center for access. The pockets at times are in pairs and were fastened around a women's waists with handmade tapes. They appear in both patchwork and crewel-embroidered linen and in shapes that can be practical and forthright, or elegant. The practical shapes are probably Pennsylvania-German; the elegant ones, either Pennsylvania-English, such as Quaker, or Moravian. We must remember that the Quakers and the Moravians more than likely were better educated.

There is also a great variety of needle cases, some flame-stitch and others of early cotton materials and initialed. They roll up into a cylindrical shape when not in use. It is interesting that most of the latter type are in dark colors; subtle brown is predominant. This may be to eliminate soiling from the owners' handling.

For both ladies and gentlemen, we have located flame-stitched, cross-stitched, silk embroidery, and Queens' stitch pocketbooks, at times embellished with silver clasps. One of ours is marked by the Philadelphia silversmith, Joseph Richardson (1711-1784), on the back of the clasp. Again this refinement suggests they were made by the Pennsylvania English or by the Moravians.

In a young lady's education, there was little more important than learning her stitches by working a sampler. Samplers were often made at an early age, depicting regional symbols and including the makers' names and ages. The embroidery on samplers and on show towels is traditionally in blue and red. The embroidery colors have generally lost their strength due to the sun, since they were often hung on the walls.

We purchased our first sampler from Hattie Brunner's shop. It was followed by two which came from the Merkey estate in Strausstown, Berks County. They were a simple sampler in blue and white and another in red and white retaining the original threaded needle used to work it.

Our most important sampler depicts a spinning monkey and was embroidered in the Oley Valley, Berks County.[11] Later the girl graduated to finer workmanship, such as our Moravian silk embroidery of flowers, or our Philadelphia needlework picture on silk with diverse forms of stitchery forming a pleasant friendship scene similar to the memorials to departed loved ones, which are far more common than this scene. The finely detailed faces of a woman and child on the Philadelphia piece are finished in watercolor on paper.

There are also pin cushions, which come in all shapes and sizes: stars, circles, rectangles, and balls. Many were used by women working at the quilting frame. We have found five of these made of crewel-embroidered silk or wool at household sales in the Oley Valley, Berks County. In the Chester County area, we have discovered similar examples with silver bands signed with the owners' names or initials and dated in the late 18th or early 19th century.

John Weber doll cradle, 8¼" l. × 5" h., with quilt of print cottons 4½" sq., machine stitched. Collection of Richard and Rosemarie Machmer.

Wooden sewing boxes and rye-coil, oak-splint, or rod baskets were all used for storing sewing materials. Many are found with attached pin cushions as well as spool holders that keep the thread in an orderly manner and make it easy to pull off.

One of the rarities in sewing artifacts is the iron buttonhole cutter, seam ripper, or thread pick. They can be found from time to time in southeastern Pennsylvania. Here one encounters some of the finest skills of the whitesmith, a worker in highly filed iron or steel. These small hand tools were probably made for seamstresses and tailors. The width of the cutter blade determined the size of the buttonhole.

In these years, we also put aside quality examples of homespun linens and woven coverlets from the looms of the many 19th-century weavers from this region. Homespun linen was used in a wide range of subtle colors and patterns. In an early 19th-century ledger from the village of Drehersville, (now in Schuylkill

Tin patterns by Samuel Christ, 2-14" h. Collection of Richard and Rosemarie Machmer.

County, but then in Berks), Daniel Bensinger, a notary public and one of the founders of Schuylkill County, noted the payment of 14 cents per yard for the weaving of blue and white homespun on his looms.

In 1980, we enhanced our collection of linens by purchasing from Mrs. Helen Janssen Wetzel's collection, which included 35 different patterns of colored bed ticks and five examples of patterned white linen.[12] She also sold two bolts of white homespun, 50 yards in length, as well as a three-colored table cover.

The blue and white linens were indigo-dyed with imported materials. The brown and white, on the other hand, used local walnut shell dye, which made the linens less expensive. Therefore, the thrifty Pennsylvania Germans used the brown and white, while the blue and white were often stored in chests. Today the monetary value has logically reversed itself. The combination of brown, blue, and white is the ultimate in Pennsylvania homespun.

Also at the Wetzel auction there were more than 100 show towels, an item which now has seemingly disappeared from the marketplace. The decorated show towel usually hung on pegs on a door to cover the family's simple hand towel of homespun. One of our show towels depicts the unique form of a tavern with its stag sign, all in brown counted cross stitch. The towels are often edged, top and bottom, with patterned drawn work. This is ornamental openwork made by pulling threads of fabric and forming, by needlework, various patterns with the remaining threads.[13]

Thus have the Pennsylvania Germans turned "Rags into Riches." Perhaps with patience and time you can do the same.

End Notes

[1]The Cunninghams were one of the earliest active quilt dealers with tie-ins to the New York City trade. They also collected and sold Pennsylvania cookie cutters as well as a general run of local antiques including furniture. The Levengoods were mainly collectors who did an occasional flea market with a general line of area antiques.

[2]Jolie Kelter later established a business with Michael Malcé on Bleecker Street, Greenwich Village, New York City. They expanded from quilts into American Indian artifacts, folk art carvings, and varied collectibles.

[3]Kate and Joel Kopp also began as dealers in quilts in New York City. They rapidly expanded into quality folk art: paintings. carvings, hooked rugs, and pottery as well as American Indian accessories. Greenstein and Woodard, also New Yorkers, concentrated mainly on quilts and other textiles, but later on dealt in decorated furniture and garden ornaments.

[4]In the 1960s period, all of these dealers were buying mostly patch-work quilts. Each one of them had a number of pickers in the various source areas. Only on rare occasions did they personally compete at the local public sales. Through the years they were purchasing whatever types market popularity dictated. Often E. P. Dutton's annual quilt engagement calendars, published in New York, pictured a heavy percentage of quilts from the New York shops, perhaps serving as an arbiter of popular taste. The dealers gave the calendars as gifts to their customers as well as to their pickers.

[5]Sandra Mitchell bought a very wide range of quilts — both in pattern type and cost — often bringing midwestern quilts into our area for sale at the twice annual York Antiques Show in York County. She has also offered Pennsylvania quilts for sale at those shows. She has remained active in the market and presently owns the Midwest Quilt exchange in Columbus, Ohio. She has always sold quality American Indian artifacts.

Morris Finkel, as well as his father, Judith, had operated separate antiques shops in Philadelphia. In the mid-1970s Amy Finkel joined her father, Morris, adding a quilt gallery upstairs to his furniture and art department, as well as the name "and Daughter" to his business.

[6]See fig. 107 in *The Pennsylvania Germans/A Celebration of Their Arts*, Philadelphia: Philadelphia Art Museum, 1982 and fig. 3 in Patricia T. Herr's "What Distinguishes a Pennsylvania Quilt?" *In the Heart of Pennsylvania/Symposium Papers,* Lewisburg, PA: Oral Traditions Project, 1986, 31.

[7]See Fox, Sandi, *Small Endearments* (New York: Charles Scribner's Sons, 1980; Johnson, Bruce, *A Child's Comfort*(New York: Museum of American Folk Art, 1977); and Woodard, Thomas and Blanche Greenstein, *Crib Quilts,* (New York: E. P. Dutton, 1981).

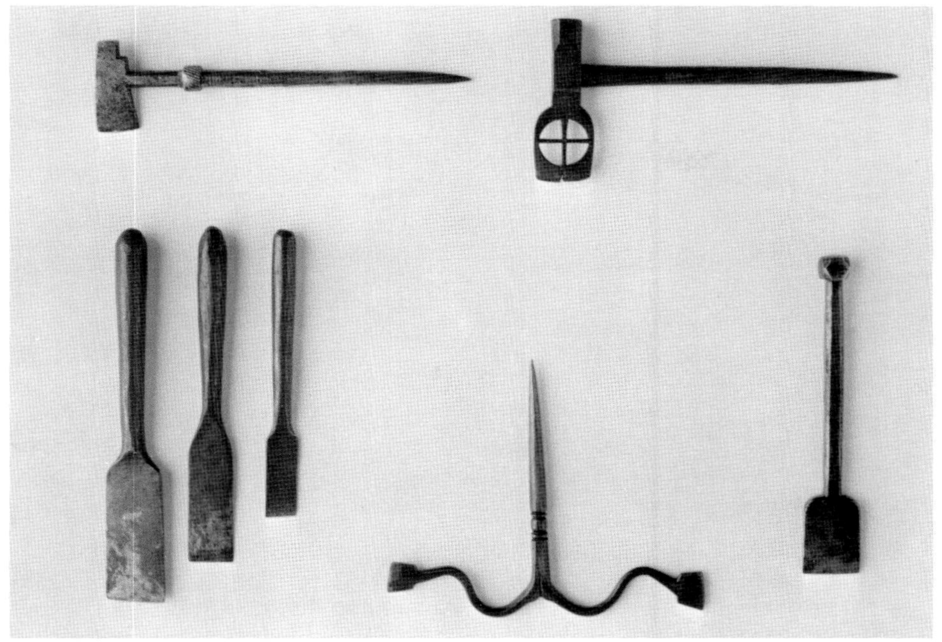

Forged button holers and seam rippers or thread pickers:
3¼-5⅛"h. Collection of Richard and Rosemarie Machmer.

[8]See Keyser, Alan G. "Beds, Bedding, Bedsteads ,and Sleep," *Quarterly of the Pennsylvania German Society, Der Reggeboge* (The Rainbow),12:4,1-16, October 1978, Breinigsville, PA and reprinted in *Pieced By Mother/Synposium Papers*, Lewisburg, PA: Oral Traditions Project, 1988, 23-34

[9]See Tandy Hersh, "The Evolution of the Pennsylvania-German Pillowcase," *Bits and Pieces/Textile Traditions*, Lewisburg, PA: Oral Traditions Project, 1991, 38-47.

[10]See cover of *Bits and Pieces*.

[11]See Hersh, Tandy and Charles Hersh, *Samplers of the Pennsylvania Germans*, Birdsboro, PA: Pennsylvania German Society, 1991, p. 171, figs. 4-60.

[12]Wetzel, Helen Janssen, sale catalog. October 5, 1980, Sotheby's New York, held at Tulpehocken Farms, Spring Township , PA.

[13]See Gehret, Ellen J., *This is the Way I Pass My Time*, Kutztown, PA: The Pennsylvania German Society, 1985.

Richard and Rosemarie Machmer are collectors who were featured in "Berks County Collections," the Magazine Antiques, *October 1990. It noted that "Over the past two decades they have constantly evaluated and upgraded the metals, textiles, fraktur, furniture, carving, and pottery in their collection. Thus it is hardly surprising that many of their objects have been included in important exhibitions and published as prime examples of the Pennsylvania-German tradition." These shows have been at the Museum of American Folk Art, the Los Angeles County Museum of Art, the Heritage Center of Lancaster County, the Reading Art Museum, the Historical Society of Berks County, the Allentown Art Museum, and the Philadelphia Museum of Art among others. They researched and wrote* Just for Nice/Carving and Whittling Magic of Southeastern Pennsylvania *(1991) as well as curated the accompanying exhibit at the Historical Society of Berks County.*

All In and All Done?

The Pennsylvania Vendue

Alan G. Keyser

While the men watched the farm tools sold, the women waited for the household goods to follow. Visiting among the crowd was natural and the auctioneer would have to silence the crowd from time to time. Here, nearly fifty wait on the porch for the auctioneer to get to the doughtray, washing machine, wash tubs, window shades, rag carpet, and other household items. Winslow Fegley photograph. Courtesy of the Schwenkfelder Museum and Library, Pennsburg, Pennsylvania.

John Updike commenting on his mother's passing said, "Most of a person's world flies apart when they die."[1] This dispersal was promoted in times past by the age-old institution of the vendue, now called an auction or public sale. The word vendue, pronounced by the Pennsylvania Dutch in English as "van'doo," comes from French, while the institution seems to have had its origin in the British Isles.

The earliest documents in Pennsylvania concerning the vendue are to be found in the archives of the offices of the Register of Wills in the three oldest counties — Bucks, Chester, and Philadelphia. Here filed with the person's original will, the estate inventory, and all the accounting records necessary to settle an estate, one may also find a copy of the vendue record or bill.

Although death was one reason for holding a public sale, it was not the only reason. Some people held auctions when they retired from farming in preparation for a move to smaller quarters in a village or town. Some held them for the same reason people now hold yard or garage sales — too much unwanted stuff.

Real estate auctions were used to sell undeveloped woodland, mills, farms, houses, as well as properties seized by the sheriff, and various commercial properties. Many real estate vendues were held at a tavern in the locale rather than at the property just so the owner could treat the prospective buyers to the proper levels of liquid refreshment, and thereby realize a higher price for the property. A happy buyer is a generous spender.

By the 19th century the occupations of cattle dealer and horse trader had developed to the extent that livestock sales became popular. Here cattle or horses imported from the West were auctioned off at a profit, and farmers got the chance to improve their herds by the introduction of new blood lines. Sheep, turkeys, geese, and pigs were also sold at auction. By the 20th century two more types of sales were created and now draw a large following — the antiques auction and the quilt auction.

Quilt auctions are held, for the most part, as fund raisers for not-for-profit institutions and church programs. Various Mennonite churches have taken up making and auctioning quilts as an acceptable method of raising money while still shunning carnivals and raffles used by some churches for the same purpose. At these auctions high levels of competition develop, and as a result quilts bring far higher prices than would be realized on the open market. In the early period, quilts were not part of the Pennsylvania-German household and so were not sold. The earliest reference found so far is the estate sale of weaver Henry Wismer of Bedminster Township, Bucks County. On November 4, 1813 the heirs sold "a Bed quilt" for 8 shillings.[2]

The advent of the internal combustion engine and the automobile allowed antiques collectors from nearby cities easy access to the countryside and its sales. One broadside from Richlandtown, Bucks County, begins with large numbers and says "1, 2 & 3 Generation old Household Outfit Saturday August 3, '18," and goes on to tell everyone that "everything put up will be sold. Members of the immediate family will not bid on anything put up for sale, and only a few things have been reserved for keepsakes."

High prices cannot be hoped for at an auction that few attend. For this reason, even from the early part of the 18th century, vendues were widely advertised in newspapers and on broadsides. Both types of advertisements yield valuable information about auctions in years past. Even the earliest ones were not too different from the newspaper ads and the auction hand-outs of today. They gave the date, time and location of the sale as well as a description of the real estate, and other items to be sold. Because of the cultural mix, many

The sequence of a farm sale remains essentially unchanged from the time Winslow Fegley took his series of photographs in the early 1900s. The auctioneer stands above the crowd so they and he can see each other easily. He maintained a steady patter of dialect asides and tried to encourage spirited bidding in order to get the highest pieces possible. Success depended on his rapport and control of the crowd which was exclusively male when he was selling the farm tools, equipment, and livestock. Courtesy of the Schwenkfelder Museum and Library.

of the broadsides in the 18th century were bilingual. Later, as the Germans displaced those of British Isles heritage, the language of the broadside became German and even later all English.

Both the broadsides and the newspaper ads frequently contained a woodcut of some sort, as an eye catcher. But at times the woodcut had little to do with reality. In the 1860s the standard cut of a two-story brick house was used in one instance to announce the sale of a frame railroad station warehouse and on another broadside the same cut was used to illustrate a one-story log house. One sale bill advertises "a good stone house" and uses a large woodcut of a forest tree.

General farm sales used various small cuts at the beginning of the notice. A single issue of the Sumneytown "Bauern Freund" in 1845 used these to illustrate various auction ads: a pig, two different renderings of a horse and man, a cow with and without a woman milking, a sheep, and an auction scene complete with auctioneer and crowd.

By studying the broadsides and newspaper ads a clearer picture emerges and shows that vendues were held nearly any time of the year except during haymaking and harvest. But the most popular season was in late winter, a time when farmers were less pressed by the annual routine. Since it was most convenient to move to a new farm before the spring planting was begun, by far the greatest percentage of real estate transactions were made just prior to or on April 1. As a result April 1 was the traditional moving day. Normally the season from mid-April to the last week in August was sale free. It was also wedding-free except for the occasional emergency.

Apparently starting time of a vendue depended on the quantity of items to be sold, but 1 o'clock in the afternoon was certainly the most popular. A few began at 9 and 10 am, but these were the exceptions.

One of the things about vendues that seems to have changed little is the order in which the items are sold. On the 18th-century sale bills the first items listed were of the same type as are sold today in Pennsylvania — things of low value displayed on the wagon at the barn. In the early days the scrap iron was sold first, next the hand tools of low value. The litany proceeded to the more valuable farm equipment, wagons, plows and harrows, and further to the livestock and field crops. From there it went to the household goods, the furniture, then the cooking equipment, and finally the linens and bedding. The broadside mentioned above from Richlandtown makes the statement that the "sale will start with the workshop tools and things around the bar. Quilts, spreads, feather ticks and other things in that line will be sold last of all." This order has been kept for more than 200 years.

Of the number of people needed to operate an auction smoothly, only the vendue crier, now called an auctioneer, and the clerk were paid in the early days. The runners were, and in many cases still are, unpaid. Today the auctioneer is paid a percentage of the gross proceeds of the auction. Formerly he was paid a daily wage as if he had helped cut grain in the harvest field. This was a higher wage than average for day laborers but was by no means the large sum collected today. In the tax list for Upper Hanover Township, Montgomery County, Pennsylvania, one person was listed as a vendue crier and fiddler during the 1790s. This fellow made certain that he had several sources of income, for crying sales was really not a reliable way to earn a living.[5]

At the end of the last century and the beginning of this one a number people filled the position of penny man. These men went to sales to buy the items that no one else wanted for the grand price of one cent each. It is related that George and Henry Landis, the founders of the Landis Valley Museum, were often penny men and by this means emassed the large museum collection that they left to the Commonwealth of Pennsylvania. Other penny men were not quite as shrewd in their purchases, and when they went on to their reward, only a huge pile of trash and unsalable goods remained.

Rural inhabitants had few chances to gather and as a result took the slightest opportunity to socialize. Because of this, the Sunday morning church service or meeting held a greater significance than it does now. If the funeral became a bright spot on the social calendar, it is no wonder the occasional public sale held even higher social status. Travel was limited in the time before the automobile and people often spent entire lives within several miles of their birth place.

Some people really knew how to throw a vendue. As at funerals it was a generally accepted practice to serve a full course sit-down meal.[3] And during the auction alcoholic beverages were available either at a low cost or free. One auctioneer at the turn of the century commented that "large public sales in Berks county . . . resemble a small fair. Besides big dinners and free cider, some farmers in selling out employ a brass band and have music before the sale begins."

In the last century venders of all sorts came to any kind of public gathering, ranging from a church organ dedication to the public sale. They set up their stands and hawked lebcakes, candy, nuts, and the famous oyster stews. Although some people reported that each oyster stew had "only one or two weasand [sic] oysters drowned in it," and that the broth was nearly as blue as the sky, others eagerly anticipated the great flavor and warming effect.

Young children also looked forward to going to a sale because most fathers gave their children a small amount of money to buy candy. One woman told of the first vendue she and her three sisters attended. She related, "father gave me a nickel for the four of us to spend on candy. We bought one cent's worth of candy for each of us, and we saved a penny."[4] This was their first lesson in the legendary Pennsylvania-Dutch thrift.

Besides the chance to visit with neighbors and see people they did not see regularly, the older boys played corner ball while the auction was going on[5]. This game is a combination of catch, tag, and king of the mountain. It is played by two teams of four on the manure pile in the barnyard. First the manure pile is covered with fresh straw. Then one team of four takes each of the four corners, while the other four stand on the top of the manure pile. The corner team throws a homemade leather covered cotton string ball to each member of their team. Each person must catch the ball. The last one then throws it at the group standing on the pile trying to hit someone. All try to dodge the ball with all kinds of contortions. Once hit that person is retired until all are hit. When all the players in the middle of the square were retired, they became corner men, and the corner men became middle men. Scoring was kept of the number of winning innings and the losers had to buy the winners oyster stew. The ball was owned by one of the hucksters and was a means of selling a few more oyster stews.

Fresh oyster stew was often served at sales where today corn soup or ham and beans is common. Winslow Fegley photograph. Courtesy of the Schwenkfelder Library.

Not all vendue entertainment was as innocent as corner ball. Most communities had bullies who, like the hucksters, followed the public events circuit to all the battalion days, fair days, election days, and public sales.[6] Every bully had his following. Each tried to show his abilities at fighting. They did not follow the Marquis of Queensbury rules. Anything went. Sometimes the encounters were boxing matches, sometimes a good hair pulling, and at other times they were brutal engagements where gouging and general mayhem took place. However, they seldom resulted in criminal prosecution or law suits. They were forerunners of the modern boxing and wrestling matches and provided yet another kind of entertainment at the public vendue.

Vendue List of the Goods and Chattels of Joseph Schnee late of Freeburg, Union County Deceased, held by Philip Shnee and Jacob German Administrator of the said Dec^d On the 26 day of November AD 1838

Philip Schnee	Stove pipe &c	"	9
George German	3 Corn Hoes	"	18
Philip Schnee	4 Straw Covers or lids	"	11
Jacob Wilmer J. Son	Shovel &c	"	11
Jacob German	Lot of Iron	"	6
Philip Schnee	Basket with Sundries	"	8
Widow Schnee	A Fork & Spade	"	25
George Snyder	" Hand Saw	"	61
Jacob Steffy	2 Scythes	"	20
Simon Hezold	2 D^o	"	15
Frederick Stahl	A Chain	"	39
William Schnee	" Hatchet & Drawing knife	"	31
Jacob German	" Grubing Hoe	"	65
Simon Strawser	" Hayfork & Straw knife	"	24
David Moyer	" Grubing Hoe	1	02
Jacob Menges	" Mason Hammer	"	65
Jacob Weller	" Wooden Sledge	"	16
Isaac Weller	" Water Bucket	"	37½
Henry Boyer	" Rake Whip	"	16
John Bickel	" Pump & Anvil	"	28
Widow Schnee	3 Hogs	1	50
Philip Schnee	2 D^o	1	25
George Glass Junr	1 D^o	3	00
Solomon Straub	1 Sheep	1	56
George Snyder	1 D^o	1	75
D^o D^o	1 D^o	1	60
D^o D^o	1 D^o	1	75
John C Moyer	1 Plough	6	25
Jacob Reichenbach	1 D^o	5	50
Eli Hains	1 Double tree	"	90
Henry Rine	1 Shovel Plow	"	50
William Hughs	1 Sled	1	00
George Glass	1 Slay	3	10
John German	1 pair Runners	"	6
William Hughs	A Lot of Ba[illegible]	"	80
Henry Straub	" Lot of Bl[illegible]	1	00

Vendue listing for weaver Joseph Schnee of Freeburg, Union County, Pennsylvania taken written on November 26, 1838. Courtesy of the Archives, Union County Courthouse, Lewisburg, Pennsylvania.

The auctioneer, too, did his part in entertaining the crowd. Sale after sale, year after year, the auctioneer cracked the same time-worn jokes and one liners. And just as predictably the crowd, duty bound, laughed at the old well-rehearsed humor.

Money was scarce on a farm in the era before banks became prevalent. So each sale holder gave the conditions under which credit would be granted. To quote one set of conditions from the Boyertown, Pennsylvania area: "Conditions of this Present Public Sale helt this 14th Day of March 1863 at the resitance of the Subscribers as follows to wit[:] The Heighest and besd bidder to be the purchaser[.] All persons bying to anney Sums not exceeding Two Dollers to pay cash[,] and all Sums Suceeding and over to have a Cratit of six month with sufishent Security if required by the subscriber[.] No cash goods to be remuved untill paid[.] Anney person bying at this present sale who can not comply with the fore going Condition shall give up the goods before the sale is over[.] So Saith Tobias Koch" Not all sellers granted credit. One storekeeper stated in his sale ad that "because the undersigned is moving out of the area, everything will be sold without credit."

At times the seller of a property reserved rights to a portion of the crops as did Benjamin Tyson of Skippack and Perkiomen townships, Montgomery County in November of 1832: "All the grain in the Ground is excepted with Privilage to harvest and stack it on the beds where the subscriber usually did stack his grain with privilage to thrash it in the barn."

Both buying and selling at an auction required a high level of expertise. First the prospective buyer sought to conceal any interest in the items really desired. The buyer when bidding tried his best not to let other bidders know that he was bidding at all. He signaled his bids to the auctioneer by one of any number of moves. The auctioneer had to be alert for a bid which consisted of nothing more than the bidder putting his thumb in a certain button hole in his coat. Or perhaps a bid would be made by scratching the left ear or any of a number of almost moves. This way one would not bring undue attention to oneself. All this was done to avoid inciting an unnecessary case of "bidding fever" in an opponent.

The auctioneer, on the other hand, was looking to get the bidding to proceed at a feverish rate. He tried to get people to bid high prices on items that they absolutely would not use. For instance he would seek to induce a vigorous young woman to buy a crutch, lest she should need one some day, and an old woman to buy a cradle for a great-grandchild she did not have. All of these maneuvers belonged to the old vendue.

Through the years many changes have occurred at the auction. Where once Pennsylvania Dutch was the language of the auctioneer and crowd alike, it became a mixture of Pennsylvania Dutch and English. Now English prevails and only rarely does the auctioneer use Pennsylvania Dutch. At the beginning of the last century the whole country changed from pounds, shillings, and pence to dollars and cents. This transition took several decades to complete. The United States began its own coinage in 1792 in the present monetary system but Pennsylvania farmers thought and spent in the old English system consistently until the second decade of the 19th century.

The brass bands have long since disappeared from the sale scene, as have the free drinks and the free dinners. Oyster stew is no longer sold and has been replaced by vegetable soup and in Lancaster County by chicken corn soup. Of course the old prices will never be back either. But on the bright side, auctions are alive and well in Pennsylvania, and are still a great way to spend a day. They are not all in and all done.

End Notes

[1]John Updike, "Safe in the bosom of Ursinus," *Ursinus College Bulletin*, 82:2, (Spring 1991), 10.

[2]Manuscript sale bill of Henry Wismer of Bedminster Township, Bucks County, Pennsylvania. Privately owned.

[3]"The Public Sale Sixty Years Ago," *Pennsylvania Folklife*, 18:4, (Summer 1969), 50.

[4]Interview with Sadie Krauss Kriebel, February 21, 1992.

[5]C. M. Bomberger, "Vendues," *The Pennsylvania Dutchman*, 2, 5, (July 1950), 7.

[6]"Vendue — Dutch Style," *The Pennsylvania Dutchman*, 3:16, (January 15, 1952), 7.

Alan G. Keyser is a student of Pennsylvania folk culture. He has published some of his research in the Pennsylvania German Society's quarterly where "Beds, Bedding, Bedsteads and Sleep" first appeared (then reissued in the Oral Tradition project's Pieced by Mother/Symposium Papers *in 1987). He has also co-authored the book* The Homespun Textile Traditions of the Pennsylvania Germans *(1976) with Ellen J. Gehret and worked with Ellen Gehret and Tandy Hersh on* This is the Way I Pass My Time/A Book About Pennsylvania German Hand Towels *(1985). He has shared his vast knowledge with others including acting as consultant to Winterthur and the Philadelphia Museum of Art when they researched and mounted the Pennsylvania-German tercentenary exhibition in 1983. A member of the Goschenhoppen Historians and curator of their museum in Green Lane, he is usually found boring out logs at their annual Folk Festival.*

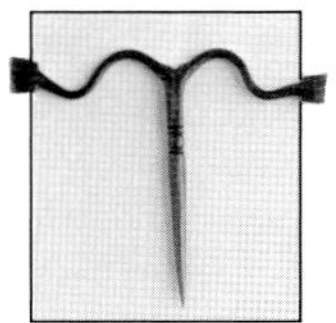

Fabric and the Amish Quilt

Tradition, Sources and Change

Eve Wheatcroft Granick

Nine Patch Variation made of rayon cotton blend in Mifflin County, PA ca. 1920-1930. This material was very popular with Amish women in Mifflin County for both clothing and quilts. It appears in the Mifflin County area somewhat earlier than other communities and was often purchased from the American Viscose Corporation's factory outlet in Lewistown.

Diamond in the Square made of plain weave wool batiste in Lancaster County, PA ca. 1920. This type of fine quality dress wool was used by Lancaster Amish women for both their dresses and for quilts.

In discussing fabric and Amish quilts there are two communities in Pennsylvania that this essay will focus on: the Old Order Amish in Lancaster County and the "Big Valley" Amish located near Belleville, Mifflin County. The particular textiles found in each of these settlements as well as the larger historical events that have influenced the selection and changes in materials used by women in these two communities will be examined.

The Lancaster County community is the oldest, continually occupied community of Old Order Amish in the United States. This is a unique and ever evolving community with a very distinctive tradition in both the textile and folk arts. The quilts and other textiles made in this community are among the most clearly distinctive of all Amish quilts. But before looking at more recent examples of Amish textiles from this community we need to understand about the textiles produced in this settlement prior to the "quilt era" to show that the changes seen in the 20th century also have a parallel in the 19th century.

There are quite a number of documents which describe the types of materials and textile items owned by Amish men and women in the late-18th and early 19th centuries as well as a few rare items made prior to 1840 that have survived. In the years between the 1840-1880s we continue to rely primarily on documents with an increasing number of objects that can be examined as we move toward the 1880s. It is in the years between the 1880s and the 1950s that Amish women became heavily involved in quiltmaking and where we have a large body of textile items to examine and compare.

For the colonial and early 19th-century Amish, as well as other Americans, the production of textiles was a time consuming project — labor intensive and critical to the well-being of the family. The ownership of large quantities of textiles was indicative of wealth and prosperity and inventories taken after death are careful to list both the quantity and types of all textiles found in the home of the deceased.

For example, Abraham Kurtz emigrated to America in 1749 and was the first landowner in Earl Township, Lancaster County. He later moved to Salisbury Township where he died in 1782. He was a minister in the Lower Pequea area. His inventory was taken in 1782 following his death. Christian Beiler who died in 1804 also left textiles for appraisal.

Until the 1820s, the home manufacture of materials was an integral part of both American and Amish farm life. For the Pennsylvania Germans the growing of flax for linen and tow, was central to the yearly work schedule. Inventories list tools for planting and harvesting flax, for transforming it into linen and tow and then finally the finished products are listed by lengths in final inventories and are given high monetary value. Until the 1820s most American families depended heavily on the materials they cultivated and processed themselves. While there was a small variety of manufactured materials available they were expensive and included things like wool broadcloth and cassimere as well as nankeen, corduroy, jersey (a knitted wool), serge , linsey-woolsey, flannel, and muslin.

In the years between the 1820s and the 1840s, the predominance of home-produced goods diminished rapidly as the importance of factory-made textiles increased. In the 1820s-1840s, factory-produced fabrics included such things as cassimere, satinet, and Kentucky jean as well as finer goods such as cashmere, merino and delaine. The inventories of Amish families in this period suggest that the Amish were perhaps more conservative than others and continued to produce some materials at home into the 1850s and early 1860s. Changes were clearly occurring in these years

Abraham Kurtz
Lancaster County
1782

his wearing apparel
25 bags
a great coat
48 lb of hackled hemp
5 spinning wheels
bed, bedcloath and bedsteat
4 blankets and old wagon cloath
old table cloath
bed with bedcloath
bits of linen
60 yds of flax linen
60 yds of hemp linen
26 yds of flax linen
11 yds of drilling
10 yds of bed ticking
ash cloath
195 wt of tow

Christian Beiler
Lancaster County
1804

his wearing apprel
quantity of linen
7 yrds of linen
11 1/2 yds of linen
4 yds of linen
12 yds of tow
7 1/2 yds of flax linen
5 yds of of blane fustian
5 3/4 yds woolen cloth
5 3/4 yds worsted lincy
11 yds lincy
worsted lincy
planket
7 yds of planket
table cloath
bedcase and bedsheet
7 towels
heckled flax
woolen yarn
linen yard
hemp seed
spinning wheel
flax and hemp

however. A number of Amish women interviewed mentioned that their grandmothers who were born in the 1840s and early 1850s had learned about how to produce and dye cloth but they had not continued this skill into adulthood, indicating that the Amish community like the larger American community also saw the benefit of giving this time-consuming task over to industry and manufacturing. Inventories in the 1840s and 1850s list materials such as drilling, muslin, flannel, cassinet and home-made cassinet, linsey, and woolen cloth.

So both inventories and oral histories confirm that Amish families continued to produce some fabrics through the 1840s and 1850s. By the 1860s however, this traditional job was replaced completely by the purchase of materials from local shopkeepers and travelling peddlers. The local dry goods dealer alone offered an extensive variety of imported and domestically produced textiles by the mid-19th century.

In the last half of the 19th century, American life changed in very radical ways. The population of the United States grew at a remarkable rate, thanks in part to the constant influx of immigrants. As the population grew and the migration westward continued, the Indian lands to the west continued to shrink. New technologies, inventions, and the growth of the American industrial base added to the changes in American life. Finally, the Civil War and far-reaching effects saw the emergence of a truly national sense of identity in America. The isolation of small farm communities and very localized economies was gradually replaced by a economic and emotional connection to the larger national scene. While the Amish resisted many aspects of encroaching modernism, the old Pennsylvania-German textile traditions did fade away and were replaced by new traditions, including quiltmaking.

Just as materials changed, so too did the tools used in the household. When the mass marketing of sewing machines began in 1856, it did not take long for Amish women to join in. Here was a piece of technology that was quite acceptable to the Amish community. Even the earliest Amish quilts that date from the 1870s and 1880s are pieced on the treadle sewing machine.

The inventories of Amish families in the last decades of the 19th century reveal the decline and disappearance of home-produced fabrics and the decreased value of textiles in general. As the older generation passed away, spinning wheels and flax hatchels were replaced by sewing machines and quilting frames. From the 1870s onward Amish families list quilts among their possessions with increasing frequency in each decade. The extensive listing of linen and flax material is gone as are the detailed descriptions of yardage of each type of fabric. Clothing and bedding materials no longer head the inventories nor do they have the high monetary value they held in the earlier years of the century.

Mennonites in both the Lancaster and Mifflin county areas, who embraced changes more rapidly show a greater number of quilts in inventories in the 1840s and 1850s. The very earliest examples of quiltmaking that we have found to this point in the Lancaster Amish community date from the 1860s. This change from more Germanic forms of bedding to "English" influences also coincides with the end of home-produced fabrics. Among Lancaster Amish inventories there are only two or three references to quilts in the 1850s and no extant examples until 1869. There is one very early example from Mifflin County dated "1849." This is the earliest known Amish quilt.

The very early examples are whole cloth or plain quilts, fabric of one color quilted together with no pieced design. Another early example of Lancaster quiltmaking, only one step removed from the simplicity of the plain quilt is a Center Square quilt dated "1875."

By the 1880s and 1890s the numbers of quilts listed in inventories as well as the known examples increase sharply (although it is important to remember that in comparison to other types of American quiltmaking the numbers of Amish quilts are quite small).

From the time that Amish women in Lancaster County began to make quilts in any noticeable number the choice of materials used was influenced by the availability of fabrics in the marketplace. Lancaster women from the late-19th century through the 1940s preferred above all else to use a fine dress weight wool for their quilts. Such fabrics as a fine plain weave wool batiste and wool twill cashmere or challis were purchased primarily from three different sources: the local dry goods stores, travelling peddlers, and from mail-order catalogs such as Sears. These fabrics were purchased for clothing and also specifically for use in quiltmaking.

While the women in Lancaster expressed a very strong preference for fine wools, a different picture emerges in Mifflin County. There the more midwestern tradition of using either wool or cotton in early quilts and the heavy preference for cotton, cotton sateen and a cotton rayon fabric, which was locally produced, became the predominant choice of materials for quiltmaking.

Like their cousins in Lancaster, women in Mifflin County obtained their materials from local stores, travelling salesmen, and mail-order businesses. In addition there was an outlet store for the American Viscose Corporation in

Lewistown that was quite popular with Amish women for material. Established in 1921 this factory produced a variety of rayon and rayon mixed materials. Most frequently used by the Big Valley Amish was a soft mixed cotton rayon material with a dull, smooth finish.

In Lancaster, frequently cited local sources for fabric were W.L. Zimmerman and Sam Rubinson in the New Holland area. Zimmerman's was established in 1909 as a general store with a grocery, hardware, and dry goods. Eventually the grocery, hardware, and oil delivery divisions became more important to the business and about a decade ago they stopped carrying dry goods. For nearly 70 years however Zimmerman's store sold piece goods to local Amish women. In an interview with Mr. Zimmerman he noted that the big changes in Lancaster came in the period around World War II and in the post-war years. He mentioned that Amish women would complain a great deal about the poor quality of war-time materials but had little choice. In the post-war period many of the older women really lamented the lack of fine quality wools but gradually the younger generation came into the market and preferred cottons and then polyester fabrics.

Sam Rubinson was the other frequently mentioned local source of fabric in interviews with Amish women. He operated a department store in New Holland that was opened in 1914. Advertisements from the store show the kinds and prices of materials popular with the Amish in the first half of the 20th century.

century in America, the ready-made clothing business was growing steadily. In the Amish communities however, peddlers found ideal customers. Here were women who purchased vast amounts of fabric on a yearly basis. They had large families and made almost all of the family clothing themselves. They bought fabric every year but their needs were limited to specific types of fabric and they were not particularly interested in the latest fashions or a myriad of choices. The network of friends and family in the Amish community meant that introduction to a new household was facilitated and a few peddlers found they could make an entire business of supplying Amish women with materials. Both sides were satisfied; Amish women were consistent and easy to deal with as customers. From the Amish point of view these men offered materials at good prices, often below those sold by local merchants because the peddlers sold what is known as remainders and closeouts, fabrics available from textile jobbers in the cities at a fraction of the cost paid by standard wholesale purchasers.

One of the early peddlers in Lancaster County was a man by the name of Jack Barsky. He was a man with a prodigious memory for names and calculating numbers in his head with accuracy. A few Amish women told stories of Jack Barsky spending several hours with their families adding and subtracting, bargaining over materials all the while chatting about the local news and socializing with the family. There were three other men who also developed a large business in the Pennsylvania and Ohio communities: Nathan and Sam Greenburg and their cousin Isaac Korsch. These three men began as peddlers working door-to-door in the 1920s and 1930s. In the 1940s when their children came into the business they continued the door-to-door sales but also enlarged to include mail order as well. In the years from the turn of the century to the 1960s peddlers and in particular these few men and their families who followed in the business, supplied a great deal of the material that went into Amish quilts.

Peddling was not particularly easy work; it required good bargaining skills, stamina, and a sense of humor. These men genuinely en-

---

Whatever you need in Amish Dress Goods - Amish clothing - Amish hats and shoes. Write to the biggest Amish store — Get samples and our low prices.

Write for samples of

All wool batiste, men's suiting, cottanade pantings, moleskins, corduroys, blue and black denim, blue bell shirting, all wool flannels, all wool crepes, apron gingham, cotton flannels, mohairs, pebble crepes, ticking, shawl goods, cap goods, rayon flat crepes, silk flat crepes, Indianhead linens, muslin, sheeting, half wool crepes, poplins, charmeuse, broadcloth, linings, hemstitched sheets, pillow cases, bolster cases and dust cloth.

Some of the items listed for sale in the advertising of Sam Rubinson's store in New Holland, PA ca. 1925

Travelling salesmen have long been figures in both American history and folklore. Travelling from one rural community to the next with their stock of trade they brought goods for purchase as well as bits of gossip and news from the neighbors and other communities. Before the advent of nationally-run chain stores and standardized advertising, Amish women purchased many things including dry goods from traveling business-men.

The peddlers best remembered in the Amish communities are the ones who came beginning in the early part of this century. The men who happened upon the Amish communities of Lancaster and Mifflin counties recognized a good thing when they saw it. By the turn of the

---

Christian Hertzler
Caernavon Twp
Lancaster County
1842

1 flax heckel
flaxen and tow linen
woolen goods
flax in bundle
spinning wheel and reel

Michael Yoder
Mifflin County
1843

3 yards of cotton flannel
8 yards of drilling
8 yards of ticking
1 1/2 yards of muslin
2 remnants of flannnel
7 yards of blue muslin

David Hartzler
Mifflin County
1844

3 coverlets, 3 haps
7 feather ticks
9 bolsters and 2 pillows
3 spinning wheels
1 large wool wheel and reel
2 blankets and 11 sheets
1 1/2 yards of cassinet
7 1/2 yards of cassinet
2 1/2 yards of flannel
4 1/2 yards of homemade cassinet

Joseph Beiler
Leacock Twp
Lancaster County
1857

10 bedstead and bedding
tablecloths and towels
lots of linen
bedstead and chaff bed
wollen yarn
table linen sheets
feather beds, pillows
lots of linen yarn
chaff bed
wheels, reels, lots of flannel
sattinet

Sam J. GREENBERG Co.

5646 Arlington St. - Philadelphia 31, Pa.

"Plain Goods for Plain People"

We want to advise you to continue listing your children still living at home. We still feel that the larger the family, the more goods you use and the greater a discount you deserve. So we'll continue to give you a 1% discount per child but find that we must limit the discount on pants goods to 10%. A 10% DISCOUNT WILL ALSO BE GIVEN ON ALL GOODS BOUGHT FOR RELIEF.

60-Inch Double Width
GENUINE SILVER MIX
MEN'S SUITING

100% Virgin wool. The kind you've been waiting for for years.

SPECIAL $5.95 YD.

Fast Color DARK GREEN
CRAVANETTE

36-in., Sanforized. This material in a slightly heavier weight and different color makes the best of knockabout suits. As strong and soft and easy to sew as any material around. Regular 98c yd. In 1-10 yards.

SPECIAL 59c YD.

60-Inch 100% Virgin Wool
Black Melton Coating

The softest & finest around. A genuine $5.95 quality sponged and shrunk. Cut from the bolt.

SPECIAL $3.95 YD.

All-Wool NAVY BLUE
Coating Remnants

60-Inch. In 1 to 4 yd. pieces. Some Meltons, some Fleeced Shetlands. Reg. $3.95 and $4.95 values.

SPECIAL $2.95 YD.

36-Inch Fast Color
Cotton Gabardine

From the bolt. In DARK WINE and DARK GREEN. Regular 59c value.

SPECIAL 39c YD.

45-INCH JAPANESE BATISTE FROSTED

One of the most "lumerick" and finest of wrinkle-resistant batistes. In just exactly the most beautiful colors. We've tested out the goods in Lancaster County and we've found that it's highly recommended because it wears so well and gets nicer each time it's washed! In BEAUTIFUL NAVY, OXFORD GREY, LILAC, DARK BROWN, RUST, GRAPE WINE, DARK YELLOW GREEN, DARK BLUE GREEN. This lot was especially made for us. Reg. 79c yard.

SPECIAL 59c YARD

Friends, we have the greatest bargain in crepes we've ever offered. These are in remnants which sell for over $1.00 a yard and are usually too expensive for us to handle in full pieces. They are in 1 to 4 yard pieces, all matchable, and we've put them up into 15 to 20-yard bundles. This is what you get:

1. The most beautiful Amish colors.
2. Each bundle contains 2 colors—3 to 4 suits.
3. You tell us the colors you want and we'll see that you get one of your choices, at least.
4. Let us know what yardage, between 15 and 20 yds. you want.
5. Every Bundle Unconditionally Guaranteed!
6. THE PRICE? A SUPER

SPECIAL 49c YARD!

Your choice of the best in pants goods:

Regular width, full bolts.
9-OZ.
Deepest Blue Denim

SPECIAL 49c YARD

10-Oz. DEEPEST BLUE
DENIM

Regular width, full bolts.

SPECIAL 54c YD.

36-Inch, 12-Oz. Black Stripe
Herringbone Weave COTTONADE

Full bolts.

SPECIAL 79c YARD

45-Inch Black Granitco
MELROSE CREPE

Reg. 79c yard.

SPECIAL 59c YARD

36-Inch, 12-Oz.
Pepperrill Rayon Mixed Whipcord

From full bolts. DARK OXFORD GREY, BEAUTIFUL BLUE.

SPECIAL 69c YARD

36-INCH
8-Oz. GREY DENIM

3 to 20 yard pieces.

SPECIAL 49c YD.

(We also have this in 1 to 3 yd. pieces)

SPECIAL 10 YDS. 43c YD.
SPECIAL 20 YDS. 39c YD.

All the above pantings are Sanforized.

MOSS CREPE

BLACK, DARK BROWN. Reg. 79c yard.

40 - 42-INCH PREMIER PEBBLE CREPE

Can be either dry cleaned or hand washed. Although the regular price is 79c yard, you bought loads of it from us last year at the special price of 59c yd. We were fortunate enough to get another supply at the same price! In beautiful shades of GLEAMING BLACK, BEAUTIFUL NAVY, BEAUTIFUL DARK BROWN, MEDIUM DARK GREY, EMERALD GREEN.

SPECIAL 59c YD.

35-Inch Fast Color
SPORT DENIM

You're missing a great bargain if you pass this up. Excellent for any everyday use. From the bolt. WINE, MED. BLUE, DK. BROWN, DK. TAN, RUST. Reg. 39c Yd.

SPECIAL 29c YARD

60-Inch Double Width
CRAVANETTE

50% wool, 50% Rayon. You have always liked this so well for your best "go to town" suits because it wears and cleans so good. In NAVY BLUE, BEAUTIFUL DEEPEST BLACK.

SPECIAL $1.99 YD.
10 YARDS $17.50

36-Inch Sanforized
Sunbeam Broadcloth

The finest! SNOW WHITE, DK. GREEN, DK. BROWN. Reg. 59c Yard.

SPECIAL 49c YARD

36-Inch, Sanforized
Indianhead Linene

From the bolt in beautiful shades of ROYAL BLUE, NAVY. Reg. 79c Yard.

SPECIAL 59c YARD

38-Inch, 12-Oz.
BLUE DENIM

From bolt. Sanforized. Your choice of plain back or white back.

SPECIAL 59c YARD

36-Inch Excellent Quality
DRESS CHAMBRAY

In full bolts. The kind you've bought loads of from us in the past at the same old low price. For good knockabout dresses, shirts, quilting, etc. In DARK GREEN, MEDIUM GREY.

SPECIAL 39c YARD

TWO YARD WIDE
WHITE SHEETING

Heavy quality muslin. Fr[illegible] bolt.

SPECIAL 79c YARD

56-Inch, 100% Virgin Wo[illegible]
BLACK SHAWLING

Also good for children's mantles.

SPECIAL $1.39 YARD

The lowest price in eve[illegible] day shirting in years!

36-Inch, 320 Weight
Heavy Covert Shirting

BLACK & WHITE. Reg. [illegible] Yard.

SPECIAL 39c YARD

36-Inch Pepperrill
Heavy Chambray

The DARK BLUE you've always liked so well. Re[illegible] 49c yard. Both Sanforized.

SPECIAL 39c YARD

We're listing only the[illegible] serges because we got the[illegible] at a very special price an[illegible] we think they're just wh[illegible] you'll want.

60-Inch Double Width
Stillwater Serge

"Gold Medal" quality. I[illegible] the exact shade of DAR[illegible] OXFORD GREY most Amis[illegible] have always wanted. Re[illegible] $7.95 yd.

SPECIAL $5.95 YARD

60-Inch Double Width
Regular Stillwater

$5.95 quality. In REGULA[illegible] NAVY BLUE ONLY!

SPECIAL $3.95 YD.

The finest, silkiest, softest o[illegible] the market!

36-Inch, Sanforized
DRESS CHAMBRAY

In beautiful SEA GREEN o[illegible] COPEN BLUE. Sunday quality. Reg. 79c yd. From bolt.

SPECIAL 59c YARD

The softest, most perfect of
SUEDE FLANNELS

at way below regular price. Excellent for shirts, linings, comforts, etc. DARK GREEN, DEEP WINE, LIGHT BLUE, BEAUTIFUL AQUA, LIGHT TAN. Previous low prices were 49c yard. From the bolt.

SPECIAL 39c YARD

45-INCH
Teka Batiste Frosted

Exactly the same as the plain Tekas but with the frosted appearance. LIGHT BLUE, TAN, AQUA, MED. GREY, COPEN BLUE. Reg. 69c yd.

SPECIAL 54c YARD

42-Inch Burlington Mills
ALPACA

The finest of wrinkleproof, full bodied, soft finish crepes. In beautiful shades of DARK BROWN, DARK GREEN.

45-Inch, The Very Finest o[illegible]
SWISS ORGANDY

Nelo's best. Won't thick[illegible] or curl. A beautiful eve[illegible] weave. SNOW WHITE, a[illegible] BEST BLACK. Reg. $1.39 y[illegible]

SPECIAL $1 10 YARD
(5 Yards for $5.00)

45-Inch Summerweight
BLACK ALPACA

Regularly 79c yard.

joyed dealing with the Amish and returned year after year, witnessing the birth, childhood, and coming of age of thousands of children. Many Amish women commented that the materials for their wedding dresses were gifts from the traveling salesmen. One women from Indiana noted that she had eight daughters and Sam Greenburg seemed to know when it was about time for a wedding because he would always show up with just the right goods and present them to the girl as a gift — a smart business tactic designed to insure a new customer every time.

In the late-19th century and early 20th century, mail-order catalogs were an important fixture in the lives of rural families, including the Amish. For those living in the countryside away from central markets or the shops on main street, the mail-order catalog became an essential part of consumer life as well a form of entertainment. The two kings of the catalog trade were Sears & Roebuck and Montgomery Ward. Amish women mentioned these two companies frequently in interviews when they were asked about sources for materials.

Montgomery Ward's first catalog appeared in 1872. It was a single page of about 50 different dry goods all priced at one dollar or less. It sold out immediately. Sears & Roebuck began with pocket watches and jewelry but by 1895 they too had entered into the dry goods business. Sears offered an extensive variety of materials popular among Amish women: colored henriettas, domestic and imported serges, alpacas, and cashmere wools in different widths, colors and prices. Cotton batting was also sold through the catalog in 16 ounce rolls 7 feet long and 36 inches wide. Cotton flannels and printed cottons found frequently on the back of Lancaster quilts were also available.

By the turn of the century Sears and Montgomery Ward's had developed a considerable audience. Dry goods listings included: cashmere, henriettas, mohair, brillantine, heavy serges, plain and fancy dress fabrics, black dress goods, colored wash dress fabrics, sea island batiste cottons, mercerized sateens, and a large assortment of cotton battings, thread, and notions. The wool batiste so prevalent in Lancaster quilts was sold in solid colors such as royal blue, green, cardinal, brown, gray, pink, and black.

During the first two decades of the 20th century the types of materials offered by the catalogs remained largely the same though there was a yearly increase in the prices. In the years around World War I there were some shortages and a steep climb in the price of available goods. For example, the plain colored chambray Amish women used for quilt backings jumped in price from 9 cents a yard in 1915 to 29 cents a yard in 1918. All wool batiste available in a wide selection of colors for 42 cents in 1915 was 98 cents a yard in 1918 and only available in pink, lavender, light blue or navy.

The textile industry in the United States in the early 20th century had grown tremendously but it was still heavily dependent on the Europeans and the years of World War I meant shortages and a disruption of services and access to technologies. The United States relied in particular on the German dye industry so heavily that in those years there were incredible shortages in all items requiring colored dyes from stamps to paint to fabric. In the post-war period there was a very concerted effort to eradicate this problem and develop a national industry. The Dupont company which would later be instrumental in the creation of new types of fabrics was heavily involved in this effort.

In the early 1920s the American economy restabilized and started to develop more rapidly than ever before. In the post-war period certain changes in fabrics begin to appear. The once standard and ubiquitous henrietta woolens all but disappeared from the catalogs. As wool became increasingly expensive, new part wool fabrics gained in popularity. Rayon also came into the marketplace heavily in the 1920s. Known as "Artificial Silk" in its first years, it could be found in a variety of fabric types and blends after the mid-1920s.

In the mid-1920s the traditional woolens and cottons preferred by Amish women were still abundant and once again they were less expensive than during the war and post-war period. The variety of colors was extensive and in these years we see some of the most dazzling and richly colored Lancaster quilts.

The decade of the 1930s brought new changes. New blend fabrics such as washable half wool-cashora and non-shrinkable half wool crepe and wool rep as well as the increased use of rayon in mixed woolen fabrics appeared. Sears "best all wool batiste" was still available through 1933 but by 1935 it too had gone the way of other traditional and Amish preferred fabrics such as mohair, brillantine, alpaca, and henrietta. By the end of the decade only creped and suiting wools can be found in the catalog.

As the 1930s wore on the increasing severity of the Depression meant the introduction of more inexpensive fabrics and the disappearance of high quality wools. The Sears catalog of the mid-1930s is filled with a variety of wool-rayon combinations and weaves: pebble crepes, rayon flat weaves, and wool-rayon blends.

World War II managed to end the Depression in the United States but it also introduced a period of shortages in domestic and consumer goods. Every Amish woman who is old

Advertisement in The Sugarcreek Budget *1954, a national newspaper that served the Amish and Mennonite communities throughout Pennsylvania and the Midwest. Sam Greenburg sold both as a door to door salesman and through mail order.*

Wear What the Stars are Wearing . . . the Exact Designs Worn in the Picture by Scarlett, Melanie, Careen, and Bonnie Blue. Exclusively by Mail at Sears

"GONE WITH the WIND" Prints

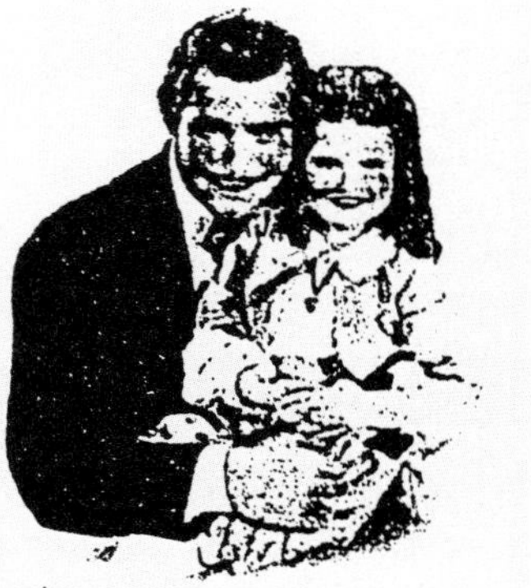

Scene from the Picture "Gone With the Wind" as produced by David O. Selznick and released by Loew's Inc.

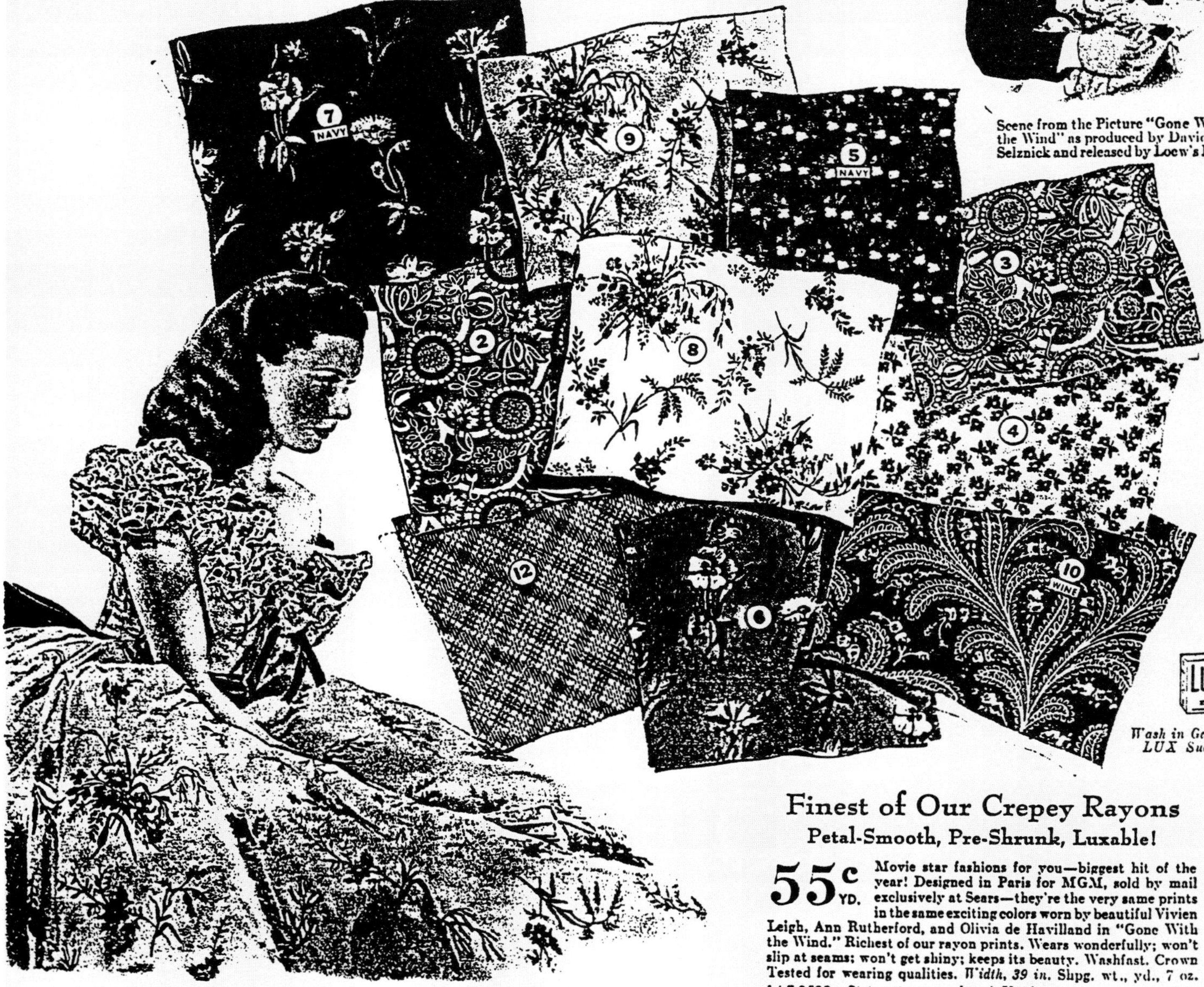

Wash in Gentle LUX Suds

Finest of Our Crepey Rayons

Petal-Smooth, Pre-Shrunk, Luxable!

55c YD. Movie star fashions for you—biggest hit of the year! Designed in Paris for MGM, sold by mail exclusively at Sears—they're the very same prints in the same exciting colors worn by beautiful Vivien Leigh, Ann Rutherford, and Olivia de Havilland in "Gone With the Wind." Richest of our rayon prints. Wears wonderfully; won't slip at seams; won't get shiny; keeps its beauty. Washfast. Crown Tested for wearing qualities. *Width, 39 in.* Shpg. wt., yd., 7 oz.
14 E 8539—*State pattern number.* A Yard 55c

Bouclé Semi-Sheer

77c YD. For the Easter dress you'll wear all 4 seasons of the year! Smartest new semi-sheer, delicately nubbed, so fine it's almost like a crepe; a triumph for rayon. Radiant washfast colors; use *Lux.* *Width, 38 inches.* Shpg. wt., yd., 6 oz.
14 E 8316—*State color.* A Yard 77c

Sweet 'n Lovely

59c YD. Finest rayon crepe we've ever seen! Close-textured, strong, smooth, decidedly luxurious . . . and so wonderfully soft. Perfect for your best dresses, for fine undies. Newest washfast jewel colors. *Width, 38 inches.* Shpg. wt., yd., 6 oz.
14 E 8345—*State color.* A Yard 59c

Rayon Crepe Romaine

77c YD. A texture too beautiful ever to go out of fashion. Smooth, delicately cross-grained surface, and a remarkable quality of Celanese Rayon. Resists sagging, stretching, crushing. Dry cleans. *Width, 38 inches.* Shipping weight, yd., 6 oz.
14 E 8384—*State color.* A Yard 77c

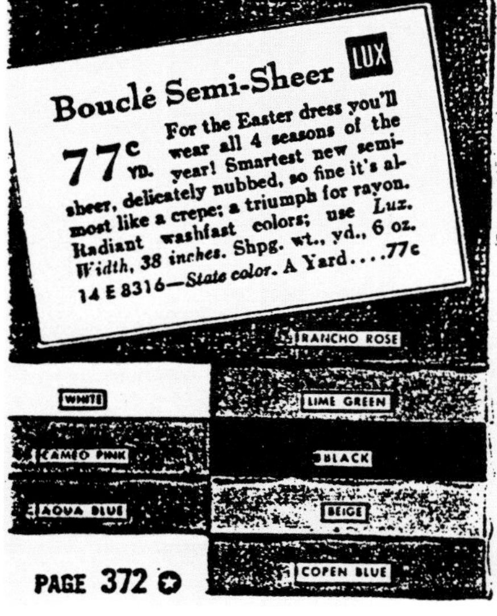

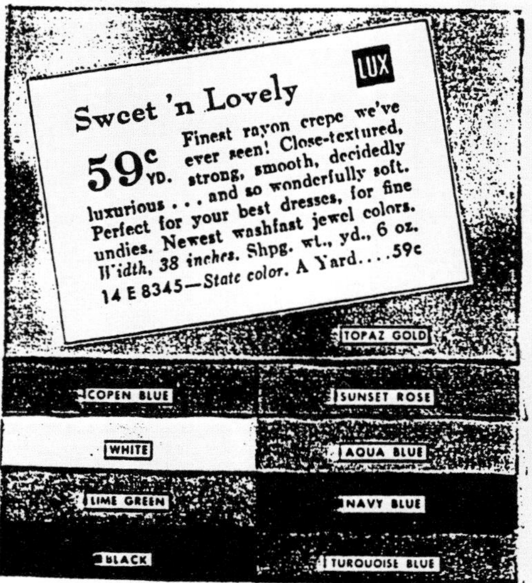

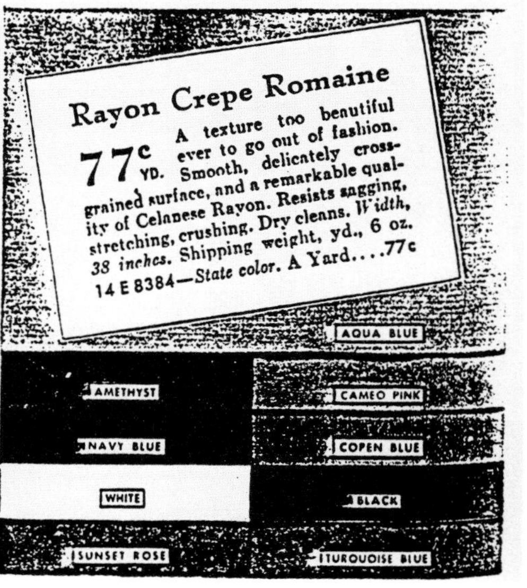

enough to remember those years will tell you that at that time you "made do with whatever fabrics you could get." Between 1940-1944 the listing of fabric choices declined every year and in 1945 Sears did not offer any fabrics in its catalog.

When the war ended a post-war economic boom began. In 1946 and 1947 the wartime economy and manufacturing effort was converted to the production of consumer items. Sears advertised in 1947 that they had "good quality percales back again—the biggest value in years." The optimism of the catalog was perhaps a little premature as these cottons were only available in medium blue or rose and little else beside rayon and cotton chambrays were advertised. Wools and part wool fabrics appear in very limited colors at relatively high costs. The 1950s saw the full revival and new growth in the American economy. Textiles were once again plentiful and inexpensive. Alpaca-type rayon, rayon romaine, rayon crepes, and rayon gabardine as well as percales, broadcloths, and chambray fabrics were offered by Sears in a rainbow of colors.

The textile section of the Sears catalog emphasized synthetic and synthetic blend fabrics. There were no traditional wool offerings. Polyester appears in the late-1950s and was first used primarily in combination with other fibers. By 1961 quilters could buy 100 percent dacron polyester batting weighing 1½ pounds in sheets that measured 72 inches × 92 inches for $3.93. Glazed white quilting cotton was still a better and lighter buy at one pound for $1.27. By the mid-1960s polyester had been improved in quality and price, virtually replacing the traditional cottons until their revival in the new quilt era of the 1980s.

From the 1880s - 1960s the changes in textiles and textile production methods changed as radically as they had in the early and mid-19th century when fabric production moved from the home to the factory. The changes that occurred in both of these centuries are reflected in the clothing and home furnishings created by Amish women in both of these periods. The information gathered from inventories, catalogs, advertising, interviews, and observation of specific textile objects is useful in helping to clarify the specific changes in Amish textiles as well as the larger issues of societal and cultural change. Despite the efforts of the Amish to remain "in the world but not of it," the effects of American social, scientific and economic history have all had as large an influence on the appearance and style of Amish quilts as the sect's principles of religious faith and its guidelines affecting community aesthetics.

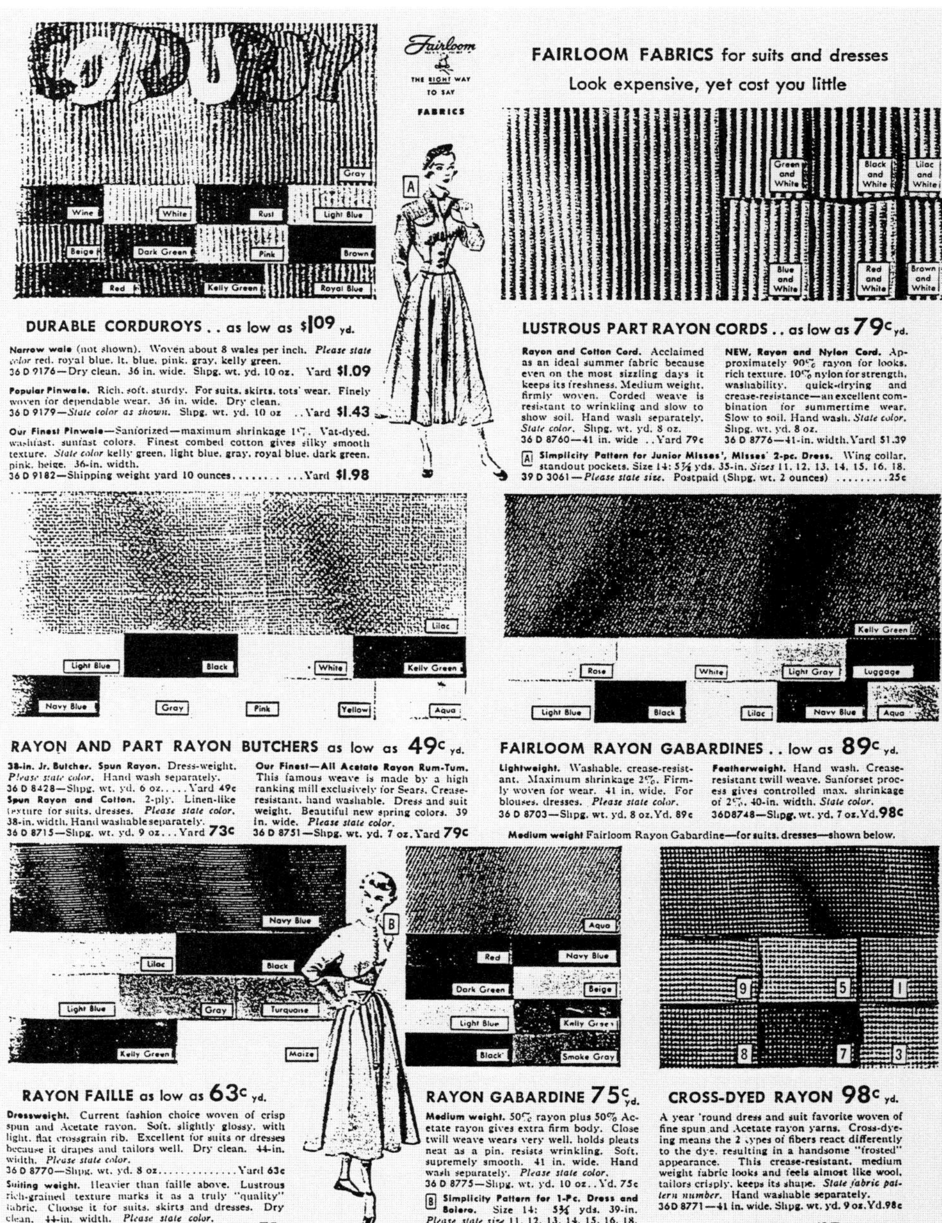

Sears catalog 1950

Eve Wheatcroft Granick made her paper and publishing debut at the Oral Traditions first symposium in 1985 where she presented the paper, "A Century of Old Order Amish Quiltmaking in Mifflin County," packed with information gathered first hand by herself and her husband, David Wheatcroft, both MFA degree recipients from the University of Iowa. She has gone on to make numerous presentations and to write the book on Amish quilt traditions, aptly and simply titled The Amish Quilt *(Intercourse, PA: Good Books, 1989).*

Sears catalog 1940

Quiltmaking on Chesapeake Plantations

Gloria Seaman Allen

Detail of laid and embroidered counterpane, 105" × 98", attributed to Mary Willing Byrd (1740-1814) and Elizabeth Bassett Harrison (b.1730), Westover and Berkeley Plantations, James City County, Virginia, 1780-1800. The laid areas are appliquéd with buttonhole stitches, a technique found on Tidewater Virginia quilts and counterpanes. Collection of the Valentine Museum.

Women living on plantations or large farms in the Chesapeake region during the antebellum period made quilts as one of their almost daily textile activities. Quiltmaking in this area and at this time was communal and social, and the activity of quilting brought together women of different ages, social classes, and races. Women within the plantation family, from neighboring plantations, or from more remote areas came together for the purpose of quilting a bedcover after it had been put in the frame.

Focusing on two rare Chesapeake plantation diaries, this paper looks at the activity of quiltmaking in the context of daily plantation life. The study also addresses the process of female association and reliance. The first diary covers only one year, 1797. The author was Frances Baylor Hill, a young Virginia woman, who lived with her parents and did not have responsibility for managing a plantation household. The second diary is that of Martha (Ogle) Forman, a mature woman, who managed the domestic side of a large Maryland plantation and kept a series of diaries with almost daily entries throughout her married life. Her records span the years 1814 to 1845.

Since both plantation diaries were written by white women, they describe the quilting activities of other white women. Frances Baylor Hill rarely mentions the more than 70 servants and slaves who lived on Hillsborough plantation. While Martha Forman frequently records the textile work of her female slaves or "house girls," she only specifically connects them with quiltmaking in two diary entries. This paper will conclude with a look at quiltmaking by slaves on Chesapeake plantations as described in slave narratives recorded after the Civil War.

The diary of Frances Baylor Hill of Hillsborough covers the period from January 1 to December 31, 1797.[1] The diarist was the daughter of first cousins Edward Hill (1746-1816) and Frances Brock (Baylor) Hill (1748-1802). Fanny, as she was called, was probably born at Hillsborough around 1780. Hillsborough, in Tidewater Virginia, included an 18th-century manor house and various outbuildings on 1200 acres of land along the Mattaponi River, a tributary of the York River.

Frances Baylor Hill commences her diary on New Year's Day, 1797 and resolves that "Having a bad memory I write this Journal that I may with pleasure at the end of the year know who & what I have seen, where I have been & what I have been employed about, & c & c."[2] Three hundred sixty-five days later she closes her diary with the following comment — "And now [I] make a conclusion of my journal which has been rather more tedious than I suppos'd it would have been when I first began."[3] It is fortunate for us that Frances Hill persevered and kept to her diary. Her comments are rich in detail and they are an excellent source for understanding the range of domestic activities and the level of interaction among white women living on Chesapeake plantations at the end of the 18th century.

During the course of her diary Fanny seldom mentions her parents. Fanny's mother never appears to work with her daughter on textile projects, yet we read that on several occasions Fanny made aprons and caps or hemmed handkerchiefs for her mother. Usually Fanny sewed with her sister, Nancy, or with relatives and friends from nearby plantations. It was exceptional for her to work alone. On those days Fanny sadly notes in her diary — "saw no company."[4] Frances Hill's textile work was often reciprocal. She visited other plantations to work on quilts as frequently as visitors came to Hillsborough to help with Fanny's quilts and counterpanes.

Almost every diary entry includes a reference to textiles. Textile work was never-ending, and young Fanny Hill had acquired the skills necessary to undertake almost any task. She wove cloth, tape, and bindings; she wound cotton thread, but does not appear to have done spinning; she knitted, hemmed, sewed, and embroidered; she reworked old garments, and she cut out and sewed new garments such as aprons, coats, robes, short-gowns, shifts, pockets, and caps. Fanny generally attended to knitting and mending in the early morning before breakfast or in the late evening by candlelight. She reserved the better part of the day for more social activities such as visiting and quilting. She always worked on several things at the same time and frequently started and stopped a tedious project like her counterpane. When Fanny went visiting, she took sewing or knitting with her in case her hostess did not provide something for her to work on.

Frances Hill's companions in textile work included mature women and their daughters from neighboring plantations, but they also sometimes included young men. In the winter months Fanny wound spun cotton for her weaving. On January 16 she recorded that three young men helped and made sport of betting a bowl of punch on the total length of cotton thread they had wound. Only the day before, Fanny had wound 465 yards.[5] In July while Fanny worked on a quilt with female relatives and friends from nearby plantations, she was distracted by the presence of Sam Garlick and Cousin John Hill who "plagued" the ladies.[6] Two days later the energies of the young men were put to use on the quilting project. Fanny notes that "Cousin John Hill, Sam Garlick, & Cousin Ben Temple draw'd on the quilt."[7] Probably they were marking the quilting lines for the women to stitch. Four years later Fanny would marry cousin John Hill.

Fanny's diary only covers a year, but it includes several active periods of embroidering and quilting. The diary clearly reveals how plantation women depended upon each other in order to complete their major textile projects. In April, probably when the dirt roads had become drier and more passable, Fanny increased her visits to other plantations along the Mattaponi River. She first walked to the home of Gregory Tunstall where she, sister Nancy, and Sally Garlick helped Mrs. Tunstall "sew on her bed quilt."[8] The young ladies were given dinner and put up for the night. About three weeks later, on May 5, Fanny and Sally walked to Major Buckner's to help quilt and were again put up for the night. The next day Fanny and the Buckner's daughter, also named Fanny, went on to Mr. Kay's and spent the day working on Mrs. Kay's quilt. The following week Fanny Hill was back at the Buckner's quilting. On this occasion she was joined by Mrs. Kay, who presumably had finished or put aside her own quilt.

On May 24 Fanny resumed work at Hillsborough on a counterpane she had started some time before. She worked on her counterpane almost daily until June 10. During that time period Mrs. Buckner and her daughter came to visit on three separate occasions and helped Fanny with the counterpane. The work was then put away until the end of August when Fanny writes that she had four visitors who stayed for three days and helped sew leaves on the counterpane. After the guests left Fanny continued with her counterpane embroidery for only one more day and then set it aside. Fanny did not enjoy working alone. She writes — "I felt very lonesome after the girls went away, & set down to my work & stuck close at it the whole day."[9] In December Fanny once again took up her counterpane and this time was assisted by her sister, Nancy. With the onset of cold weather and the seasonal decline in plantation visiting, her sister may have been the only available help. The two girls finally finished the counterpane on December 30. The next day Fanny would write — "I finished my counterpane on Saturday which has been about 3 year[s]."[10]

Frances Hill's counterpane, unlike the quilts she would work on, was a very time consuming project. It was probably white on white embroidery. The only clues Fanny gives us as to the counterpane's appearance are references to working "leaves." On June 10 she worked "a great many leaves,"[11] and on August 23 she records that "the young Ladys still continu'd to work for me they fill'd up a great many leaves very pretty."[12] Probate inventories taken in nearby York County suggest that the majority of counterpanes made prior to 1810 were either white or made from "Virginia cloth," which was probably left undyed.[13]

Photograph of Hillsborough by H. Bagby, Historic American Building Survey, 1936. Collection of the Library of Congress.

Quilting was a popular activity at Hillsborough during the months of July and October. July had been a hot month, and Fanny cited the temperature as a reason for her reduced textile work. However, on July 11 Fanny started work on an appliqué quilt. She records that "Sister Hill laid the middle of my bedquilt."[14] Fanny probably used the term "laid" to signify the laying out of pieces of chintz or calico on a ground cloth preliminary to the appliquéing process. We learn no more of this quilt, but on July 24 we find "Aunt Temple very busy fixing her bedquilt in the fram."[15] Quilting continued without interruption over the next five days. During that period Fanny and Aunt Temple were joined by ten other women who came in for a day or more to quilt. Several stayed overnight. The women quilted, gossiped, and feasted on watermelons, peaches, biscuits, and cakes. They may have even consumed spirits. Fanny notes that "we spent the day agreable eating drinking and quilting."[16] This was a "merry" period of social interaction and cooperation among women of different ages but of the same social class and related by blood, marriage, or business connections.

In October Fanny was a principal contributor to two quilts for other people. On the 24th she "made the middle of a bedquilt for Cousin Hillyard,"[17] and on the 27th she exchanged textile work with Cousin Gwathmey. Fanny writes — "Cousin Gwathmey & I changed work I began a bedquilt for her & she knit for me . . ."[18] Fanny was a fast worker when she wished to be; two days later she could report — "I sew'd on the quilt it want'd only two borders to be large enough . . . Cousin Gwathmey finish'd my stockings . . ."[19]

We have an idea of what Fanny's quilts may have looked like. A quilt in the collection of the Valentine Museum was made at Hillsborough and has been attributed to Fanny and her mother. The printed linen and cottons used in this quilt date from about 1790 to 1820 so it is unlikely that Fanny's mother worked on the quilt before her death in 1802. The quilt may be the collective work of Fanny and friends. The quilt is in the laid or appliquéd style, and the center flowering tree and figurative scene is surrounded by a series of borders. The variation in buttonhole stitches used to hold the laid pieces in place suggests the work of several people.

The style of the Hillsborough quilt is similar to other quilts and counterpanes from Tidewater Virginia. A counterpane from the collection of the Museum of Early Southern Decorative Arts was made in neighboring Gloucester County and dates from about 1780 to 1810. [See Gloria Seaman Allen, *First Flowerings: Early Virginia Quilts* (Washington: DAR Museum, 1987),16 or John Bivins and Forsyth Alexander, *The Regional Arts of the Early South* (Winston-Salem, NC: Museum of Early Southern Decorative Arts, 1991), 37, 44.] The block and plate-printed linens have been appliquéd to a cotton ground with buttonhole stitches. This counterpane has the diamond-square configuration often found on Tidewater Virginia bedcovers. Another counterpane from the Valentine Museum was probably made between 1780 and 1800 by members of the Byrd and Harrison families on neighboring Westover and Berkeley plantations in James City County. [Also see Allen, 17.] In addition to laid areas appliquéd with buttonhole stitches, this bedcover has extensive embroidery. The sprigs of flowers, trailing vines, and leaves have been embroidered with colored threads in satin and stem stitches. Perhaps Fanny Hill's counterpane was as ambitious as this one.

Laid and stuffed quilt, 92" × 81", attributed to members of the Hill family living at or near Hillsborough Plantation, King and Queen County, Virginia, 1790-1820. Collection of the Valentine Museum.

Pieced quilts were also made on plantations in the Virginia Chesapeake region. However, we find no specific references to piecework in the Hill diary. One pieced bedcover comes from the most famous of all Tidewater Virginia plantations, Mount Vernon. [See Allen, 29.] Martha Dandridge Custis Washington is thought to have pieced her bedcover between 1790 and 1800. This may have been one of the counterpanes purchased by her granddaughter, Eliza Law, at the Washington estate sale in 1802. The unfinished bedcover was returned to Mount Vernon in the 20th century by a descendant of Eliza Law. The Washington bedcover is similar to two others made further inland in Spotsylvania County, Virginia. Both of these coverings, also unfinished, date from the 1790s and are pieced from multicolored block-printed linens. One, privately owned, is a genealogy bedcover pieced and embroidered by Ann Taylor after the loss of her husband at sea in 1798. [See Allen, 30.] The other bedcover was pieced by Frances Washington Ball, niece of George Washington. [See Allen, 31.] Frances Ball used Indian painted cottons in addition to printed linens to create her intricate pieced design. Her bedcover is now in the textile collection at Mount Vernon.

Stylistic similarities are readily apparent in extant early Virginia bedcovers. Strong, angular borders surround a dominant central motif. In the appliquéd quilts and counterpanes, the laid pieces are held in place by narrowly spaced buttonhole stitches, and embroidery is sometimes used to augment areas of printed fabric. The pieced bedcovers follow the same bordered central motif design. The piecing is often complex and combines an unusual selection of block- and plate-printed textiles. When the bedcovers are quilted the work is fine, often 16 to 18 stitches to the inch.

We now turn to a series of diaries by Martha Ogle Forman (1785-1864), written at Rose Hill plantation in Cecil County, Maryland between 1814 and 1845.[20] The first diary begins on May 19,1814, Martha's wedding day. Martha Brown (Ogle) Calendar, a 29-year-old childless widow, had just married General Thomas Marsh Forman, a 56-year-old widower with one grown child. Forman was well regarded as a hero of the American Revolution, hero of the War of 1812, and master of an extensive plantation, known as Rose Hill, and other tracts of land on Sassafras Neck. The Forman diaries are day by day accounts of time management and plantation life at Rose Hill where General Forman and his wife lived with their "black family" of about 50 slaves. Since no diaries dating prior to the wedding are known we can assume that the General suggested to his new wife that she keep a daily record of her activities. During her absences to visit sick relatives, he often took over as diarist.

Detail of reprint of Simon J. Martenet's 1858 map of Cecil County, Maryland. Rose Hill is located on the Sassafras River, designated on the map as the "Est. of Gen. Thos. Forman." Courtesy of the author.

During the 31 years Martha Forman kept a diary, she made quilts during at least five years. Martha records in her diary the quilting process and directly or indirectly refers to the people who helped her quilt. Unfortunately, Martha fails to mention any of the steps she took to make her quilt tops prior to putting them in the quilting frame. There are no references to the cutting, laying out, and sewing of pieces of chintz or to the piecing together of new or scrap fabrics. Yet Martha frequently described the routine chore of cutting out chemises, frocks, trousers, jackets, and other clothing for the Rose Hill slaves.

One might wish for greater detail. Nevertheless the Forman diaries are invaluable in that they provide evidence of the rhythm and context of quiltmaking and the necessity of relying on others in the plantation community for assistance with quilting. As Martha grows older her work routine scarcely diminishes but her quilting assistants do vary from young unmarried women on neighboring plantations, to out-of-town houseguests, hired sewing girls, and "house girls," or female slaves who came under Martha's supervision at Rose Hill.

Martha Forman first mentions quilting in 1818, four years after her marriage. Martha is now 33 and childless. The "General," as she refers to her husband, is 60 and "without ache, pain, or debility."[21] The Formans are the only two permanent white members of the Rose Hill household, but during the course of the year they would entertain guests for the day and/or overnight on at least 105 occasions. On some days Martha entertained as many as 20 people for tea or dinner. Among the frequent visitors to Rose Hill were the Wards and the Pearces. The Wards occupied the plantation of Woodlawn on Sassafras Neck, and they were probably the Formans closest friends. The two families' houses were within walking distance of each other and they frequently exchanged mutual assistance in the many areas of plantation management.

(The manor houses of the two plantations are today separated by several miles of road, but there may have been a shorter route across the fields.) Martha referred to the Wards as her "obliging neighbors." With an almost 30-year age difference between Martha and the General, it is likely that the senior Wards were closer to the General in age and that Martha had more in common with their four daughters who were probably in their twenties. The two older daughters, Eliza and Susan, were frequent visitors to Rose Hill. They provided companionship for Martha during the General's absences and may have served as surrogate daughters or younger sisters to Martha. The Ward girls could be counted on to lend Martha a helping hand with such routine, tedious chores as reattaching fringe to bed and window curtains after washing.

Two Ward daughters along with Anna and Emma Pearce, daughters of Matthew Pearce of nearby Poplar Neck plantation, assisted Martha with her quilting in 1818. On Wednesday, December 2 Martha records that she put her bedquilt in the frame and Eliza and Susan Ward came to quilt. The Ward sisters stayed overnight and left for home the next morning. Mrs. Vansant, the overseer's wife, stopped by the house the same day and may have spent a few hours quilting. On Saturday, the two younger Ward daughters came to visit, but did not quilt. On Monday the Pearce girls, along with their houseguest the 20-year-old Miss Martha Levy from Philadelphia, came over to help quilt. They spent the night and stayed all the next day. After their departure Martha did not return to quilting again until the following Saturday when Mrs. Vansant came to help finish the quilt. As the wife of the white overseer, Mrs. Vansant was not a social equal to the Formans, even though her husband might have been, as was frequently the case, the landless younger son of a well-to-do planter. Miss Levy, on the other hand, was the daughter of a prominent Philadelphia merchant, and Martha was flattered by her visit to Rose Hill.

The quilting process lasted from December 2 to December 12 and during that ten-day period Martha put up overnight guests on four occasions, had dinner guests on all ten evenings, nursed an injured slave, distributed the winter allotment of shoes and stockings to the people in the quarters, kept up with the routine management of the plantation household, and made preparations for Christmas visitors.

Martha next resumes her quiltmaking in 1821. On Friday, June 1 she put her bedquilt in the frame and finished the quilt a week later. Martha does not record who helped her quilt although her favorite niece, Narcissa Oldham, had been staying with her. Judging by her other diary entries, Martha was not able to devote extended periods of time to quilting. Four out of seven days she received visitors and on two days she went to church or calling on others in Sassafras Neck. Only after her husband departed for Baltimore was she able to concentrate on her needlework. On that day, June 6, she wrote -"I am very busy quilting."[22] The quilt was finished when her husband returned from Baltimore with "a piece of dimity for bedspreads," and thus another sewing project for Martha.[23]

Martha does not mention quilting again until 1826. By then she was 41. She and the General remained childless, so there were no daughters available to assist her. On May 20 of that year Martha put a quilt in the frame and on June 16 she reports that the quilt was finished. During this period Martha does not identify who worked on the quilt. She cites no visitors coming specifically for the purpose of quilting. However it is likely that she already had one or more women in the household who were talented, or at least capable, needleworkers. Sally Dixon, an itinerant sewing girl, was in residence at Rose Hill from May 17 to May 24 and again from June 12 to June 19. During that time she sewed together clothes which had been cut out by Martha for the slaves. For this service she received wages of $3.62 in store credits. On June 8, Mrs. George Stiles arrived from Baltimore with her husband, two small children, and a servant. Her husband left on business a few days later, but Mrs. Stiles stayed on until June 21 and assisted Martha in cutting out frocks and trousers for the plantation children. She may also have worked on Martha's quilt. In exchange, Martha helped Mrs. Stiles make a silk dress. Martha, therefore, did not need to call in young women from neighboring plantations to help her quilt when she had at hand the services of a professional seamstress as well as those of a willing houseguest.

Contemporary photograph of Rose Hill showing the original section on the right and the wing erected in 1837-1838 on the left. Courtesy of the author.

Martha's third quilt took considerably longer to finish than her first two. The quilting process was continually interrupted by visitors and visiting. During the 26 days the quilt was in the frame, Martha went out of town for four, entertained four or more houseguests for seven days, and had dinner guests on two more occasions. In addition to cutting out summer clothing for all the slave children at Rose Hill, she supervised the whitewashing and cleaning of the bed chambers, kitchen, and house exterior, and she attended to the year's supply of hams which all needed to be washed in lye, rubbed in ashes, and placed in cotton bags to assure their preservation through the hot summer months.

Less than a month after finishing her quilt, Martha put another one in the frame. She does not record the quilting process, the people who helped her, or the date of completion, but it is likely that this quilt was intended to be used with the one finished in June.

Martha returned to quiltmaking again in 1831. At age 46, Martha's circle of friends included a number of married women, whose husbands had business dealings with the General, and who frequently came along with their spouses on visits to Rose Hill. On Monday, April 25, Martha "put in [her] bedquilt to quilt."[24] She was joined in quilting by Mrs. Craddock and Mrs. Pennington, Sassafras Neck neighbors who lived within walking distance of Rose Hill and wera able to visit unescorted by husbands or servants. On the 25th the ladies spent the day quilting and then returned to their own homes before nightfall. The next day Martha had no visitors. Instead three of the house girls, 46-year-old Rachel Antigua, 22-year old Harriot Batton, and 19-year-old Rebecca Gilmore helped with the quilting. Rachel was the most experienced flax dresser and spinner on the plantation, and Harriot and Rebecca had the responsibility of knitting stockings for the plantation family even before they were teenagers. All three women were skilled in needlework, and their household duties included sewing together garments cut out by Martha for the General and the Rose Hill slaves. The following day, Wednesday, April 27, the weather turned stormy and continued bad for several days. This gave Martha a period of time uninterrupted by visitors and the house girls a day or two devoted to indoor work. Martha writes — "Rainy and unpleasant, we are all quilting away as fast as possible."[25] Finally on Sunday, May 1, the sun came out, and Mrs. Pennington and Mrs. Craddock returned to quilt. The quilt was then set aside for a few days. On the following Wednesday, Martha and the house girls concentrated on finishing the quilt. Martha writes with some satisfaction — "We quilted a breadth and a third this day, finished the quilt and put in another but did not quilt any of it."[26] Two days later, May 6, Mrs. Pennington returned again to help quilt. She was joined on that occasion by another friend, Mrs. Francis. Although Martha doesn't specifically mention who worked on the quilt over the next few days, the house girls probably did unless their time was taken up with outside duties which included whitewashing buildings, sweeping the yard, attending to the poultry, and weeding the garden. Martha was finally able to write on Tuesday, May 10 — "Finished the second quilt in four days, we did not quilt any of it on Saturday."[27] Martha worked on neither quilt on Saturdays, but probably worked on both on Sundays. Clearly there were no moral restrictions placed on doing needlework on Sundays, but the house girls, Rachel, Harriot, and Rebecca, would customarily have had Sundays off and have been in their quarters rather than on duty in the big house. On Sunday, however, Martha had the ladies to assist her. There is no evidence in the diary entries from this period to suggest that visitors and slaves worked together on Martha's quilt. When women visited to assist with a quilting, it was a social occasion, and slave girls were not included. Yet when there were no visitors, Martha quilted and worked side by side with her slaves.

Eighteen thirty-seven is the last year during which Martha Forman mentions quiltmaking. On April 18 she prepared for quilting by dyeing her lining cloth. The next day she "put in the bedquilt"[28] and invited to dinner long time friends, Mrs. Sewall and Mrs. Ford. They probably worked on the quilt as they visited with Martha. After returning from a trip to Wilmington, Martha again takes up her quilting. On the 26th she writes — "We finished the bedquilt."[29] Here the use of "we" implies that the house girls worked on the quilt as there were no day or overnight visitors at Rose Hill at the time. Several days later Martha put another bedquilt in the frame. On May 2 she records that Miss Eliza Ward and Mrs. Richard Ford were "here to help us quilt."[30] It is not clear from this entry if Martha is using the plural pronoun "us" to refer grandly to herself or if "us" refers to Martha and the house girls. Perhaps visitors now joined Martha and the slave girls in quilting. The "Miss Eliza Ward" is the same "obliging neighbor" who, as a young lady, quilted with Martha 19 years earlier. Now, an aging spinster, she remained a friend, companion, and readily available assistant to Martha. We do not know when Martha finished her second quilt but we do know that her quilting activities continued on for several days. On May 26 she sent for itinerant seamstress Elizabeth O'Neal and together they finished quilting her petticoat. This pair of quilts may have been intended for one of the bed chambers in the new brick wing of the manor house at Rose Hill. Construction, which more than doubled the size of the old frame house, commenced in June, 1837 and continued through February, 1838.

With Martha and the General leaving no children, and with Rose Hill passing to the General's grandson who was an absentee landowner, Martha's quilts were not handed down in her family. If any of her quilts have survived their whereabouts are unknown. We have, therefore, no way of knowing what type of quilts Martha made nor what they looked like. Martha made no references to pattern or technique in her diary, but she did provide a few scattered clues about her fabrics and their sources. When Martha made her first quilt in 1818 she exercised frugality. Perhaps she was still conscious of the acute textile shortage which had occurred during the War of 1812 and which touched the lives of nearly everyone in the upper Chesapeake region. When Martha finished her quilt, she congratulated herself in her diary that she had "made a bedquilt, and covered 6 Chairs out of my window Curtains."[31] We can only speculate that these curtains were made from a large figured block-printed fabric, or chintz, which Martha either pieced together into a wholecloth quilt or cut out for laid or appliquéd work. The lack of evidence for laid work favors the conclusion that her quilt was of the wholecloth type.

In December 1825, Martha received as a gift from her husband "a piece of material for bedquilts."[32] This was the fabric she used for the two quilts she made the following summer. The quilts were probably bound with the binding which arrived from Baltimore on July 16, 1826.

In March, 1831 Martha received, along with an order of tea, brown sugar, and ginger, enough "dimity for two bedquilts."[33] This may be fabric that Martha paid for with her own earnings. When she commenced quilting in April she noted — "[I] put in my bedquilt to quilt that I bought with my poultry and eggs."[34] After finishing the two quilts, Martha still had enough dimity left over to make an easy chair cover. We can speculate that the dimity used by Martha was a white self-patterned cotton that she made up into wholecloth quilts.

The following year, 1832, Martha made another easy chair cover. In February she recorded in her diary — "I cut out an easy chair cover of chintz the same as my bedquilts."[35] Perhaps this is the same fabric she used for quilts in 1825, but it is more likely that she made a pair of chintz quilts closer to the 1832 date of the chair cover. It is also possible that the 1831 dimity quilts were actually chintz appliquéd to a dimity ground.

With the possible exception of the dimity purchased with her egg money, Martha took little part in the selection of fabrics for her quilts. Her first quilt was made from recycled curtain fabric, probably purchased long before she became mistress of Rose Hill, and her other quilt fabrics were selected and purchased by her husband on trips to Baltimore, Wilmington, and Philadelphia. The General also bought Martha's dresses, other clothing articles, and household furnishings.

General Forman probably purchased bedcoverings for Rose Hill to supplement the homemade quilts. Martha refers in her diaries to Marseilles quilts on several occasions. It is likely the General obtained the woven fabric, or Marseilles loom quilting, which Martha then made up into bedcovers. On December 28, 1823 she wrote — "I bound one of the Mersails quilts and fringed it."[36] In addition to traditional quilts and Marseilles quilts, coverlets were also used on Rose Hill beds. One local weaver, Henry Patterson, wove coverlets out of wool grown at Rose Hill, spun by the house girls, and dyed by Martha.

The diaries of Martha Forman provide some evidence for the care of quilts on Chesapeake plantations during the early decades of the 19th century. Rose Hill was located on the Sassafras River, a swampy estuary of the Chesapeake Bay. Summers were long, hot, and humid. Mosquitos, flies, fleas, ticks, and other vermin were a continuing health problem. To minimize bug damage and infestation Martha followed an annual routine that was probably typical for the Tidewater area. Each spring, in late May or early June, all floor carpets were taken up and replaced with grass matting, all bed and window curtains were taken down and stored, looking glasses and paintings were covered with gauze, bedsteads were taken apart and inspected, bedding was aired, blankets and quilts were folded and put away, and finally bed chambers and downstairs rooms were scoured and whitewashed. From late September to early November, the process was reversed, and the house was put back in order. Walls and ceilings were again cleaned and whitewashed, floor matting was taken up, carpets put down, and curtains rehung. Blankets were shaken and aired, and quilts and counterpanes were washed and placed back on bedsteads for winter use. During some years Martha also had the quilts washed in the springtime when they were taken off the beds. The all-white Marseilles quilts frequently required washing.

Martha Forman's quiltmaking activities were sporadic and not nearly as intensive as those recorded by Fanny Hill. However, as plantation mistress she had many more responsibilities and less time for needlework than the young Miss Hill. In addition to the continuous entertaining of visitors and lodging of itinerant artisans, Martha performed

Photograph of Martha Forman (1785-1864) ca. 1855. Collection of the Historical Society of Cecil County.

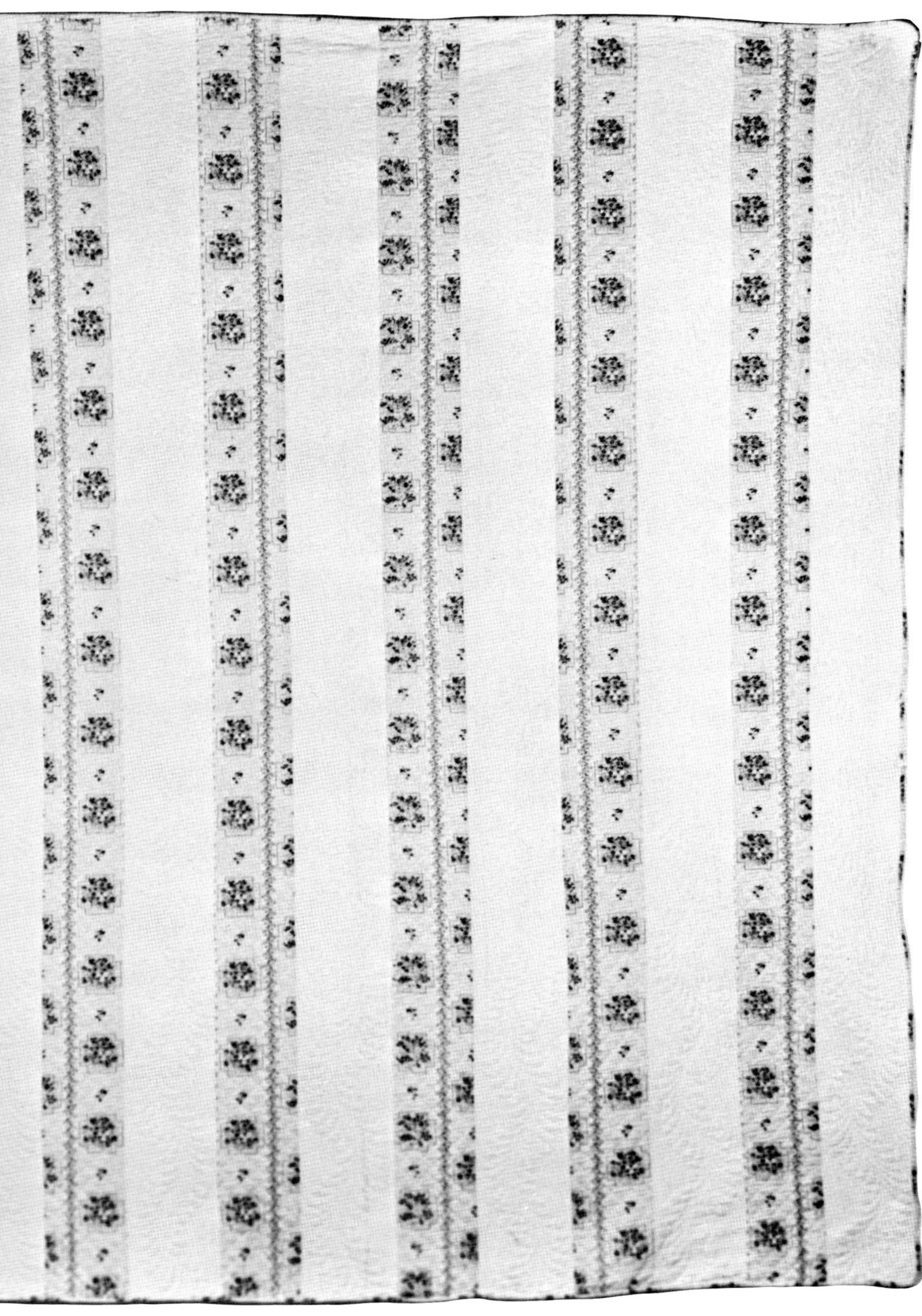

Detail of pieced quilt, 94" square, made by Elizabeth Willis Kennard (1808-1871), Galena, Kent County, Maryland. Collection of Mrs. Robert L. Bryan. Courtesy of the DAR Museum.

the seasonal chores required by a plantation economy. Often she did so when she was ill. Martha frequently came down with fevers and chills as she remained throughout the year in the unhealthy Chesapeake lowlands, an area which knowledgeable and sophisticated Philadelphians avoided from June until the November frost.

Martha's seasonal routine varied little over the years. During the winter months she supervised the hog slaughtering and cutting, salting, smoking, scrubbing, and drying the years supply of pork. After the slaughter she spent long hours rendering tallow and lard and making sausages. In addition she cut out all the woolen clothing and blankets for the 50 or more slaves on the plantation and supervised the sewing. She also measured and cut out cloth for tablecloths, towels, sheets, pillow cases, and bedticks. Most of the cloth cut out by Martha came from Rose Hill. Thus, she oversaw the house girls through the various stages of turning cut flax into tow thread ready to go to the weaver and then to the bleach yard.

In the spring the clothing process was repeated, and Martha cut out all the tow or light weight clothing for the plantation family in addition to taking the house apart for the hot months. In the summer she set about preserving each fruit crop as it ripened and supervised the harvest, washing, spinning, and dyeing of wool for the winter clothing. In the fall preserving continued as the house was put back in order. Throughout the year she supervised candle making, stocking knitting, the cleaning of plate, glass, and china, and attended herself to the baking of pies, cakes, and puddings and the processing of butter, eggs, and poultry for market. In spite of her own illnesses and chronic fatigue, Martha attended to the sick on frequent occasions. Sick family members, visitors, and slaves required Martha's care and the services of doctors who came and went, but who often needed lodging at Rose Hill for a day or more.

We can conclude that Martha Forman's life as mistress of Rose Hill was fairly typical for large plantations in the Chesapeake region. The letters of Rosalie Stier Calvert (1778-1821), mistress of Riversdale plantation in Prince George's County, Maryland, echo many of the diary entries of Martha Forman.[37] Rosalie, in writing to her father and other relatives in her native Belgium, detailed her duties as the wife of a plantation owner during the first two decades of the 19th century. She described Riversdale as both a manor and a factory which she ran as a joint economic venture with her husband. Rosalie Calvert was responsible for the "house family" which consisted of 21 people, and her duties included making cloth, candles, soap, jams, cider, sausage, and other preserved foods. She cut and pieced all the plantation family clothing, linens, curtains, and slipcovers, but rarely sewed them. She supervised the cooking, washing, ironing, and cleaning and oversaw the maintenance of the garden, dairy, carriage and horses. She educated her children, prepared medicines for the sick, and fed and lodged visitors and hired laborers. Like Martha, Rosalie made butter for market. In 1805 she noted, "I am also a dairymaid and make $7 a week from my butter at a quarter of a dollar a pound . . ."[38] Rosalie, unlike Martha, had the assistance, or perhaps extra burden, of young children. She complained frequently to her father of being overworked, and undoubtedly she was more frank than Martha who shared her diary with her husband. Rosalie wrote at one point — "My servants are very negligent and my husband does absolutely nothing other than manage his lands."[39] It is not at all surprising that Rosalie Stier Calvert found no time to make quilts.

Very few Maryland quilts have survived from the early 19th century. MESDA recorded a Harford County quilt dated 1798, and the Maryland Association for Family and Community Education, who conducted the state quilt documentation project, recorded a Frederick County quilt dated 1803. No whole cloth quilts, which are probably what Martha made, have been documented from the upper Eastern Shore of Maryland.

A pieced strip quilt by Elizabeth Kennard comes closest in time and location to Martha's quilts. It was made near Galena in Kent County, just across the Sassafras River from Rose Hill. The quilt dates from the 1830s, and the emphasis here is on fine quilting rather than intricate piecing. This quilt resembles the simple quilts suggested by Martha Forman's diary. Her quilts were most likely of the whole cloth type, or simply pieced. They were made to be used, and not intended for special occasions such as a marriage or a gift of friendship. Although the quilting process brought Martha together with friends who were her social equals, it was also one of the many chores of plantation life which she shared with the house girls or with hired itinerant seamstresses. Martha expressed no regrets when she gave away a quilt to the wife of the General's horse trainer when he left his employment at Rose Hill.

Quiltmaking, as described in the diaries of Frances Hill and Martha Forman, needs to be placed in context. Probate inventories from a comparable time period and geographic area provide evidence of the material possessions of a broad spectrum of society. For the Hill diary we look at 213 probate or decedent inventories recorded in nearby York County, Virginia between 1780 and 1810.[40] From these records it is immediately apparent that the quiltmaking activities of Fanny Hill and her friends were not typical. Of the 213 people who lived and died in York County during that time period, only 16 percent owned any quilts at all. Of the women who died during that period, quilt ownership was considerably higher at 38 percent. When a man died his wife's quilts and other bedding might be set aside as part of her dower portion, or they might be sold at vendue as part of his estate. Many a widow had to purchase back her own quilts from her husband's estate. When a widow died, sometimes her children purchased her quilts, but usually they were purchased by men who may or may not have been related to the family. George Washington purchased quilts at a neighbor's vendue for use at Mount Vernon, and General Forman purchased several coverlets at estate sales. In Cecil County, it was not uncommon for free black men to purchase quilts. Perhaps they wanted something to remember a former mistress by, or they purchased a quilt made by kinfolk.

York and King and Queen Counties, both agrarian based, relied heavily on slave labor. Edward Hill, Fanny's father, may have had more slaves than most, but York County inventories reveal that 69 percent of the decedents owned slaves. Since slaves were an expensive commodity, slave ownership implied wealth. These well-to-do planters could afford to supply the women in their households with imported textiles for their quilts. They could also provide house servants to either work on the quilts or take on other chores and thus allow the white women time for fancy needlework. Therefore, it is not surprising to find that 78 percent of the people who owned quilts also owned slaves. These statistics suggest a correlation in Tidewater Virginia plantation society between quiltmaking and slave owning. In later decades this correlation weakens as planters continued to shift from tobacco to grains and slaveholding declined in the region.

Two hundred probate inventories taken in Cecil County, Maryland between 1838 and 1847 reveal very different statistics from York County, Virginia.[41] Of the 200 decedents, 133, or 67 percent, owned one or more quilts. Of the female decedents, 82 percent owned quilts. Therefore Martha Forman's quiltmaking activity was typical for the area.

Planters and farmers in Cecil County had diversified their agrarian production during the late 18th century. This shift away from tobacco towards grains and other economic ventures, combined with the presence of a large number of Quaker landowners in the northern part of the county, contributed to the reduction in the number of slaveholders in the area. Out of 200 decedents, only 20 percent owned slaves, and then usually only one or two at a time. Of the quilt owners, 23 percent owned slaves. The Formans were the exception with their ownership of approximately 50 slaves. Since no inventory was taken of General Forman's estate when he died in 1845, there is no precise record of the number of slaves he kept at Rose Hill in later years. We do know from Martha's diaries that certain slaves had died or were elderly and several had been leased out to work on other plantations or in Baltimore. However, the General appears to have maintained a substantial labor force. Martha's use of house slaves to help with quilting was not typical of other Cecil County residents in the 1840s, although it may have been more so in 1818 when she first made quilts at Rose Hill.

We now turn briefly to the role of African American women in quiltmaking on Chesapeake plantations. Fanny Hill never mentions slaves at Hillsborough in connection with domestic work. Martha Forman acknowledges on one occasion that the house girls, Rachel, Rebecca, and Harriot, helped her quilt. She may have inferred their presence on other occasions when she used the plural pronouns "we" or "us" to describe her quilting activities. It is not until nearly the end of the diaries that Martha refers to her slave girls quilting on their own. On December 26, 1838, she writes — "Harriet and Rebecca had a quilting party."[42] (Rachel Antigua had died a few years earlier.) This party was probably timed to coincide with the four day holiday between Christmas and New Years customarily given to slaves in the Chesapeake region. We know that Harriot and Rebecca were competent needlewomen, and we know of their responsibility for sewing clothes for the Rose Hill family. We are also aware that other slaves at Rose Hill were expected to sew. Once Martha cut out the cloth for the winter and spring clothing, it was distributed to the house girls as well as to female field hands with young children to clothe. A great deal of sewing took place, not in the big house, but in the slave quarters after daily chores were completed. A Virginia lady, Letitia Burwell, recalling her girlhood in the 1850s, wrote — "Confined exclusively to a Virginia plantation during my earliest years, I believed the world one vast plantation bounded by negro quarters. Rows of white cabins . . . negro women sewing, knitting, spinning, weaving, housekeeping in their cabins . . ."[43]

Slave narratives confirm what we can only read between the lines in the Rose Hill and other diaries. Histories of some former slaves were recorded shortly after the Civil War, and then in greater numbers in the 1930s as a project of the Works Progress Administration. Unfortunately very few narratives were taken down in Maryland and Virginia. Therefore, we have only a small number of references to quiltmaking and other textile activities to help us understand what took place in slave quarters on Chesapeake plantations.

Martha Forman may have taught her house girls to quilt. Slave women probably initially learned to quilt from the plantation mistress, although this instruction was no doubt passed

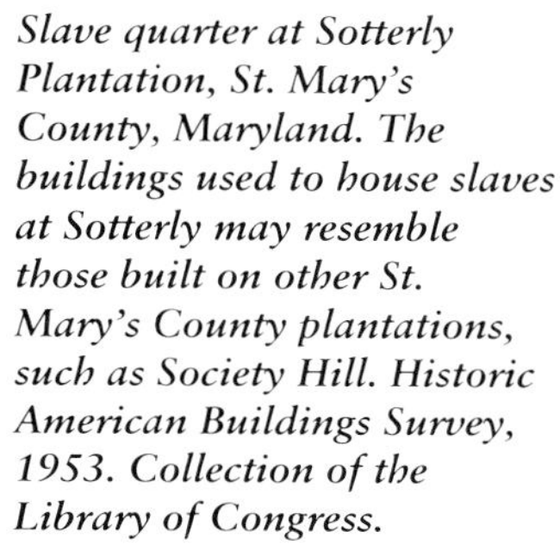

Slave quarter at Sotterly Plantation, St. Mary's County, Maryland. The buildings used to house slaves at Sotterly may resemble those built on other St. Mary's County plantations, such as Society Hill. Historic American Buildings Survey, 1953. Collection of the Library of Congress.

on as mothers instructed their daughters. Nan Stewart, who lived on a plantation in western Virginia, recalled that her mistress taught her to sew and piece quilts,[44] and Annie Wallace, another former Virginia slave, recalled that "old Miss," who had to take in sewing after her husband died, taught her to piece quilts from scraps left over from her dressmaking fabrics.[45]

Quilts were a familiar furnishing in slave cabins. James Dean of Charles County, Maryland, told his WPA interviewer — "We slept on a home-made bedstead, on which was a straw mattress, on which we used quilts made by my mother to cover."[46] Nancy Williams told her interviewer that she made so many quilts that her father built shelves in the cabin specially for them. Nancy was such a talented quilter, she was able to sell her quilts off the plantation and keep the money she earned by her sewing. She reported that she "Sol' one quilt for ten dollars, sol' one for six, one fer four."[47] Quiltmaking probably took place most evenings in the quarters. Mariah Hines described her life on a plantation in Southampton County, Virginia. "Evenings we would spin on the old spinning wheel, quilt, make clothes, talk, tell jokes . . ." Mariah also went on to give her view of a plantation mistress. "Missus didn't have to do nothing, hardly. Dare was always some of us round the house."[48] Rosalie Calvert would not have agreed.

Fannie Berry, another former Virginia slave, told her interviewer about how one woman put a quilt to unexpected use. "There wuz an' ol' lady patching a quilt an' de paddyrollers [patrol] waz looking fo' a slave name John. All at once we heerd a rap on de door. John took an' runned between Mamy Lou's legs. She hid him by spreading [the] quilt across her lap and kept on sewing an', do you kno', dem paddyrollers never found him?"[49]

Although quiltmaking was a routine chore, it was also a social activity for Chesapeake plantation slaves. Martha Forman mentioned the holiday quilting at Rose Hill, and Letitia Burwell wrote that the negro "amusements were dancing to the music of the banjo, quilting parties, opossum hunting . . ."[50] Marrinda Singleton noted that slaves on her plantation in southern Virginia were allowed to visit other plantations in the evenings. Their entertainment included "molasses candy pulls, quiltin's and maybe a little dancin' by de tune of an old banjo."[51] Sis Shackelford recalled "Cox's Snow," the great blizzard of 1857, because it prevented her from going to a "quilting spree" on a neighboring plantation. Her mother had made "a stack o' pies" and wrapped them in a table cloth in preparation for the festivities.[52]

Probably one of the most unusual references to quiltmaking by an African-American woman comes from a runaway Maryland slave, Harriet Tubman. Recalling her operation of the Underground Railroad in the 1850s, she described the daylight hours spent hidden in the woods when she would bring out her "patchwork" and sew together tiny bits of fabric. Later, these pieced covers would be made into comforters for fugitive slaves in Canada.[53]

True slave-made quilts are difficult to document. Many were lost or destroyed during the Civil War and most were used until they were used up. Histories associated with slave quilts are often vague and unsubstantiated. Some quilts, published as slave quilts, contain fabrics which postdate the Civil War. The Maryland state quilt project has documented a quilt which may have been made by slaves on a large plantation in St. Mary's County on the lower Western Shore of Maryland. The quilt dates from the mid 1840s and is especially interesting in that it does not quite fit in with other Maryland quilts. The printed fabrics, laid or appliquéd technique, and fine quilting are usually associated with big house

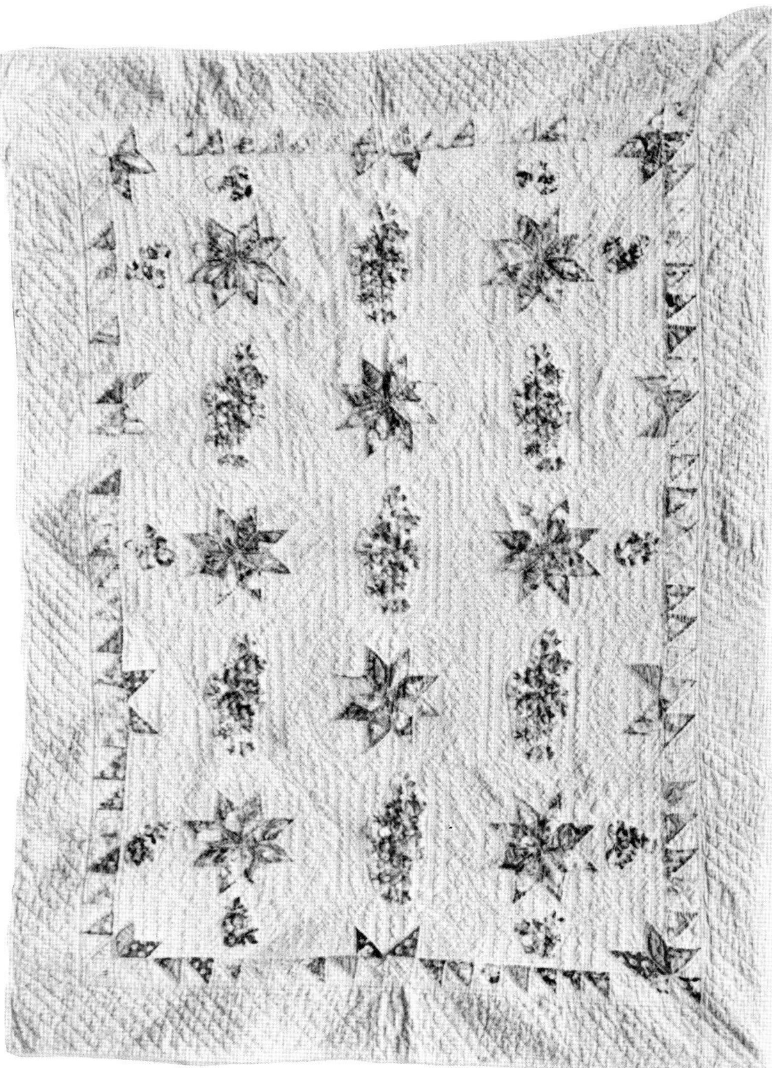

Pieced and laid cradle quilt, 49" × 36", attributed to one or more slaves living at Society Hill Plantation, St. Mary's County, Maryland, ca.1845. Collection of Mrs. Joseph M. Gough. Courtesy of the author.

quilts, but the design differs from what we would expect to find in other quilts from the region. John Vlach, noted folklorist at George Washington University, describes this quilt in terms of cultural rebellion where the maker was "compliant without compliance." In other words she complied with white folk standards by making a big house quilt, but she brought to her quilt her own sense of aesthetics.[54]

From the gleanings of two diaries and several slave narratives, we can draw some conclusions about quiltmaking on Chesapeake plantations. Quiltmaking was generally a social activity, but sometimes a routine chore, which involved several women. The women usually came from within the plantation community and might vary in age, class, and color. Quilting provided social interaction and companionship for women, both white and black, free and slave. From our knowledge of who came and went to quilt, we learn of the tightly knit social network of the Chesapeake region and the strong reliance on family, neighbors, and bound labor. For young women like Fanny Hill, who did not have the responsibility for managing a household, quilting was a pleasant task. It was festive and reciprocal. Her quilts, and those she worked on with friends and relatives on other plantations, may have been more decorative than utilitarian. For Martha Forman, quilting could be an excuse for socializing, but it was also her responsibility to keep Rose Hill supplied with bed coverings. Her quilts were intended to be used by family, visitors, and hired laborers and they were subject to frequent washing. Slave women assigned to the big house worked on quilts as one of their household duties, but they also quilted in their cabins for their families, their friends, and sometimes for profit. For slaves quilting could be a tiresome chore at the end of a long day, or it could be a form of entertainment.

In the Chesapeake region quilting was usually seasonal and confined to the spring and summer months when good weather facilitated communication between plantations. Rainy or cold weather, bad roads, and rough waters could deter quilting or change the participants from white visitors to black house girls. The demands of the plantation economy could also affect the rhythm of quilting. Martha Forman rarely made quilts in the winter when she was occupied with the pork slaughter and cutting out clothes for the plantation family. Plantation holidays, traditionally granted to slaves after Christmas, Easter, and harvests, called for festivities and provided leisure time for quilting, singing, and dancing.

Although few antebellum quilts have survived from the Chesapeake region, the diaries and narratives of plantation women, combined with probate inventories, tax assessments, and census records, provide us with an understanding of the rich and complex tradition of quiltmaking on Chesapeake plantations.

End Notes

1William K. Bottorff and Roy C. Flannagan, eds., "The Diary of Frances Baylor Hill of 'Hillsborough, 'King and Queen County, Virginia (1797)," *Early American Literature Newsletter* vol.2, no.3 (Winter 1976).

2Ibid., 6 (January 1, 1797).

3Ibid., 53 (December 31, 1797).

4Ibid., 51 (December 20, 1797).

5Ibid., 9 (January 16, 1797).

6Ibid., 38 (July 26, 1797).

7Ibid., 38 (July 28, 1797).

8Ibid., 25 (April 19, 1797).

9Ibid., 41 (August 24, 1797).

10Ibid., 53 (December 31, 1797).

11Ibid., 31 (June 10, 1797).

12Ibid., 41 (August 23, 1797).

13Gloria Seaman Allen, *First Flowerings: Early Virginia Quilts* (Washington: DAR Museum, 1987), 43.

14Bottorff and Flannagan, 35 (July 11, 1797).

15Ibid., 38 (July 24, 1797).

16Ibid., 38 (July 28, 1797).

17Ibid., 45 (October 24, 1797).

18Ibid., 45 (October 27, 1797).

19Ibid., 45 (October 29, 1797).

20W. Emerson Wilson, ed., *Plantation Life at Rose Hill: The Diaries of Martha Ogle Forman 1814-1845* (Wilmington, DE: The Historical Society of Delaware, 1976).

21Ibid., 65 (August 20, 1818).

22Ibid., 126 (June 6, 1821).

23Ibid., 126 (June 9, 1821).

24Ibid., 300 (April 25, 1831).

25Ibid., 300 (April 28, 1831).

26Ibid., 300 (May 4, 1831).

27Ibid., 300 (May 10, 1831).

28Ibid., 380 (April 19, 1837).

29Ibid., 381 (April 26. 1837).

30Ibid., 381 (May 2, 1837).

31Ibid., 73 (December 18, 1818).

32Ibid., 212 (December 9, 1826).

33Ibid., 198 (March 14, 1831).

34Ibid., 300 (April 25, 1831).

35Ibid., 312 (February 8, 1832).

36Ibid., 153 (December 28, 1823).

37Margaret Low Callcott, *Mistress of Riversdale 1795-1821* (Baltimore: Johns Hopkins University Press, 1991).

38Ibid., 128.

39Ibid., 351.

40Allen, 4-15, 46.

41*Inventories*, Cecil County, Maryland, vols. 22-25, 1838-1847.

42Wilson, 404 (December 26, 1839). Martha Forman was inconsistent in her spelling of proper names. She usually wrote "Harriot," but occasionally, "Harriet."

[43]Jacqueline Jones, *Labor of Love, Labor of Sorrow: Black Women, Work and the Family, from Slavery to the Present* (New York: Vintage Books, 1986), 56.

[44]George P. Rawick, *The American Slave: A Composite Autobiography* (Westport, CT: Greenwood Publishing Company, 1974), vol.16, 87-88.

[45]Charles L. Perdue, Jr., *Weevils in the Wheat: Interviews with Virginia Ex-slaves* (Charlottesville: University Press of Virginia, 1976), 293-296.

[46]Rawick, 6-7.

[47]Perdue 316-318.

[48]Ibid., 142.

[49]Ibid., 33.

[50]Jones, 56.

[51]Perdue, 276.

[52]Ibid., 252.

[53]John W. Blassingame, *Slave Testimony: Two Centuries of Letters, Interviews, and Autobiographies* (Baton Rouge: Louisiana State University Press, 1977), 461.

[54]Personal communication with Professor John Vlach, George Washington University, Washington, DC, May 15, 1993.

Gloria Seaman Allen is a researcher/writer on early American textiles and ceramics. Among her articles three were published in the Magazine Antiques: *Jacquard Coverlets in the DAR Museum, Parts I and II — New York and Pennsylvania Coverlets (1985 and 1989), "Dolz Collection of Delftware" (1986) and there will be a forthcoming one on Connecticut bed rugs; also, the exhibition catalogs:* Old Line Traditions: Maryland Women and Their Quilts *(1985) and* First Flowerings: Early Virginia Quilts *(1987). Gloria was the director and chief curator of the DAR Museum (1980-1990). She is a member of the American Quilt Study Group where she presented a paper, "Bed Coverings in Kent County Maryland, 1710-1820" which appeared in* Uncoverings 1985. *She is a member of the American Ceramics Circle from which she received a research grant in 1983. Gloria also was the recipient of a Benno Forman Fellowship at Winterthur in 1988 to do research on the Anglo-American trade in bed rugs in the 18th century. She is currently writing a book on Maryland quilts and is working on her doctorate on cloth production in the Chesapeake region 1790-1860 in the American Studies/Material Culture/Folk Life program at George Washington University.*

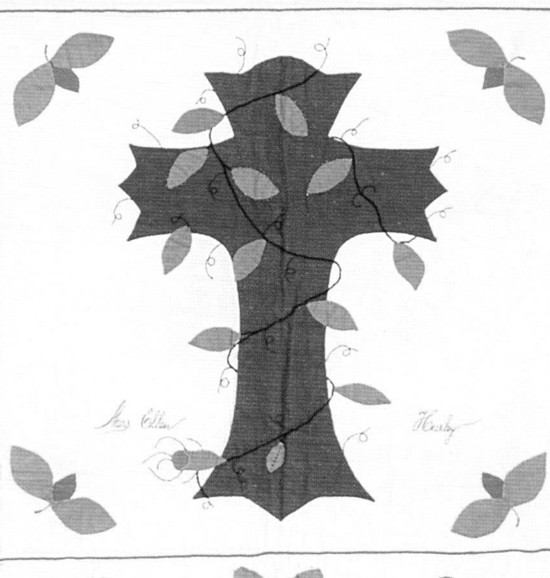

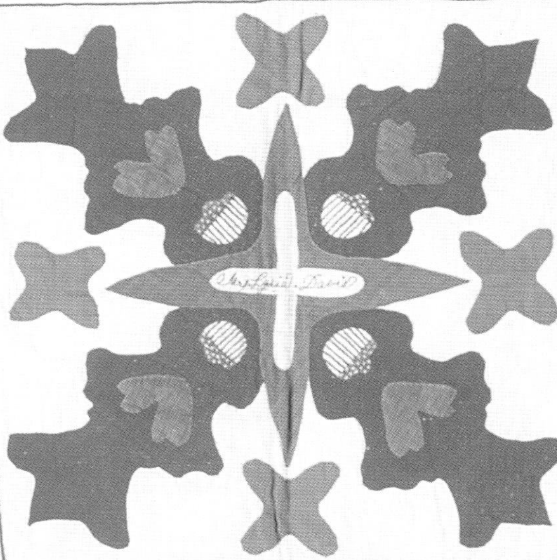

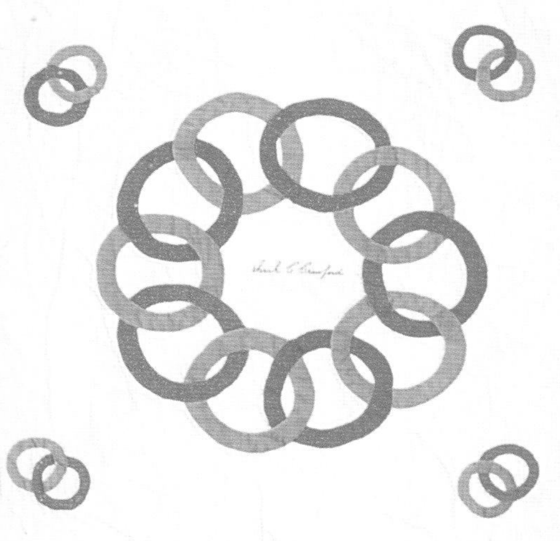

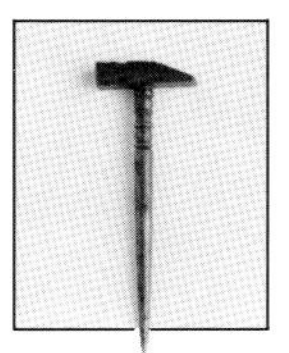

Characteristics of Signed New Jersey Quilts 1837-1867

Rita Erickson and Barbara Schaffer

Appliquéd quilt, 1867. Made by the ladies of the Old First Church (formerly Middletown Baptist Church), Middletown, Monmouth County, New Jersey. The inscription, "Presented to Reverend and Mrs. D.B. Stout, by the ladies of Leedsville Dec. 1867," makes this the latest inscribed sampler quilt seen by the New Jersey project. The quilt shows a northeastern New Jersey tendency to set more blocks horizontally than vertically. Collection of the Old First Church. Photo by Chip Greenberg.

Quilts documented by The Heritage Quilt Project of New Jersey from June 1988 to June 1991 and others that have been seen more recently show that from 1837 to 1867 New Jersey quilts were often inscribed with place names as well as dates and family names. These inscriptions make it possible to study local patterns of quiltmaking activity in the state in this 30-year period.

This essay will first present general features of 19th-century New Jersey quilts and then discuss the styles of inscribed quilts made there in the mid-19th century. It will also trace the signing of quilts from the pieced quilts popular in the southwestern part of the state in the 1840s to the appliqué sampler quilts popular in the northeastern part of the state in the 1850s and 1860s.

To understand the trends in New Jersey quiltmaking in the years 1837 to 1867, it is helpful to consider New Jersey's geographic location and settlement patterns. New Jersey's borders are formed by Pennsylvania on the west, Delaware on the south, New York on the north and northeast, and the Atlantic Ocean on the southeast. Originally, settlers to the western part of the state came by way of the Delaware River, while settlers to the eastern part of the state entered through several ports along the Atlantic Coast. In the late-1600s when the earliest settlements were being made, the area that is now New Jersey was divided into two separate colonies, West Jersey and East Jersey, along a line that ran from the natural boundaries of the Pine Barrens in the southeast to the rugged highlands of the northwest. The southwestern part was settled by Quakers, and this area retained much of its Quaker character well into the 1840s, giving it religious as well as economic ties with Philadelphia. On the other hand, the northeastern part was settled by various religious groups from the British Isles and from other parts of Europe: Methodists, Baptists, Presbyterians, and the Dutch Reformed, and had cultural and economic ties to New York City. These differences in original patterns of settlement and cultural and economic orientation are reflected in the patterns of New Jersey quiltmaking activity in the mid-19th century.

Before considering New Jersey quilts in narrow time intervals, it will be useful to point out some general features of 19th-century New Jersey quilts: block format, diagonal emphasis, and tan tape binding.

Although block-style quilts are sometimes considered a new feature of 1840s quilts,[1] block-format quilts appeared much earlier than the 1840s in New Jersey. Four of the earliest quilts seen by the New Jersey project were made in blocks. Two of these were made of wool in a simple star pattern and were assembled with alternate plain squares: the wool quilt owned by Allaire Village in Monmouth County is set square[2] while the wool quilt owned by the Wick House in Morris County is set on the diagonal.[3] Two other early block-format quilts were made of cotton: one using the Uneven Nine Patch block alternating with plain squares and the other combining the Ohio Star pattern with an Irish Chain variation.[4] Like the Wick House wool quilt, both of the cotton examples are set on the diagonal. The Uneven Nine Patch quilt is dated by family history at 1778 and is said to come from the northern border of the state. The Ohio Star/Irish Chain is attributed to 1797 and comes from Cape May at the southeastern corner of the state. During the first 40 years of the 19th century, New Jerseyans made quilts in a variety of formats including whole cloth,[5] medallion,[6] and strip, so that blocks were only one of several formats in common use. As the 1840s began, the other forms of quilts largely disappeared from the record, leaving block-style quilts as the dominant form of quilts being made throughout the state.

Diagonal emphasis is another feature that appeared early in New Jersey quilts, as three of the early block-style quilts illustrate. Diagonal placement even extended to medallion quilts. One diagonally set medallion quilt[7] incorporated portraits of the first six American presidents cut from fabrics that were printed in both France and England (one as early as 1829),[8] suggesting that the quilt might have been made in the early 1830s. In the 1840s New Jerseyans achieved diagonal emphasis in block-style quilts in one of two ways: either by diagonal set with conspicuous sashing[9] or by the choice of a block design that set up strong diagonal lines when the blocks were assembled.[10] In the 1850s and 1860s when appliqué sampler quilts dominated the New Jersey quilting scene, interest in diagonal effects seemed to wane somewhat.[11] Most of the New Jersey appliqué quilts of the 1850s and 1860s are set square, although there are a few interesting exceptions.[12] But after 1870, New Jerseyans seemed to regain their interest in using strong diagonal effects in their quilts.[13]

Tape binding woven of tan thread, often with a lengthwise blue or green stripe, was used on New Jersey quilts of the 1840s with some regularity.[14] This type of binding is sometimes called "Trenton tape" by local historical societies, but its exact source and date of manufacture have yet to be identified. It may have been used on whole cloth quilts as early as the 1820s as it is occasionally seen on pieces of glazed chintz that appear to have been part of a set of bed hangings. This type of binding does not seem to be common on quilts made after the 1840s however.

New Jerseyans of the mid-19th century generally used: 1) simple pieced blocks, 2) a limited selection of borders or, frequently, no borders at all, 3) inconspicuous styles of quilting (fancy stencil patterns, stippling, and close parallel rows of quilting are rare), and 4) a limited amount of white space (white alternate set squares and white borders are rare although white is used for backgrounds).

Generally missing from 19th-century New Jersey quilts are: 1) four-block and nine-block quilts, 2) several color schemes common even in neighboring states including two-color quilts in navy and white, scrap quilts with orange or blue backgrounds, and pink flowers in appliqué designs, 3) appliqué quilts using a single pattern (except Oak Leaf and Reel and a few other rare examples), and 4) a stairstep appliqué border often seen in Virginia and Maryland quilts.[15]

Sometimes New Jersey quilts are noticeably similar to quilts made in the adjacent areas of neighboring states of Delaware, Pennsylvania, and New York. Some of the features identified in New Jersey quilts may serve as the basis for an understanding of wider regional patterns along the mid-Atlantic coast.

For instance, the Quaker religion provided a major link between the quiltmakers of southwestern New Jersey and the quiltmakers of the Philadelphia area. The Quakers of New Jersey, Pennsylvania, and Delaware were an intermarrying social community, and this fact can be seen in the overlapping styles of their quilts as well as in the mixture of place names on several quilts.[16] Some New Jersey quilts bear Philadelphia references, while a Philadelphia marriage quilt, owned by the Philadelphia Museum of Art, bears the names of the New Jersey towns where some of the groom's relatives lived.[17] The Delaware connection with New Jersey quilts is documented by a Lone Star quilt pieced in Burlington County, New Jersey, in 1837 and quilted in Delaware in 1839. Quaker society extended well beyond the Delaware Valley, as is demonstrated by a mid-1840s Indiana quilt now owned by the Smithsonian Institution.[18] The quilt was made for or by an Indiana Quaker girl and includes blocks made by her father's relatives whose town names in New Jersey and Pennsylvania are inscribed on the blocks.

In the 1850s as the practice of signing quilts began to disappear from the southwestern counties of New Jersey, it gained popularity in the northeastern corner of the state. When this happened, Philadelphia references disappeared from New Jersey quilts and New York place names — such as Brooklyn — began to appear in their place. Concurrently, the styles of quilt being signed changed so that 1850s sampler quilts made in New Jersey cities such as Newark are more similar to an 1853 quilt probably made in Brooklyn (now owned by the New Jersey State Museum),[19] than to the quilts made in southwestern New Jersey in the 1840s.

1837 was chosen for the beginning date of this study because it is the earliest inscribed date the New Jersey project saw on a quilt's top: a Lone Star owned by The Historic Houses in Odessa, Delaware, and inscribed with the date "December 28, 1837." A later notation attached to the back of the quilt says that the top was pieced in 1837 and quilted in 1839. Family history indicates that the maker, Mary Jane Moore from Moorestown in Burlington County, New Jersey, married a Delaware man in 1838, between the year she pieced the quilt and the year she quilted it.[20] The ending date of this study is provided by an appliqué sampler quilt made for the minister of the Middletown Baptist Church (now called Old First Church) in Monmouth County. Its inscription says that the quilt was presented in December 1867.[21] The date associated with this quilt is

the latest documented on a 19th-century appliqué sampler. The two quilts that define the beginning and end of our 30-year time period come from opposite sides of the historic line that divided the state at the time of early settlement. The first quilt comes from a southwestern county and the last quilt comes from a northeastern county. These two quilts also illustrate the types of women usually associated with signed mid-19th-century New Jersey quilts: young women of marriageable age, often Quakers, and women who were members of church congregations, often Methodists, Baptists, Presbyterians, or Dutch Reformed.

More than 66 New Jersey quilts with a known time and place of construction and with inscribed dates between 1837 and 1867 have been identified.[22] Some of these quilts have both dates and place names written on the quilt itself. Others bear either a date or place name, accompanied by a strong family history providing the rest of the information. When inscribed quilts of known origin are located on maps of the state, they reveal local patterns of quiltmaking activity. Figure 1 shows four mid-19th-century time intervals: from 1837 to 1844 all the known signed quilts were made in the southern or western part of the state, clustering in Burlington County; from 1845 to 1848 is a transition period in which the making of signed quilts was scattered throughout the central counties and along the western border; from 1849 to 1857 the making of signed quilts began to cluster in the northeastern cities such as Newark and Elizabeth; and from 1858 to 1867 most of the quilts of known origin were made in northeastern counties of the state, completing the

Lone Star, 1837. Made by Mary Jane Moore, a Quaker from Moorestown, Burlington County, New Jersey. The inscription, "Mary Jane Moore/December 28, 1837," seems to reflect the quilt's date of construction, making it the earliest ink inscription on a New Jersey quilt seen by the New Jersey project. A cloth label attached to the back says the top was pieced in 1837 and was quilted in 1839. Owned by The Historical Houses of Odessa (Delaware) which are owned by the Henry Francis du Pont Winterthur Museum. Courtesy: Winterthur

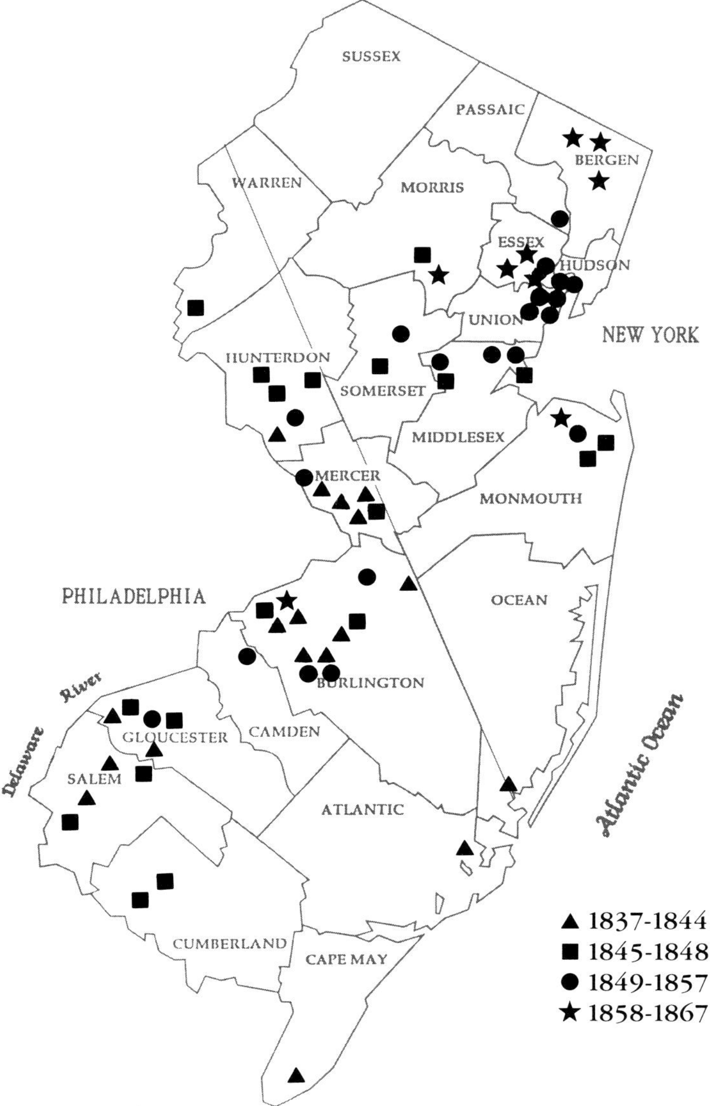

New Jersey locations where signed quilts from various time intervals have been recorded. In the earliest time interval, 1837-1844, the southern part of the state seems to have been most active in the signing of quilts. By the latest period, 1858-1867, the signing of quilts seems to have shifted to the northeastern counties. The two intervening time periods show the transition of signing from one corner of the state to the other.

shift in the signing of quilts from one end of the state to the other. Figure 2 shows the locations where pieced and appliqué signed quilts were made in the state between 1837 and 1867. This map shows that most of the pieced quilts of known origin were made in the southern or western part of the state, while about twice as many appliqué quilts of known origin were made in the northeastern part of the state.

Ink inscriptions first appeared on the front of New Jersey quilts in the late-1830s as the 1837 Lone Star, the earliest quilt in our time period, illustrates. Several 1820s and 1830s quilts were dated and initialed on the back, but in cross-stitch or embroidery, not ink,[23] and they were apparently marked as a part of the tradition of marking valuable textiles to show ownership. Although dating and initialing the back of quilts immediately preceded the use of elaborate ink inscriptions on the face of quilts, these two types of markings served different purposes. Rather than denoting ownership, ink inscriptions on the front of quilts made in the late 1830s and 1840s often conveyed sentiment of friendship or commemorated an important social event, such as the recipient's marriage or departure from the community. By 1842 ink inscriptions on New Jersey quilts were at their most elaborate,[24] and their complexity tended to decline over the next 25 years.

Again, the signing of quilts in New Jersey shows a clear regional pattern. In the early 1840s, signed quilts are seen only in the southern part of the state, but by the 1850s inscriptions had largely disappeared from quilts made in the southern counties. On the other hands, inscriptions are not seen in the northeastern counties until later in the 1840s, and they are at their height of popularity in the 1850s. Cross-stitch and embroidery are occasionally seen[25] as techniques for marking quilts on their face, particularly in the 1850s, but ink was still the most common method of signing quilts throughout the middle of the 19th century.

Starting in the 1840s, brighter fabrics, usually set against white backgrounds, made New Jersey quilts strikingly different from earlier quilts made in the more muted fabrics of the 1820s and 1830s. New fabrics in the 1840s included small scale red prints,[26] intense blues or greens,[27] and an occasional acid yellow.[28] The use of sashing, sometimes combined with diagonal set, also gave New Jersey quilts of the 1840s a distinctive look. Sashing (strips of fabric separating pieced or appliquéd blocks) was not seen on New Jersey quilts before 1840, but the idea of sashing was illustrated in tile floors pictured on furnishing fabrics of the period.[29] Once sashing was adopted in the 1840s, New Jersey quiltmakers largely abandoned the use of plain squares of fabric (alternate set) as a means of separating pieced or appliqué blocks in their quilts.

Appliqué quilts of the early 1840s that have been recorded to date contain none of the conventional floral designs such as tulips or wreaths that became widely used in New Jersey sampler quilts a decade later and in repeat block quilts made in other states. Appliqué designs on quilts dated before 1845 are limited to Oak Leaf and Reel variations, some geometric motifs, and chintz appliqué. The quilts documented to date in New Jersey confirm Barbara Brackman's suggestion that the Oak Leaf and Reel appliqué pattern was in use earlier than other familiar appliqué designs.[30] It is almost the only appliqué pattern seen as a repeat block quilt in New Jersey in the mid-19th century.[31] It is also the only appliqué design in an otherwise pieced 1842 sampler quilt from Swedesboro in Gloucester County.[32]

A second 1842 sampler quilt, made in Mount Holly in Burlington County and owned by the Art Institute of Chicago, provides a record of additional designs apparently involving appliqué that were used by New Jersey quiltmakers in the early 1840s.[33] Several blocks in the Mount Holy quilt appear to be constructed like the current Dresden Plate design in which the pieces are first joined into a circle and then appliquéd onto a square of background fabric. The piecing step may have been accomplished by the English or template method since this technique is known to have been used by Quaker women in the Delaware Valley to assemble other circular designs.[34] It is possible that some of the designs in this group may have been totally template-pieced, while others seem to require the use of appliqué. This group of patterns will be referred to as "circular designs" to emphasize their geometric, rather than floral, basis.

Circular designs are seen on a third sampler quilt made in the early 1840s, owned by the Philadelphia Museum of Art.[35] It was made for a Philadelphia bride, Charlotte Gillingham, but it contains blocks bearing New Jersey place names associated with the family of the groom, Samuel P. Hancock. One circular design, sometimes called Caesar's Crown or Fullblown Tulip, was used as the pattern for two repeat-block quilts made in southwestern New Jersey in the early 1840s. One of these quilts is owned by the New Jersey State Museum,[36] and the other can be seen in Linda Lipsett's book, *Remember Me*.[37]

The other type of appliqué quilt made with some frequency in New Jersey in the 1840s is the sampler quilt made of blocks with floral chintz cut outs. The earliest examples seen to date were made in Trenton in 1842 and 1843. One, owned by the DAR Museum, has a wide chintz border and large center wreath.[38] The other, shown in Nancy and Donald Roan's

Sampler quilt, 1841-1842. Made for Ella Maria Deacon, Mount Holly, Burlington County, New Jersey. Of particular interest are the many blocks containing circular designs that were first pieced and then appliquéd to background squares. The quilt is typical of southwestern New Jersey quilts of this period in its diagonal set, strong lines of sashing, contrasting triangles at the edges, and an absence of borders. Collection of the Art Institute of Chicago. Courtesy: Art Institute of Chicago.

book, *Lest I Shall Be Forgotten*, is set on the diagonal with contrasting sashing and natural leaves at the edges as is characteristic of New Jersey pieced quilts of the period.[39] Both of these early chintz appliqué samplers were made by or for individual young women.

All of the other Delaware Valley chintz appliqué samplers seen to date share a common format: being set square either without borders or with a plain white border. The Philadelphia Museum of Art owns at least two Pennsylvania chintz appliqué quilts similar to New Jersey examples.[40] Other New Jersey chintz appliqué samplers include a quilt made for the minister of the Mount Holly Baptist Church in 1848, owned by the Burlington County Historical Society,[41] and a quilt made for the minister of the Presbyterian Church in Perth Amboy dated 1852-1853 and owned by the Shelburne Museum.[42] All of the New Jersey chintz appliqué quilts seen to date were made on the western part of the state in the 1840s, except for the latest example which was made in Perth Amboy on the east coast in 1852-1853.

The appliqué motifs used on the backgrounds of two 1840s Lone Star quilts represent the dominant types of appliqué found in New Jersey at that time: a Lone Star quilt owned by the Metropolitan Museum has an Oak Leaf and Reel variation in the corners and along the sides,[43] while another Lone Star owned by the Burlington County Historical Society has pieced circular forms appliquéd in the corners and floral chintz cut outs appliquéd along the sides.[44]

On the other hand, a sampler quilt made in 1845 for the minister of the Amwell (now Flemington) Baptist Church and recently acquired by the New Jersey State Museum[45] is an encyclopedic example of 1840s New Jersey appliqué styles. This 72-block sampler presents every type of appliqué seen in New Jersey in the 1840s: variations on Oak Leaf and Reel, several circular designs including Caesar's Crown, chintz appliqué, and some designs incorporating natural leaves. It also includes a few rather basic conventional floral designs, making it the earliest New Jersey quilt recorded to date using the kind of stylized floral patterns that would come into wide popularity in the 1850s.

Concurrent with such appliqués, an identifiable style of pieced quilts began to appear in the central and southern counties along the Delaware River in the early 1840s: dark-and-diagonal pieced quilts developed in New Jersey's southwestern counties and then moved to the northeastern. The characteristics of these pieced quilts include dark fabrics, diagonal placement of the blocks, contrasting sashing, and half-square triangles at the edges instead of borders. An early example of this particular style is a Chimney Sweep quilt in the collection of the New Jersey State Museum.[46] It has inscribed dates of 1842 to 1844 and southwestern New Jersey place names such as Moorestown, Camden, and Mullica Hill.

However, by the middle of the 1840s, this dark-and-diagonal style was not restricted to the southwestern region. Two quilts of similar style dated 1845[47] and 1848[48] were recorded in Middlesex and Morris counties, indicating that this quilt style was moving in a northerly direction. The latter, known as the Randolph quilt, was made in Morris County from 1842 to 1848 and documented by the California Heritage Quilt Project. It is the earliest known pieced quilt from a northern county in the dark-and-diagonal style. It also features a characteristic often found in the dark-and-diagonals as well as other New Jersey quilts: the inclusion of a different center block to form a central focus. The center of the Randolph quilt is a Mariner's Compass medallion bordered with Flying Geese, while the rest of the quilt is made of up blocks in a Shoo Fly variation. Because of the diagonal arrangement of the blocks in dark-and-diagonal quilts, the Randolph quilt, like others in this style, is finished with half-square triangles at the edge. These large triangles were usually cut from one piece of either plain or printed fabric.[49] However, one variation from Monmouth County displays half-square triangles that contain half-

A Summary of Mid-19th Century Appliqué in New Jersey.

Location	Dates	Style
Burlington County and Philadelphia	1842-1843	Circular designs included in samplers (possibly combining appliqué and template piecing).
Burlington County east to Middlesex County	1842-1853	Chintz Appliqué Samplers
Burlington County northeast to Essex County	1849-1867	Conventional Appliqué Samplers (primarily stylized floral motifs)
Union County north to Bergen County	1853-1865	Original Appliqué Samplers (including religious motifs, local products, events, homes, etc.)

block designs.[50]

In contrast to quilts of the southwestern areas,[51] no dark-and-diagonal quilts have been attributed to the southeastern counties of Cape May and Atlantic during the 1840s. Instead, the quilts of this region are characterized by their square set. Some in the southeast exhibit highly contrasting fabrics and bold, graphic designs,[52] while others combine a variety of lighter-colored fabrics (both prints and solids) and present a much different appearance.[53] It is interesting to note, however, that pieced block-style quilts in the entire southern region of the state, whether set on the diagonal or on the square, are made of single repeat-block patterns that are based on squares and triangles.

In the 1850s, as the northward shift of quiltmaking activity began to take place, the central counties became a transition area where a variety of styles were tried: solely pieced, appliquéd, or made by combining the two techniques.[54] Pieced quilts of the central counties continued to use the style and set of the previous decade: diagonal set, contrasting sashing, and half-square triangles at the edges.[55] Yet, the overall appearance of these transitional quilts reflected more carefully selected colors and a much more limited number of fabrics, a trend which became characteristic of 1850s pieced quilts One of the earliest dated quilts from this decade is a Feathered Star from Monmouth County that bears the inscription, "1850 This quilt presented to William B. Mount at the age of 14 years, by his mother Mary Mount."[56] This quilt displays only four different fabrics and a red, white, and blue color scheme.

A major change in New Jersey quilts during the years 1837-1867 was the introduction of some white fabric.[57] First seen in quilts of the 1840s where it was sometimes used as background, the use of white increased in the 1850s and 1860s in both pieced and appliqué quilts, but characteristic of New Jersey quilts, no matter what the time period, is the minimal amount of white space compared to quilts from other states where solid blocks or large white spaces are filled with elaborate quilting designs. Thus, New Jersey quilts often appear to be more crowded or dense than those of other states.

In the 1850s another important change to occur in overall design was the addition of appliqué borders to pieced quilts. Circular pieced designs such as Sunburst or Starburst were often combined with appliqué borders that displayed either the more elegant swag and bow design[58] or the running vine design.[59] It is extremely rare for New Jersey quilts to incorporate elaborately appliquéd borders; however, one example from Gloucester County in southwestern New Jersey is the exception.[60] The center of the quilt is constructed of Peony variation blocks set on the diagonal and surrounded on three sides by wide borders. In the center of two of the borders is an appliquéd basket filled with flowers. A large running vine with oak leaves and peonies fills the space from the basket to the ends of each border.

New Jersey quiltmakers showed a certain interest in using natural leaves rather than stylized leaves in both their appliqué and pieced quilts. The addition of recognizable oak leaves to the somewhat stylized reel pattern set a precedent for the use of actual leaves as templates, but the idea was carried further by using identifiable leaves in the half-square triangles around the edges of diagonally set quilts,[61] in borders,[62] in other blocks,[63] and as sashing.[64]

During the 1850s and 1860s it becomes more difficult to identify the trends of pieced quilts that were made due to the disappearance of ink signatures. While the majority of pieced quilts from this time period were not signed, signatures appear occasionally on pieced quilts — one made as late as 1862. Ex-

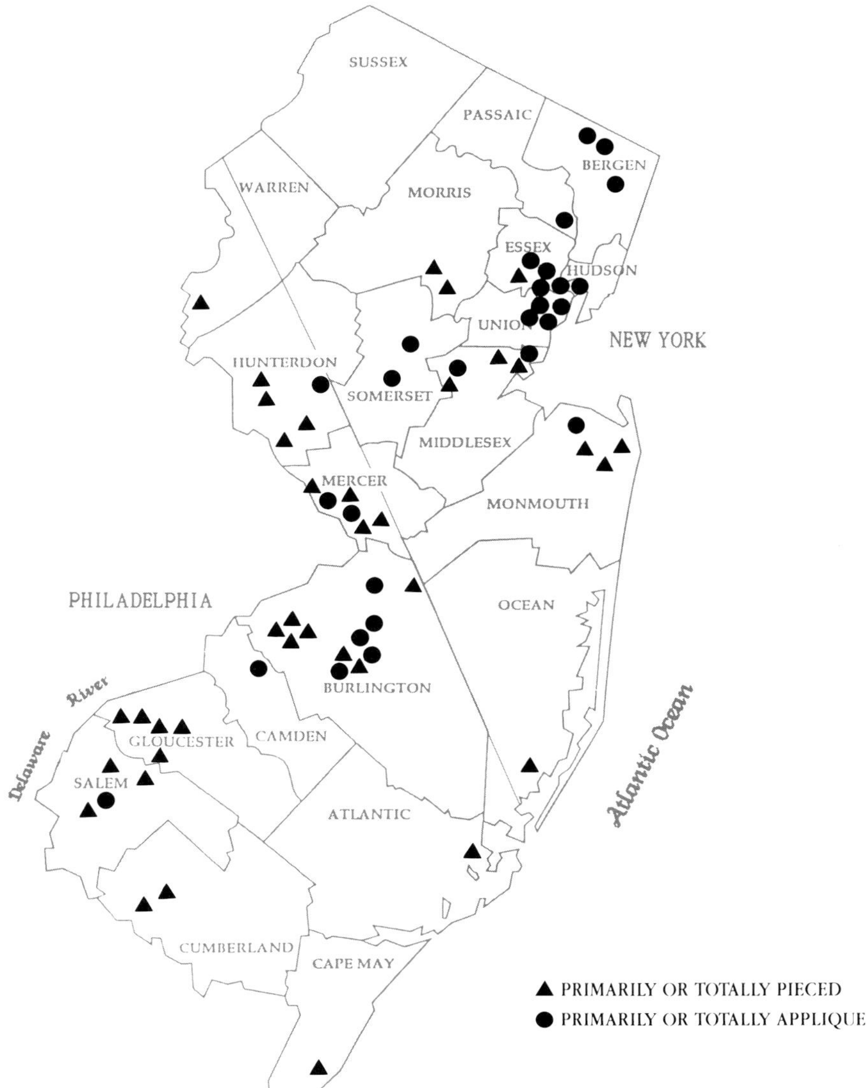

New Jersey locations where signed pieced and appliqued quilts are known to have been made between 1837 and 1867. Signed pieced quilts have more often been found in the southern/western part of the state while inscribed appliqué quilts were more commonly found in the northeastern counties.

Medallion Star with Flying Geese and Shoo Fly Variation, 1842-1848. Made by Harriet Jane Pope Randolph and her mother, Morristown, Morris County, New Jersey. The diagonal set, contrasting sashing, central focus, and edge triangles make this quilt the northernmost example of the dark-and-diagonal style of pieced quilt more commonly seen in southwestern New Jersey. Collection of Flora Jane Randolph Gorman. Courtesy of the California Heritage Quilt Project.

amples include: a Rambler variation with a signature and date of 1856 made in Burlington County;[65] a star variation in the collection of the Shelburne Museum that contains signatures in addition to information pinned to the quilt stating that it was made in South Orange, which is in the northeastern part of the state in Essex County, for J. Wickliffe Beach when he entered Yale in 1860;[66] and a basket quilt owned by the Newark Museum that contains ink signatures and a Bible verse in each block and was made in 1860-1862 for the minister of the First Presbyterian Church in New Vernon in Morris County.[67]

In the 1850s and 1860s, perhaps due to the proliferation of original appliqué designs, only one conventional appliqué pattern — the Oak Leaf and Reel — has been seen as a repeat-block quilt. One example comes from southwestern Burlington County and is signed and dated 1856.[68] It echoes the dark-and-diagonal style that was so popular in the pieced quilts of the 1840s: diagonal set, dark sashing, half-square triangles at the edges, naturalistic leaves, and central focus.

But as the northern areas became the focus of appliqué quilts during this period, diagonal set was largely replaced by square set. Wide and contrasting sashing was either eliminated or was replaced with pieced sashing, tiny piping, or embroidery over the seams where the blocks were joined. In the northern counties, appliqué borders began to appear on appliqué quilts in the mid-1840s, while the quilts of the central and southwestern areas essentially remained borderless. In the 1850s and 1860s, borders were found on some appliqué quilts made in Monmouth County,[69] but for the most part appliqué quilts were generally made without borders. However, one feature common to both the southwestern and northeastern areas is the technique of combining different appliqué styles — chintz appliqué, conventional, and original — into one quilt.[70] Sometimes in the southwestern counties even needlepoint blocks were incorporated into quilts of this type.[71]

The earliest appliqué sampler quilt from a northeastern county is dated 1845-1849 and is owned by the New Jersey State Museum.[72] It contains 25 square set blocks that feature chintz appliqué birds, chrysanthemums, and roses in addition to original appliqué designs. Signatures appear in each block and in the area above each swag in the swag and bow border. The quilt was made by members of the Methodist Episcopal Church of Elizabeth Town in Union County, an area which has been identified as a center of quiltmaking activity in the 1850s.[73] This appliqué sampler quilt closely resembles another one in the museum's collection that was possibly made in New York in 1853.[74]

Another example of this square set style is an appliqué sampler that links New Jersey quilts to Baltimore-style album quilts.[75] It is owned by the Historical Society of Plainfield and was made in New Jersey in 1857. It contains ink inscriptions of both New Jersey and Baltimore-area place names. Constructed of 30 blocks and set on the square with no sashing and no border, it resembles Baltimore-style album quilts in terms of the set and the appliqué designs, especially the blocks that feature vases of flowers, floral wreaths, and diagonal sprays. However, typically New Jersey blocks containing naturalistic leaves and the Oak Leaf and Reel pattern are also included.

Another variation found in the construction of New Jersey appliqué quilts is the sheer number of blocks. Traditionally, they range from 12 (set three across and four down) to 30 (set five across and six down). Other variations have been seen in diagonally set quilts which often contain 40 or more blocks. In two of the more urban areas of the northeast, quilts were made that contain 90 to 121 blocks. These multiple-block quilts were made by church groups as tokens of friendship and were given to the minister often upon his leaving the congregation. One example is the Cory presentation album quilt in the collection of the Shelburne Museum that was made in Perth Amboy, Middlesex County, in 1852-1853 by members of the Presbyterian Church.[76] Each of the 121 chintz appliqué blocks is inscribed with a signature and a Bible verse. Not far away in adjoining Union County, three quilts each containing 90 or more blocks were made during the same time period by members of the Methodist Episcopal, First Presbyterian, and First Baptist Churches in Elizabeth.[77] Among the many designs featured in these quilts are Bible pictures, naturalistic leaves and flowers, cut paper snowflakes, and chintz appliqué. Large cutout paisleys are also seen in New Jersey appliqué sampler quilts of this time period.

While there are identifiable styles and characteristics of New Jersey quilts, exceptions have been found. One example is an original appliqué from Mercer County which features alternate white blocks, elaborate floral vine borders, heavy quilting in feather wreaths, as well as double- and triple-line quilting, all of which are unusual for New Jersey.[78] However, this quilt does include typically New Jersey naturalistic leaves.

The early 1850s marked the beginnings of original appliqué design, and by the late-1850s and early 1860s these designs became even more personalized, especially in the northeastern counties. This new style emerged when quiltmakers began to record everyday

Appliquéd quilt, 1859. Made by Betsey Haring, Bergen County, New Jersey. Like many northeastern New Jersey quilts of the late 1850s and early 1860s, this quilt features objects that were important to the quiltmaker's life. Representing local manufacturing trades are a pair of wooden chairs and a rooster weathervane. Baskets used in the local strawberry industry are also depicted. Collection of the Bergen County Historical Society. Courtesy: Bergenfield Museum.

Appliquéd quilt, 1860-1865. Made by Emeline Dean, East Orange, Essex County, New Jersey. This northeastern New Jersey quilt is another example of the newly emerging personalized style of quiltmaking in which objects important to the quiltmaker's life were recorded. The center block is thought to show the maker, her dog, the family homestead, and her horse-drawn cart. However, the diagonal set emphasized with embroidered vines echoes the style of the quilts made in the 1840s in the southwestern counties of the state. Collection of The Newark Museum. Courtesy: Newark Museum.

activities and special events that took place in and around the communities in which they lived. Three quilts in particular — all from northeastern Bergen County — are examples of such personalized designs: the Betsey Haring quilt made in 1859, the Mowerson quilt made in 1859, and the Ackerman quilt made in 1860.

In the Betsey Haring quilt, owned by the Bergen County Historical Society, all the appliquéd items — some more familiar than others — have been identified in ink: table, pitcher, citton [sic], Butter Fly [sic], dog, buggy, etc. In particular, two items in the quilt — a rooster weathervane and a pair of wooden chairs — tie the quilt to local manufacturing trades.[79] Additionally, a woven and appliquéd strawberry basket is representative of the strawberry trade which reached its peak just before the Civil War when buyers, sellers, and pickers congregated in the inns at the strawberry centers in Ramsey and Allendale. Most of the strawberries were then transported by wagon to Paterson, Newark, and New York.[80]

The Ackerman quilt, attributed to the Saddle River area, has been documented in Sandi Fox's book, *Wrapped in Glory*.[81] Several blocks represent local figures and events or depict Bergen County's agricultural wealth. The many horse farms in Saddle River are represented in the blocks with horses which are also inscribed with men's names. One block contains a horse and rider and a tiny figure which may represent the time when P.T. Barnum and his circus spent the winter in New Jersey. Another block represents the harvests of the orchards and the fields.

The Mowerson quilt made in Ramsey, which is near Saddle River, has recently been linked to the Ackerman quilt.[82] Even though these two quilts do not display the same block designs, they do share some of the same inscribed names such as Mowerson,[83] Ackerman, DePew, Pulis, and Winter. In addition to the horizontal placement of blocks, both quilts also share several smaller shapes such as hearts and flying birds, as well as the same detailed embroidery on the horses' manes and tails. Although the designs in two of the blocks have not yet been interpreted, they are worth mentioning. One block depicts a majestic-looking horse and rider while the other displays a girl, a dog, and a boy flying a kite.

Finally, a signed quilt made toward the end of the 30-year period displays the characteristics of both the new personalized designs as well as the quilts made earlier in the survey period. The Emeline Dean quilt, dated 1860-1865 and in the collection of the Newark Museum, not only records the quiltmaker's life and home in relation to the earth and the heavens, but is also a dramatic personal statement.[84] Its center block is a small girl, perhaps Emeline, in hoop skirt and pantalettes shown with her dog on the grounds of the family homestead along with a horse-drawn cart that she received as a birthday gift. In combination with these personal images, the style and set of this later quilt continue to display characteristics that first began to appear in the early 1840s: diagonal set, central focus, half-square triangles at the edges, and naturalistic leaves; characteristics that were typical of New Jersey quilts in the 1840s and 1850s. Thus, the Emeline Dean quilt symbolizes the way in which both quiltmaking activity and style in New Jersey shifted from the southwestern counties to the northeastern during the 30-year period, 1837-1867.

The Heritage Quilt Project of New Jersey will continue to document quilt collections in local museums and historical societies as they become available for examination. A recent listing by the Museums Council of New Jersey names 130 museums and historic places. This suggests that a survey of quilts at all of the institutions will necessarily be a long-range goal. Experience to date suggests that the types of New Jersey quilts owned by museums are sometimes different from the quilts still in private hands. For example, two of the more high-style types of quilts — chintz appliqué and white whole cloth quilts — were rarely presented at public documentation days in New Jersey, although they are found with some frequency in museum collections. The project will also continue to accept mail registration of quilts through 1995.[85] Additional information from still-to-be documented sources and research into quilts from adjoining states should provide further insight into the regional patterns presented in this report.

The authors wish to thank: the Montclair (New Jersey) Craft Guild for its grant toward photographic expenses associated with this research as well as the other members of The Heritage Quilt Project of New Jersey for their continuing help in the research, analysis, and presentation of this material. They would like to thank, especially, Rachel Cochran for her skillful and sensitive editorial assistance.

End Notes

Many of the end notes refer to photographs of quilts illustrating the points made in the text. The quilts described are privately owned unless a museum is cited as the owner. The pattern names used are those in current usage and were not generally provided by the quilt owners who often referred to their quilts by a previous owner's name rather than a pattern name, e.g., "Aunt Lydia's quilt," rather than "Oak Leaf and Reel quilt."

[1]Jonathan Holstein, "The American Block Quilt," in *In The Heart of Pennsylvania Symposium Papers*, ed. Jeannette Lasansky (Lewisburg, PA: The Oral Traditions Project, 1986), 16-27.

[2]Rachel Cochran, Rita Erickson, Natalie Hart, and Barbara Schaffer, *New Jersey Quilts 1777 to 1950: Contributions to an American Tradition* (Paducah, KY: American Quilter's Society, 1992), 49.

[3]Carter Houck and Myron Miller, *American Quilts and How to Make Them* (New York: Charles Scribner's Sons, 1975), 77.

[4]Cochran, 50.

[5]Ibid., 60 and 62.

[6]Ibid., 53.

[7]Ibid., 219 and 222.

[8]Florence Montgomery, *Printed Textiles, English and American Cottons and Linens 1700-1850* (New York: Viking Press, 1970), 341. Also seen in Herbert Ridgeway Collins, *Threads of History: Americana Recorded on Cloth, 1775 to the Present* (Washington, DC: Smithsonian Institution Press, 1979), 78.

[9]Cochran, 75.

[10]Ibid., 76 and 77.

[11]Ibid., 79 and 84.

[12]Carter Houck, "Echoes of Elegant Living," *Lady's Circle Patchwork Quilts* 30 (Summer 1983): 10.

[13]Cochran, 13, 19, 115, 151, and 153.

[14]Ibid., 62. The HQPNJ originally learned about Trenton tape from Burlington County resident and national quilt lecturer Kay Lukasko who had seen several local examples.

[15]Gloria Seaman Allen, *First Flowerings: Early Virginia Quilts* (Washington, DC: DAR Museum, 1987), 18.

[16]For further information on Quaker quilts and their role in Quaker society see: Jessica F. Nicoll, *Quilted for Friends: Delaware Valley Signature Quilts 1840-1855* (Winterthur, DE: The Henry Francis du Pont Winterthur Museum, 1986); Jessica F. Nicoll, "Signature Quilts and the Quaker Community, 1840-1860," in *Uncoverings 1986*, ed. Sally Garoutte (Mill Valley, CA: American Quilt Study Group, 1987), 27-38; Patricia Herr, "Quaker Quilts and Their Makers," in *Pieced by Mother Symposium Papers*, ed. Jeannette Lasansky (Lewisburg, PA: The Oral Traditions Project, 1988), 13-22; Patricia Herr, "In All Modesty and Plainness," in *Quilt Digest 3*, ed. Michael M. Kile (San Francisco: The Quilt Digest Press, 1985); and Jack L. Lindsay, "Nineteenth-Century Appliqué Quilts," *Philadelphia Museum of Art Bulletin* Vol. 85 No. 363-364 (Fall 1989): 27.

[17]Cochran, 100. Also Lindsay, 27.

[18]Doris M. Bowman, *The Smithsonian Treasury — American Quilts* (Washington, DC: Smithsonian Institution Press, 1991), 45. Museum records show that some of the inscriptions document the making of blocks by one person on behalf of another: "Elisabeth Nicholson for her brother Coleman Nicholson." Several blocks bear the names of young children.

[19]New Jersey State Museum Accession #CH1987.38, unpublished.

[20]The Historic Houses of Odessa, Delaware, which own the 1837 Lone Star quilt are, in turn, owned by the Henry Francis du Pont Winterthur Museum, Winterthur, Delaware. The quilt is Winterthur #81.0282. This quilt was inscribed only with the maker's name and the date of construction, not messages of friendship, but several friendship quilts with dates as early as 1839 are known, including one from Bridgeton, New Jersey, owned by the Abby Aldrich Rockefeller Folk Art Museum, Williamsburg, Virginia, (#90.609.3) which is inscribed "This bed quilt commenced in 1839 and finished in 1847."

[21]Cochran, 84.

[22]Although at least 66 inscribed quilts with known date and place of construction form the basis of this study, several additional unsigned quilts from this time period with firm histories support these findings.

[23]Cochran, 47 (upper right).

[24]Ibid., 94 (top) and 99 (bottom).

[25]Ibid., 94 (bottom right).

[26]Cochran, 23.

[27]Nicholl, *Friends*, Plate VII, sashing.

[28]Cochran, 76 (lower right of photo).

[29]Mary Schoeser and Celia Rufey, *English and American Textiles from 1790 to the Present* (London: Thames and Hudson, 1989), 58, Plate 42.

[30]Barbara Brackman, "Signature Quilts: Nineteenth Century Trends," in *Uncoverings 1989*, ed. Laurel Horton (San Francisco: American Quilt Study Group, 1990), 30.

[31]Cochran, 18 and 23.

[32]Ibid., 76 (center right of photo).

[33]Christa C. Mayer Thurman, *Textiles in the Art Institute of Chicago* (Chicago: The Art Institute of Chicago, 1992), 108-109.

[34]Nicoll, *Friends*, 31. This illustration shows a circular design totally assembled over paper templates, raising a question as to which circular designs were usually constructed totally by English piecing and which were made with a combination of piecing and appliqué. Also see Tandy Hersh, "1842 Primitive Hall Pieced Quilt Top: The Art of Transforming Printed Fabric Designs Through Geometry," in *Uncoverings 1986*, ed. Sally Garoutte (Mill Valley, CA: The American Quilt Study Group, 1986), 47-60.

[35]Lindsay, 27. The same quilt is shown in Nicoll, *Friends*, Plate IV.

[36]New Jersey State Museum Accession #CH1985.4, unpublished.

[37]Linda Otto Lipsett, *Remember Me: Women and Their Friendship Quilts* (San Francisco: The Quilt Digest Press, 1985), 26.

[38]Jane Bentley Kolter, *Forget Me Not: A Gallery of Friendship and Album Quilts* (Pittstown, NJ: The Main Street Press, 1985), 22.

[39]Nancy and Donald Roan, *Lest I Shall Be Forgotten: Anecdotes and Traditions of Quilts* (Green Lane, PA: Goschenhoppen Historians, Inc., 1993), 45.

[40]Lindsay, 23.

[41]Nan Helene Mutnick, *New Jersey Quilters: A Timeless Tradition* (Morristown, NJ: Morris Mu-

seum of Arts and Sciences, 1983), 10.

[42]Celia Y. Oliver, *55 Famous Quilts from the Shelburne Museum* (Mineola, NY: Dover Publication, Inc., 1990), 31.

[43]Amelia Peck, *American Quilts and Coverlets in the Metropolitan Museum of Art* (New York: The Metropolitan Museum of Art and Dutton Studio Books, 1990), 188.

[44]Houck, "Echoes," 12 (bottom).

[45]Christie's, *Important American Furniture, Silver, Folk Art and Decorative Arts* (New York: Catalog for Auction on June 23, 1993), 49, quilt 85.

[46]New Jersey State Museum Accession #CH1986.8.1, unpublished.

[47]Mutnick, 14.

[48]Jean Ray Laury and The California Heritage Quilt Project, *Ho for California! Pioneer Women and Their Quilts* (New York: E.P. Dutton, 1990), 28 and 29.

[49]Cochran, 73.

[50]New Jersey State Museum Accession #CH1987.36.1, unpublished.

[51]Cochran, 75.

[52]Carter Houck, "A Timeless Tradition," *Lady's Circle Patchwork Quilts* 30 (Summer 1983): 22.

[53]Cochran, 97 (bottom left) and HQPNJ Archives #53-049-04.

[54]Cochran, 78.

[55]Mutnick, 36.

[56]Cochran, 96 and 97 (top).

[57]Ibid., 95 (bottom right).

[58]Ibid., 39 (plate 9).

[59]HQPNJ Archives #71-01-011.

[60]Cochran, 81.

[61]Ibid., 18 and HQPNJ Archives #52-019-03.

[62]HQPNJ Archives #52-019-04.

[63]Cochran, 79.

[64]Ibid., 80.

[65]Ibid., 77.

[66]Shelburne Museum Accession #10-419.

[67]Philip H. Curtis, *American Quilts in the Newark Museum Collection* (Newark: The Newark Museum Association, 1974), 48 and 49.

[68]Cochran, 18.

[69]Mutnick, 4 and Cochran, 84.

[70]Houck, "Echoes," 10.

[71]Mutnick, 21.

[72]New Jersey State Museum Accession #CH1980.41, unpublished.

[73]Lee Kogan, "The Quilt Legacy of Elizabeth, New Jersey," *The Clarion* (Winter 1990): 58-64.

[74]New Jersey State Museum Accession #CH1987.38, unpublished.

[75]Cochran, 79.

[76]Oliver, 31.

[77]Kogan, 58-64.

[78]Cochran, 15.

[79]HQPNJ Archives #71-001-01.

[80]John Cunningham, *This is New Jersey* (New Brunswick, NJ: Rutgers University Press, 1978), 84.

[81]Sandi Fox, *Wrapped in Glory, Figurative Quilts and Bedcovers 1700-1900* (Los Angeles and new York: Los Angeles County Museum of Art and Thames and Hudson, 1990), 92-07.

[82]HQPNJ Archives #71-004-02.

[83]Mowerson also appears as "Mowerfson."

[84]Curtis, 34 and 35.

[85]Cochran, 237-238.

Barbara Schaffer and Rita Erickson have served as president and vice-president, respectively, for the New Jersey Quilt Documentation Project since they founded it in 1987. They are two of the authors of New Jersey Quilts 1799-1950: Contributions to an American Tradition *and curated the project's traveling exhibition. A native New Jerseyan, Barbara Schaffer is currently a fine arts student with a concentration in textiles at Montclair State College and a vintage clothing dealer. She has been a quiltmaker/designer since 1974 and has had several one-woman shows. Her work has been published in* Quilting *by Laurie Swim (1991), the American Quilter's Society's* Quilt Art Calendar 1987, *and* Lady's Circle Patchwork Quilts: Editor's Choice *(1984). Rita Erickson has her BA in history from Depauw University and a MA in anthropology from New York University. She inherited quilts from both sides of her Indiana family and has taught quiltmaking for the past ten years. Her own designs have been published in Oxmoor House's* Great American Quilt *series (1988) and Joyce Schlotzhauer's* Cutting Up with Curves *(1989) and her quilts have been exhibited in juried and invitational shows:* Tactile Architecture, Quilt Images, Dreamscapes, The Design Group, *and the* New Jersey Arts Annual. *Rita has also published articles on old quilts in the* Quilter's Newsletter Magazine *and* Lady's Circle of Patchwork Quilts.

Grandmother's Authentic Early American Patchwork Quilts
Illustrations Cutting Charts Instructions
BOOK Nº23
INDIAN WEDDING RING
DRESDEN PLATE
YO-YO or BED of ROSES
FLOWER GARDEN
PRISCILLA Patchwork Book
№ 1
Published by
The Priscilla Publishing Co.
Boston, Mass.
NEW DESIGNS FOR NEEDLEART LOVERS
GOOD LUCK ISSUE
SEASON 1933
BOOK 14
HOME
2659 WA
CHICAG
Quilt Patterns ...Old and New
Patchwork Quilts
A Collection of Thirty-seven Old Time Blocks
Compiled by Clementine Paddleford
QUILTING
LEISURE HOBBY SERIES
COMMISSIONERS
CHICAGO
THE R·O·M·A·N·C·E of the VILLAGE QUILTS
McELWAIN SHOP
WISCONSIN
Old Fashioned Quilts
CARLIE SEXTON
Wheaton, Illinois
YESTERDAY'S QUILTS IN HOMES OF TODAY
POPULAR PATCHCRAFT in
Catalog of ... Quilts and Quilting
CUT, READY-TO-SEW QUILT TOPS
ATTRACTIVE, STAMPED APPLIQUE PATCHWORK DESIGNS, QUILTING DESIGNS
LADIES ART COMPANY, 38
CAPPER PUBLICATIONS
TOPEKA, KAN.
Prize Winning Designs
Many Quilt Patterns Never Before Published
Embroidered Patch-Work Appliqué
By Mary E. Fitch
Series No.14
OLD FASHIONED QUILTS
RURAL NEW YORKER
The Lure of Patch-work

Quilt Design Explosion of the Great Depression

Merikay Waldvogel

Faced with thousands of pastel-colored quilts and piles of yellowed quilt patterns and catalogs, a quilt researcher would be smart to declare the 1930s a quilt pattern explosion and leave quietly hoping someone else would do the analysis.

The task is daunting. By 1930, as the gross national product plummeted, the number of quilts skyrocketed. Companies in New York, St. Louis, Chicago, Nashville, Ohio, Indiana, and Kentucky sold thousands of patterns through the mail. Kits of pre-cut and pre-sorted pieces to make appliqué and pieced quilts were sold in department stores and through the mail. Women's magazines continued to promote quilting, and newspapers added quilt patterns to attract new readers.

What led to the quilt pattern explosion of the Great Depression? What fueled its growth? Why did it occur at a time when Americans faced one of the bleakest times in their history? In the search for answers, I assembled magazines, newspapers, quilt books, catalogs, and mail order advertising from the late-1880s through 1935. As I read, I compiled lists of patterns and counted them; then assembled them chronologically. Arranged in this way, it became apparent how one author affected quilt descriptions in later publications or, how a pattern innovation was incorporated into later, multiple patterns.

I discovered two streams of quilt style development closely paralleling the two main divisions of quilt construction — pieced and appliqué. The source for patterns of pieced quilts seems to have originated in the reader exchange columns of farm journals in the *Hearth and Home* group of the late-1880s. Then Ladies Art Company of St. Louis offered 400 patterns in 1898 which are similar to the ones appearing in the *Hearth and Home* group.[1] The Ladies Art Company group of patterns, in turn, was adapted, copied, and renamed in various quilt pattern pamphlets and booklets — especially the farm magazines of the 1920s and 1930s such as *Rural New Yorker*, *Successful Farming*, *Progressive Farmer*, *Southern Agriculturalist*, and *Capper's Weekly*. By and large, these pieced patterns were not unlike those we see in extant quilts of the late-1800s.

Early 20th-century quilt pattern publications. From Mildred Dickerson Collection owned by the author.

Appliqué quilt patterns, on the other hand, showed much more innovation — in layout, color, and theme. For example, they do not always contain the repeated block arrangement common in quilts of the late-19th century. The new appliqué quilt style often had a center medallion surrounded by floral borders made up of solid pastel cloth. Borrowing from the needlework designs for bedspreads, the quilt designers created a sophisticated style suitable for the bedrooms of the modern home or apartment. Clothing and household furnishings patterns employing embroidery, tatting, appliqué, and crochet were commonly sold through the printed media. With lining, cotton batting, and quilting to hold the layers together, such embroidered spreads were transposed into a quilt by the magazines' needlework editors.

What happened during 50 years preceding the great quilt explosion of the 1930s? What might have affected the quilt pattern development?

As American cities industrialized in the early 1900s and hundreds of thousands of new immigrants entered society, one might expect the quiltmaking tradition to be diluted by an infusion of large groups of people who had no quiltmaking traditions in their native culture and an aesthetic distance from America's past.

America moved rapidly from a mainly agricultural country to an urban one. This phenomenon, too, might lead one to think quiltmaking would die out when transplanted to an urban setting. In fact, we know the opposite occurred. Quiltmaking was repackaged, revamped, and revived during the 1920s. Urban women, lured by the advertising disseminated nationally by the popular press, incorporated the old-fashioned designs in the modern decorative styles. The Colonial Revival aesthetic allowed all Americans — multi-generational or newly immigrated — to decorate their homes alike if they wished.

The interest in colonial (or pre-industrial) America gained strength at the 1876 Centennial Exposition in Philadelphia where American antiques and artifacts were displayed alongside the latest inventions. Americans looked with pride at their early ancestors' artistic endeavors. Following the 1876 celebration, quiltmaking experienced a revival of interest.

The opening of exhibits of American antiques in prestigious museums hastened the collecting of antiques including quilts. The 1924 opening of the Metropolitan Museum of Art's American Wing devoted to American antiques and the installation of period rooms at the Brooklyn Museum heightened the interest in America's colonial past. A January 1922 article in *Ladies' Home Journal* proclaimed "old-fashioned quilts are the new-fashioned quilts, and there is no touch quite so modern in the present-day bedroom as that lovely relic of grandmother's time." This nostalgic theme seeped quite naturally into descriptions of quilt patterns. For example, in the August 1929 *Modern Priscilla* "favorite old quilt blocks" Dove at the Window, Hickory Leaf, Mill Wheel, and Gentleman's Fancy are described as good patterns for an heirloom quilt, but advised choosing the new "fast color fabrics and good sturdy materials."

Paralleling the Colonial Revival, the Arts and Crafts Movement affecting architecture and the decorative arts began in mid-19th century England and spread to the United States in the 1880s. It emphasized the use of natural, unadorned materials, good workmanship, and simple designs. By the early 1900s, women's magazines were promoting tastefully simple designs reflecting the strength of this artistic movement. Marie Webster's quilts, for example, were described in the early 1900s as having "achieved a new and artistic note for hand-made quilts of applied patchwork."

Later, the Modern Movement in painting, graphics, architecture, and industrial design paid homage to the beauty of the machine. In Art Deco, as it came to be known, art imitated machines rather than nature. Designs incorporated straight lines, hard edges and motifs of zigzags, rays of light and checkerboards.[2] Ruby Short McKim's quilt block series *Mother Goose* and *Nursery Rhyme* running in newspapers from as early as 1917 contain embroidered illustrations with an Art Deco style. Later, Kim's *Poppy* block used an unusual oblong block and recommended machine-piecing.

With an understanding of the decorative arts movements and a chronology of the publication of quilt books, catalogs, magazine articles, kits, and newspaper columns, the steps leading to the great explosion of patterns in the 1930s is easier to follow.

The publication of Marie Webster's quilts in *Ladies Home Journal* in 1911 and 1912 marked the beginning of a period of innovation — a breaking with traditional color choice, fabric use, and construction. I was not able to find any printed sources of appliqué quilt patterns similar to Webster's designs prior to 1911 although some may have existed. Suffice it to say, due to the national exposure her designs received through the *Ladies Home Journal* articles, Marie Webster stands as an important figure in the development of innovative appliqué quilt designs associated with early 20th-century quilts.

Webster's quilts featured in *Ladies Home Journal* in January 1911, reflected a refinement of the decorative aesthetic — return to classic forms, elimination of excessive and distractive frilliness, and softening of the color palette. In keeping with the aesthetic of the day, the editors called the hand-made quilts "artistic." The aim was to make the quilts practical as well as beautiful by the use of fast-color linens of good quality. The designs came from nature. *Snowflake* reminded the viewer of "the sharp glistening snowflakes against a background of blue sky," Iris was "designed so as to make it consistent with its natural growth," and *Wind-Blown Tulip* brought "a breath of springtime in form and color."

One year later in the same month, *Ladies Home Journal* featured four more quilts by Webster. This time the quilts were described in design terms — the *Poppy*'s "naturally irregular shape of the stems lends itself to the center motif as well as the borders." The *Sunflower* is "a very realistic bold design of vivid coloring, but well-balanced in its relation to space. The border, too, is harmonious." The *Morning Glory* was praised for its duplication of "the natural grace of the growing vine."

In August 1912, Webster presented six baby quilts described in terms of their uses. She suggested the pictorial *Bedtime* quilt and the *Sunbonnet Lassies* quilt would become sources for storytelling at bedtime. For the two floral quilts *Wild Rose* and *Morning Glory* she suggested colors to harmonize with other decorations in the child's room specifically "a bedstead of white enameled wood or iron."

Webster created a quilt style consistent with the Arts and Crafts decorative arts movement — use of natural forms, straightforward use of the materials, elimination of excessive decoration, and balance between form and line. The object's use and longevity were paramount.

Marie Webster's original quilt designs appeared in* Ladies Home Journal *in January 1912. Mildred Dickerson Collection owned by the author.

The New Flower Patchwork Quilts

Designs by Marie D. Webster

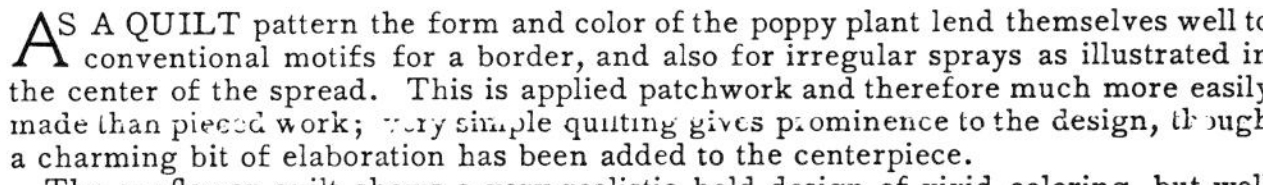

AS A QUILT pattern the form and color of the poppy plant lend themselves well to conventional motifs for a border, and also for irregular sprays as illustrated in the center of the spread. This is applied patchwork and therefore much more easily made than pieced work; very simple quilting gives prominence to the design, though a charming bit of elaboration has been added to the centerpiece.

The sunflower quilt shows a very realistic bold design of vivid coloring, but well balanced in its relation to space. The border, too, is harmonious, suggesting a firm foundation for the stems. The quilting in the center is noticeably attractive in a design of spider webs, leaves and flowers.

MORNING-GLORIES, in one of their many beautiful and delicate varieties, were chosen for this quilt, and while the design is conventional to a certain extent it holds much of the natural grace of the growing vine.

The dogwood quilt offers another good choice in flower designs and one of unusual delicacy and coloring. The full-grown blossoms on the green background remind us delightfully of the beauty of trees and flowers in early spring.

Any of these designs are suggestive for stencil decorations for friezes, couch-covers, cushions, portières or table-covers. Mrs. Webster will be glad to answer inquiries if a stamped, addressed envelope is inclosed.

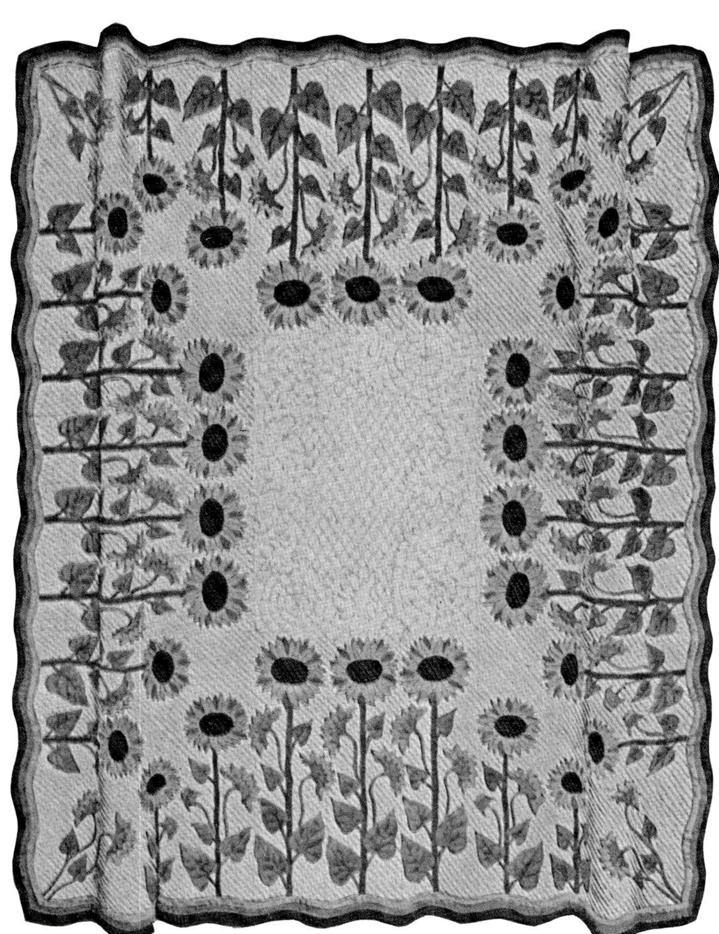

Page from scrapbook contains quilt patterns clipped from farm magazines in the Hearth and Home *group published in the 1880s in Augusta, Maine. The scrapbook compiled by Lottie R. Mollette of New Milford, Connecticut is in the collection of Barbara Halgowich.*

In 1905 (six years before Webster's quilts appeared), *Ladies Home Journal* had tried unsuccessfully to revamp America's quilt styles. They commissioned five artists to create original quilt patterns. Though extremely innovative, the patterns were too difficult to reproduce in fabric and not many were sold or made.[3] In contrast, Webster's patterns, grounded in the American needlework tradition coupled with classic artistic design, must have thrilled both long-time quilters and newcomers to the art.[4] *Ladies Home Journal* was deluged with requests for the patterns for Webster's New Patchwork Quilts even though the magazine had not planned to offer them. Her family began a mail order pattern company to fill the requests.[5]

Ironically, another Marie Webster milestone, the publication of America's first quilt book *Quilts: Their Story and How to Make Them* (1915) may have slowed the changes she envisioned for American quilt styles. In her book, Webster researched European and Middle Eastern roots of traditional quiltmaking and styles. By doing so, she equated the efforts of American quiltmakers with those of fine craftsmen of centuries past. By praising the stalwart efforts of pioneer quiltmakers in the United States — creating artistically strong quilts when limited by available fabric, time and space — she fed the Colonial mystique developing around the quiltmaking process and traditional quilt styles. Her writings also encouraged thousands to protect their heirloom quilts, and for thousands of others, having none, "to go ahead and make one."

Ruth Finley with the publication of *Old Patchwork Quilts and The Women Who Made Them* (1929), like Webster, lauded our foremothers' efforts working with certain basic principles of design. In the growing Colonial Revival movement of the 1920s, she singled out quilts as being peculiarly adaptable, offering always interesting contrasts in color and form.

Finley believed the year 1880 marked the end of the golden era of American patchwork. She bemoaned

> the rapid multiplication of machinery that eliminated the need for hand-work. The wonder and novelty of mechanical construction, quite apart from its ease and rapidity, exalted bad taste; men wanted to see just how intricately materials could be worked up by their power-driven tools.

However, she continued, at about the same time, educational and career opportunities for women opened up and women "closed the gate at the end of many a road. [Their] journey . . . along the trail of her patchwork was finished."[6]

Ironically, the publication of Finley's book (which took 16 years to write) came at a time when the "gate to the patchwork trail" was open wide again partly due to time-saving tools produced by the despised power-driven machines. By documenting the patterns, detailing the steps in the process, and providing stories Finley fed the pattern-hungry masses of long-time quiltmakers and put quilts in an historical continuum.

Finley's book focuses on traditional pieced and appliqué blocks — their origins, names, and construction. For women rediscovering their grandmothers' quilts in attic trunks, this information helped authenticate family stories. For women wishing to duplicate these old quilts, Finley provided the means to do so.

Carlie Sexton, of Iowa and later Wheaton, Illinois, writing for a rural audience, encouraged women to take up quilting. Her first booklet *Quaint Quilts*, published in 1922, was followed in 1924 by *Early American Quilts*. It was a nostalgic personal account of visits to her grandmother's to see her 19th-century quilts. Writing for farm magazines, Carlie Sexton took an approach similar to that found in the 1880s farm magazines, "There is something homey about quilts and quilt lovers and you, no doubt, have a favorite pattern that makes you feel just a bit sentimental, haven't you?" She provided her readers with rudimentary information about the construction and design of quilts along with photographs of quilt blocks.

Sexton wrote two other booklets: *Old Fashioned Quilts (1928) and Yesterday's Quilts in Homes of Today* (1930). Both tell of trips to visit quiltmakers or attempts to rescue old quilts. Patterns in these booklets were available through Sexton or her publisher for 25 cents.

In contrast to these few full-length quilt books published prior to 1930, the mail order catalogs of quilt pattern companies reached a much broader clientele. The oldest company offering a line of quilt patterns was the Ladies Art Company, owned by J. H. Brockstedt of St. Louis, Missouri. The earliest extant 1898 catalog, entitled *Diagrams of Quilt Sofa and Pin Cushion Patterns*, was the 11th revised edition and included over 400 quilt patterns — many of them taken from the rural farm women's magazines published by the *Hearth and Home* group of Augusta, Maine. No credit was given to the contributors.

Practical Needlework: Quilt Patterns, a catalog produced by Clara Stone of Boston (ca. 1905) also included several pieced patterns which appeared in late-1800s farm magazines such as *Farm and Home*, *Hearth and Home*, and *Home Queen*. In fact, Clara Stone along with Eva Niles and others may have established a quilt column syndicate in the late-1880s which provided quilt block illustrations with a short description to the *Hearth and Home* group of magazines.[7]

A HEXAGON QUILT PATTERN.

PATCHWORK FOR SOFA-CUSHION.

This design is of old-gold and maroon colored satin. The pieces must be lined with paper muslin before they are embroidered.

Use light blue real Scotch linen floss and red on the maroon blocks, and on the old-gold ones use darkest shade of olive-green. This design will also be pretty for bedspreads.

FANTASTIC PATCHWORK.

A NEW QUILT PATTERN.

One more design for bedquilt blocks, pattern for which will be furnished by the publishers of FARM AND HOME, is shown herewith. No 3 is known as the "lost ship." The illustration shows one-quarter of the design, and is several sizes smaller than the pattern offered for sale.

NO 3. LOST SHIP PATTERN.

The whole block is made by sewing together four pieces cut according to this design, the four pieces all occupying a similar position; that is, the large white space being in the upper right-hand corner. The material may be blue on a white back-

CHIMNEY SWALLOW.

Our Quilt Blocks.

"Charlie's Choice" has a romantic history, being the pattern which "Charlie" selected for his mother to make a quilt to send his bride by. The corner half squares and the pieces joining, which meet in the center, were of a golden brown sateen, with a tiny dot of a lighter color in it. The center half diamonds were a lovely shade of blue, and the light pieces cream with an orange figure. All were of a very

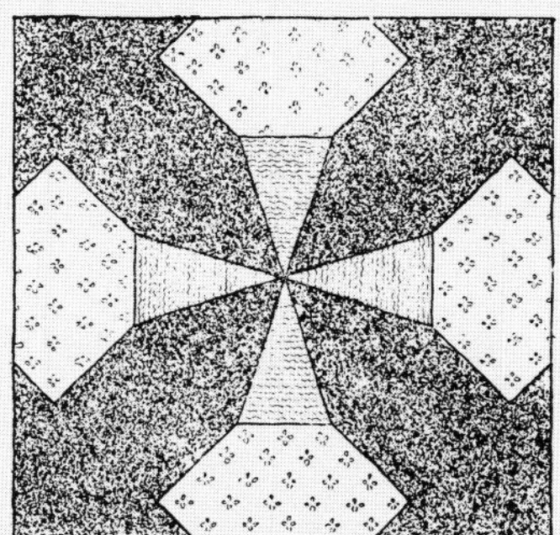

Charlie's Choice Quilt Block.

fine sateen. Every one who saw that quilt praised its beauty and, no doubt, it won the bride's love for her clever mother-in-law. It might be made of four colors, having the corner half squares different from that adjoining, which, when set solidly, would make a square.

Mosaic quilt blocks are always odd and striking if a pretty combination of colors is used. They are certainly cheerful, for bright colors seem to be called for in them, the only thing

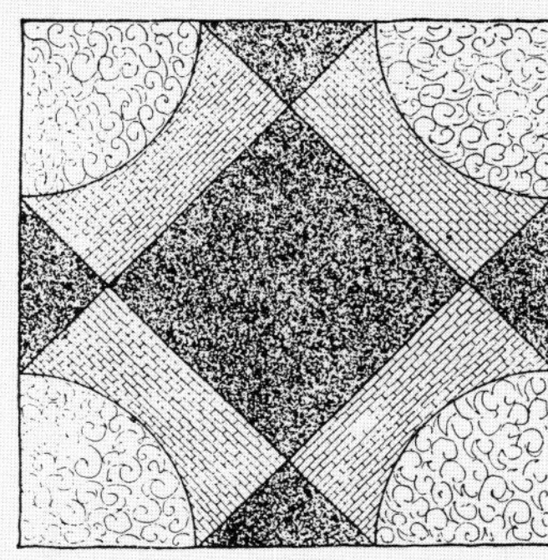

Mosaic Quilt Block.

being to have those which will contrast well and avoid those which "fight." It should be set solidly, as sashwork will utterly destroy the effect, and each square must be exactly like every other square in the quilt. J. S. A.

* * *

JEWEL PATCHWORK.

This is sewed on to a cloth foundation, and is made of two shades only. It may be easily worked from the design.

LINCOLN'S CABIN.

This very interesting quilt block is called Lincoln's cabin. A full-size pattern by

LINCOLN'S CABIN.

which to cut this design, which is No 5 in the F & H series, will be furnished on receipt of 10c and the coupon which accompanies this article, properly filled out. The shaded portions indicate material of a colored or figured pattern, the other pieces white. Directions accompany the pattern.

Similar block drawings appear in the Ladies Art Company catalogs, *The Patchworker's Companion* printed in 1911 by the Joseph Doyle Company of Hoboken, New Jersey, and *Aunt Jane's Prizewinning Quilt Designs* printed in 1914 in Springfield, Ohio by *Household Journal*. The blocks were traditional patterns probably gathered from seeing 19th-century quilts and corresponding with quiltmakers.

Another source of quilt patterns in the early 1900s was the slick women's magazines aimed at the growing urban middle class. Magazines such as *Modern Priscilla*, *Woman's Home Companion*, *Needlecraft*, *Ladies Home Journal*, *McCall's*, and *Good Housekeeping* competed fiercely for readers. Most included regular columns written by needlework designers which enriched and refined the pattern offerings available to quiltmakers. The magazines continued as a source of information about old quilts, but they also set new standards for design aesthetics by introducing innovative styles.

Modern Priscilla, more than the other women's magazines, experimented with the quilting medium. Their *Red Cross* quilt in 1917 has been featured often in recently published state and regional quilt documentation books and exhibits. In 1918, *Modern Priscilla* also offered patterns for sateen quilts called "puffs." In 1920, the magazine featured the Wilkinson Sisters of Ligonier, Indiana who had a cottage industry producing sateen monogrammed boudoir quilts. In 1921, *Modern Priscilla* included patchwork patterns based on tile floors in villas in Italy. In 1923, the magazine presented a *Bambino* spread, in 1924 a *Christmas Tree* Quilt, and in 1925 appliqué wall hangings called "appliqué photography." In 1927 one could order *Wings of Victory* in honor of Charles Lindbergh's flight. In 1929 *Modern Priscilla* included an article about quilted palampores. As the 1930s opened, the magazine sold 20 stamped blocks in the theme, *League of Little People from This Wide World Around*.

Page from pamphlet The Wilkinson Art Quilt published by the Wilkinson Sisters, Ligonier, Indiana in 1921. Mildred Dickerson Collection owned by the author.

Good Housekeeping, with its needlework editor Anne Orr in place from 1919 through 1940, concentrated on traditional needlework patterns — crochet, tatting, embroidery, and knitting. Quilt patterns (based on traditional patterns) appeared about once a year. With the magazine's publication of a group of quilt patterns in 1932, Anne Orr's name became closely associated with fine quilt design. Floral themes, rich and harmonious color choices, and a balance between all design components in her quilt designs helped raise Anne Orr to the level of Marie Webster.

In 1931, Marie Webster herself offered a new catalog of 13 quilt patterns, most of which were offered as cloth kits. Interestingly, pre-cut or pre-stamped quilt kits were not uncommon in the 1920s. Many imitated the quilt layout and themes advocated by Marie Webster. The *Rose Quilt* featured in a 1920 *Modern Priscilla* catalog is a close copy of Webster's Dogwood quilt. The $5.00 quilt kits showed a high standard of design and certainly streamlined the process, but few examples of these quilts survive.

Cuesta Benberry, in an article on "Quilt Kits Present and Past" for *Nimble Needle Treasures*, pointed out that while the quilt kits represented the commercialization of the craft of quiltmaking, the design represented in the kits, especially those of the 1920s, was innovative and might have enriched the quiltmaking heritage further if the distribution of the kits had been better.[9]

As the 1920s came to a close, quiltmakers had a rich resource of patterns to choose from. New appliqué quilt styles (such as those of Anne Orr) based on familiar needlework designs and construction were available through the mail and at department stores. Pieced patterns, most based on late-19th-century blocks, were available through farm magazines and catalogs. Even ready-to-make quilts (like Marie Webster's) with pieces cut and sorted were available. However, the daily newspaper bringing a different quilt pattern several times a week probably did more to heighten interest in quiltmaking than any magazine, book, catalog, or kit.

The earliest syndicated newspaper quilt pattern I was able to find was the Art Deco style *Mother Goose Quiltie* series of outline embroidery blocks designed by Ruby Short McKim for the *Omaha Daily News* in 1917. The series of 20 quilt blocks, which ran on Sundays for several weeks, was a clever innovation. The small blocks could be worked on at odd moments of free time and did not require a large work space as Marie Webster's central medallion designs did. Since they appeared weekly, a challenged seamstress might finish the current week's block before the next one appeared, and before she knew it, she had enough blocks to make a quilt. By 1928, Ruby Short McKim produced single quilt block patterns which appeared in the *Kansas City Star*. Later these were carried by newspapers throughout the country.

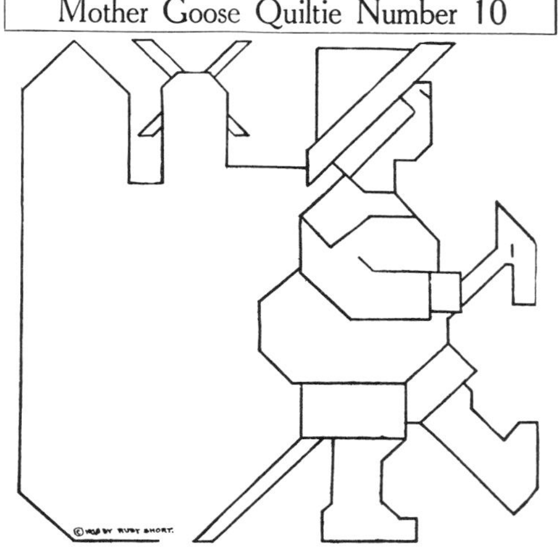

Block #10 in Mother Goose Quiltie series designed by Ruby Short McKim which exhibits an Art Deco style. From Mildred Dickerson Collection owned by the author.

In 1929, the Nancy Page quilt series premiered in newspapers around the country. The first series, a set of 24 embroidered and appliqué *Alphabet* blocks, ran for several weeks from the fall of 1929 to the spring of 1930. To encourage readers to complete the quilt, the newspaper often sponsored a contest. In Chicago, the completed *Alphabet* quilts were shown at a downtown hotel. Bertha Stenge, who eventually became one of the top quilt contest winners of the 20th century, entered that contest as did her two young daughters. Bertha Stenge's quilt did not win because the colors were not acceptable to the judges, according to her daughter Prudence. More importantly, Bertha Stenge (and hundreds of other novice quiltmakers) may have been inspired to make quilts by such contests.

Nancy Page writers also added individual block patterns to the once-a-week series pattern. By 1935, quilt patterns appeared in newspapers and farm magazines throughout the nation. Other early 1930s syndicated quilt columns were Laura Wheeler, Jane Alan Grandmother's Quilt Blocks, Aunt Martha, Margaret Techy in *Cleveland Plain Dealer*, Nancy Cabot, and the Home Art Studio. Quilt patterns from newspaper sources number in the thousands.

A prominent quilt supply company writing to their retailers reported in 1934 that,

> recent surveys show that at least 400 metropolitan newspapers are publishing quilt material regularly. A Gallup survey in six large cities shows further that the quilt article is the most popular Sunday feature — 32 percent of the women reading it.[10]

Capitalizing on the increased interest in obtaining quilt patterns, some magazines, notably *Needlecraft* and *Woman's World*, answered their competition by offering free sets of stamped quilt blocks as an incentive for readers to get new subscribers. For every new subscription, the reader got a set of stamped blocks suitable for embroidery or appliqué. The give-away sets changed frequently.

One of the best-known marketing schemes involving quilt patterns was the free quilt pattern printed on the reverse side of the wrapper for Stearns & Foster's Mountain Mist cotton batting. Over 120 patterns appeared in this way: both traditional patterns, adaptations of Marie Webster and Anne Orr patterns, and original designs. As an indication of Stearns & Foster's aggressive marketing scheme, a 1934 brochure aimed at buyers for department stores, proclaimed,

> Today quiltmaking has a universal appeal . . . . Mountain Mist is keeping pace with this interest in quiltmaking. It is helping you to make the most of this vogue, through the sale of the most complete of quilt patterns; through the finest of cotton batts; and through the complete pattern inside the wrapper of every roll.[11]

In the same brochure, Stearns & Foster summarized their new national advertising program in six magazines (with a total circulation of 9,845,938), "Two out of every five women will see Mountain Mist advertising."

Stearns & Foster also urged merchants to sell more Mountain Mist and other quilt materials through "A Quilt Show." They presented testimonials from large urban department store owners who reported thousands of women coming to the store to see such exhibits.[12]

The most successful one-time campaign to get people to quilt would have to be the 1933 Sears National Quilt Contest. Sears, Roebuck & Co. had used contests successfully in the past to improve their corporate image within the communities of their far-flung family of customers. Contests to locate the best ear of seed corn and the best stalk of cotton in America enabled Sears to reward their customers who used modern farming methods. The good will generated by such contests helped Sears educate their customers about better crop yields. Their customers' improved living standard meant more business for Sears.

Seeing the large numbers of quilts entered in quilt contests in the late-1920s sponsored by newspapers and department stores in Chicago, the Sears officials chose a quilt contest to promote the 1933 Chicago World's Fair. They offered an enormous prize: $1000 with a $200 bonus if the top quilt was made in the theme of the Chicago World's Fair. More than 24,000 people entered quilts from all across the country — rural and urban.

The exhibit of 30 quilts shown at the Sears Pavilion at the 1933 Fair represented the final round of hundreds of local and regional showings of the quilts — each receiving extensive newspaper coverage and each open to the public for two or three days.

The 1933 Sears Contest entries reflected the number and variety of quilt patterns available at the time. The quilts attributed to the contest are a mixture of traditional patterns, adaptations of traditional patterns, and new center medallion appliqué floral quilts. The judges were impressed by the craftsmanship and skill of the quilts — not necessarily the design. Quilts entered in a special category commemorating the Century of Progress theme reflected the imaginative creativity brewing under the surface. Unfortunately, these quilts were generally overlooked by judges.

Following the 1933 Contest, the Chicago Park District set up regular quilting classes and staged quilt exhibits involving many new immigrants. Etelka Galbraith and Mary Fitzgerald, following Marie Webster's lead, gave lectures on quilt history to women's clubs and designed their own quilts. They also helped to establish Chicago area quilting clubs.

The Stearns & Foster Company featured a quilt pattern with actual size pieces, yardage, and instructions on the inside of the Mountain Mist batting wrapper. Collection of Margaret Seebold.

Advertisement in Chicago Tribune *January 6, 1933 announcing the Sears National Quilt Contest.*

Winning prizes and making money became common themes in quilt pattern catalogs of the Great Depression. Quiltmaking might be a life saver for someone faced with absolutely no family income.

In conclusion, the revival of quiltmaking obviously reached well back into the late-19th century and began in earnest in the early years of the 20th century with campaigns to preserve antiques and historic homes. Marie Webster's innovative quilts, grounded in the Arts and Crafts aesthetic of the day, generated interest among a new group of quilters and quilt enthusiasts. Although the styles were not generally accepted possibly due to the limited distribution and affluence needed to create the quilts both in terms of work space and materials, elements of the Webster style — notably the center medallion floral theme in pastel colors surrounded by borders and a sculpted edge — were incorporated into hundreds of other quilt patterns published in the 1930s.

With the introduction of syndicated quilt columns in newspapers and farm magazines in the late 1920s, new inexpensive patterns reached the traditional quilting community as well as the novice quilters. The designers for those quilt columns, most of whom are nameless, incorporated elements of the new quilt styles, but remained rooted in traditional appliqué and pieced quilt construction. This cross-fertilization of old and new ideas produced a strong new quilt type as reflected in Grandmother's Flower Garden, Dresden Plate, and Wedding Ring — each based on a 19th-century pattern, but modernized with pastel-colored cloth, new prints, and scalloped edges.

Without the quilt pattern design explosion and the industry's ability to entice women to take up quilting, the quilt revival of the 1930s might have sputtered leaving women with only their grandmothers' 19th-century quilts to duplicate or dozens of quilt kits to finish. Instead, we have inherited a distinctive body of quilts — Depression Era Quilts.

End Notes

[1]Wilene Smith. "Quilt History in Old Periodicals: A New Perspective." *Uncoverings 1990* ed. Laurel Horton. San Francisco, CA: American Quilt Study Group, 1991, 188-213.

[2]For an explanation of decorative arts movements read Penny McMorris and Michael Kile. *The Art Quilt*. San Francisco: The Quilt Digest Press, 1986.

[3]Ibid., 28.

[4]For examples of Webster's quilt designs see color plates 1-29 in Marie Webster. *Quilts: Their Story and How to Make Them*. Santa Barbara, CA: Practical Patchwork, 1990.

[5]Ibid., 209.

[6]Ruth Finley. *Old Patchwork Quilts and the Women Who Made Them*. Reprinted by McLean, VA: EPM Publications, 1992, 197.

[7]Smith, 202-203.

[8]For more information on boudoir quilts read Virginia Gunn. "Quilts for Milady's Boudoir." *Uncoverings 1989* ed. Laurel Horton. San Francisco, CA: 1990, 81-101.

[9]Cuesta Benberry. "Quilt Kits — Present and Past: Part I." *Nimble Needle Treasures* Spring and Fall 1974, 6:2 and 3.

[10]Joel Sater, *The Patch Work Quilt*. Ephrata, PA: Science Press, 1981, 117.

[11]Ibid.

[12]Ibid., 118.

Merikay Waldvogel has been a resident of Knoxville, Tennessee since 1977 where, until recently, she has taught English as a second language. She joined the American Quilt Study Group in 1982 and is currently a board member who heads production aspects of their publications. She has had three papers printed in their journal, Uncoverings*: first on the WPA quilts of Milwaukee, Wisconsin (1985); on southern linsey quilts (1988); and on the needlework designer, Ann Orr (1991). Merikay is also co-author with Bets Ramsey of the* Quilts of Tennessee *(1986) and with Barbara Brackman of* Patchwork Souvenirs of the 1933 Chicago World's Fair *(1993) Merikay is also the author of* Soft Covers for Hard Times: Quiltmaking and the Great Depression *(1990. Each book was accompanied by a traveling exhibition. She is currently working on an exhibition of the quilts from the SPINEA collection to be held at the Museum of Our National Heritage in summer/fall 1994. Merikay has also been involved in serious discussions with the Smithsonian regarding their licensing practices on quilts in their collection and sits on an advisory panel to that institution.*

A Marie Webster Dogwood *quilt pattern with tissue paper appliqué placement chart, swatches of suggested fabric, and photograph of one quarter of the completed quilt. Collection of the author. Photography by the author.*

Anne Orr needlework patterns with copyright forms. Collection of J. Scott Grigsby. Photography by the author.

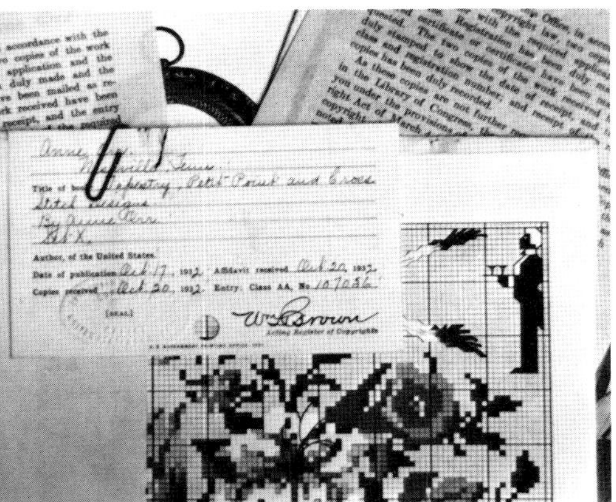

Time Line

This time line, compiled by Cuesta Benberry, Wilene Smith, and Merikay Waldvogel, attempts to list in chronological order all known published quilt pattern sources, 1900-1939. Readers are encouraged to contact the authors with corrections and additional sources.

The time line is divided into four sections: Books, Pamphlets, and Catalogs; Magazines; Newspapers; and Syndicated Features. Each is arranged chronologically with the exception of Magazines which are arranged alphabetically within each decade.

Books, Pamphlets, Catalogs 1900-1909

1901-1906. *Diagrams of Quilt, Sofa, and Pin Cushion Patterns*; 420 designs. Ladies Art Co., St. Louis, MO.

Ca. 1905-1910. Mrs. Wheeler Wilkinson. *Revival of Old-Time Patchwork and Applique.*

Ca. Spring 1906. Clara A. Stone. *Quilt Patterns*, vol. 3, no. 2, of *Practical Needlework*.

1906-1909. *Diagrams of Quilt, Sofa, and Pin Cushion Patterns*; 450 designs. Ladies Art Co., St. Louis, MO.

Books, Pamphlets, Catalogs 1910-1919

1910-1919. *Diagrams of Quilt, Sofa, and Pin Cushion Patterns*; 450 designs. Ladies Art Co., St. Louis, MO.

Ca. Jan. 1911. *Patchworker's Companion.* Joseph Doyle & Co., Hoboken, NJ.

1913. McConnell & Sutherland. *Old Fashion Patchwork.*

1914. *Aunt Jane's Prize Winning Quilt Designs.*

1915. Marie Webster. *Quilts; Their Story and How to Make Them.*

1916. Charles E. Bentley. *Artamo Colonial Patchwork Quilts, Coverlets, Etc.* Book No. 2, Artamo Thread Co.

Ca. 1916. Sophie T. LaCroix. *Martha Washington Patch Work Quilt Book.* Book No. 12.

1918. Mary E. Fitch. Brookline, MA. *Embroidered Patchwork Applique Series 14.* Distributed by F. W. Woolworth.

Books, Pamphlets, Catalogs 1920-1929

1920-1922. *Diagrams of Quilt, Sofa, and Pin Cushion Patterns*; 450 designs. Ladies Art Co., St. Louis, MO.

1920. *Priscilla Patchwork Book.* Priscilla Publishing Co., Boston, MA. Revised in 1925.

1920s. *Clark Art Embroidery.* Cleveland, OH. A forerunner to Rainbow Quilt Block Co. catalog.

Ca. 1921. The Wilkinson Sisters [Ona and Rosalie]. *The Wilkinson Art Quilt.*

1922. *Book of Applique Patchwork*, by Deaconess. *Quilt Pattern Book; Patchwork and Applique*; 500 designs. Ladies Art Co., St. Louis, MO.

1922. Carlie Sexton. *Quaint Quilts.*

Oct. 1922. *Comfort's Applique and Patchwork Book.* Winning designs from *Comfort*'s 1921 contest.

Ca. Jan. 1923. Carlie Sexton. *Old-Time Patchwork Quilts.*

1924. Carlie Sexton. *Old Fashioned Quilts.* Aka *Early American Quilts.*

1925. *Patchwork Quilts and How to Make Them. Farm and Fireside.* 25 designs.

1926. *Art Needlework*, Catalog 26. Frederick Herrschner, Chicago, IL. Annual catalog.

1926. *Style Book of the New Bucilla Embroidery Packages.* Bernhard Ulmann Co.

1927. *Olde Kentucky Quilts.* Louisville Bedding Co., Louisville, KY.

1927. Prudence Penny. *Old-Time Quilts.*

Ca. 1927-1928. Margaret Whittemore. *Quilting—A New-Old Art.* Capper Publications, Topeka, KS.

1928. *Quilt Patterns; Patchwork and Applique*; 510 designs; reissued with 530 designs. Ladies Art Co., St. Louis, MO.

1928. Carlie Sexton. *Old Fashioned Quilts.*

Ca. Sept. 1928. Clementine Paddleford. *Patchwork Quilts; A Collection of Thirty-seven Old Time Blocks. Farm and Fireside.*

Fall 1928. *Royal Society Embroidery Package Outfits.* H. E. Verran Co., Inc., NY.

1929. Ruth E. Finley. *Old Patchwork Quilts and the Women Who Made Them.*

Ca. 1929. Ethel M. McCunn. *Needlecraft Book of Patchwork and Quilting. Needlecraft Magazine.*

1929. *Woman's World. The Book of Patchwork.*

Ca. Feb. 1929. Clementine Paddleford. *Patchwork Quilts; A Collection of Forty-one Old Time Blocks. Farm and Fireside.*

Ca. Sept. 1929. *Patchwork Quilts. Farm and Fireside.* More than 55 designs.

Ca. Oct. 1929. Leonore Dunnigan. *Quilts. Farmer's Wife.*

Late 1920s. Rainbow Quilt Block Co., Cleveland, OH. Catalog of sheets of Rainbow Quilt Blocks.

Ca. 1929 or 1930. McKim Studios. *Adventures in Home Beautifying.* General needlework catalog.

Books, Pamphlets, Catalogs 1930-1939

1930s. *Quilt Patterns; Patchwork and Applique*; 530 designs. ©1928. Ladies Art Co., St. Louis, MO.

Ca. 1930. *Catalog of Quilts and Quilting: Attractive Applique Patchwork Designs with Border.* Ladies Art Co., St. Louis, MO.

Ca. 1930s. *E-Z Patterns for Patchwork and Applique Quilts.* Robert Frank Needlework Supply, Kalamazoo, MI.

Ca. 1930s. Della Harris; Waco, TX. Title unknown.

Ca. 1930s. *Heirloom Quilts.* F. A. Wurzburg and Son, Grand Rapids, MI.

Ca. 1930s. *Master Quilting Album; 101 Favorite Quilting Designs*, by H. Ver Mehren for Needleart Guild, Grand Rapids, MI.

Ca. 1930s. *Needlecraft Book of Patchwork and Quilting.* Revised edition.

Ca. 1930s. *Quilt Patterns—Old and New. Illinois Farmers Guide.*

1930s. Rainbow Quilt Block Co., Cleveland, OH. Catalog of sheets of Rainbow Quilt Blocks.

Ca. 1930s. Title unknown. Published by *Royal Neighbor* magazine.

Ca. 1930s. Emma S. Tyrrell. *Patchwork Patterns. Wallace's Farmer.*

1930. Stella Jones *Hawaiian Quilts* Honolulu.

1930. Carlie Sexton. *Yesterday's Quilts in Homes of Today.*

1930-1931. McKim Studios. *Designs Worth Doing.* General needlework catalog with additional editions for 1931; Fall-Winter 1931-1932; ca. 1932; and ca. 1933.

1931. *Grandmother Clark's Patchwork Quilt Designs*; Book No. 20. *Grandmother Clark's Oldfashioned Quilt Designs*; Book No. 21.

1931. *Mary King's Pattern Key.* Embroidery House, Chicago, IL.

1931. Ruby Short McKim. *One Hundred and One Patchwork Patterns.* A compilation of eight quilt pattern pamphlets created in 1930 and 1931.

1931. *The New Bucilla Embroidery Packages.* Bernhard Ulmann Co.

1931. Marie Webster. *Quilts & Spreads.*

1931. *Woman's World. The Patchwork Book.*

Ca. Jan. 1931. *Patchwork and Quiltmaking.* Joseph Doyle & Co., Newark, NJ.

Ca. Feb. 1931. *A New Easy Way to Make A Quilt.* Unsigned Aunt Martha.

Ca. July 1931. Orinne Johnson and Eleanor Lewis. *Quilts; The Farmer's Wife Book of Quilts.*

Ca. Oct. 1931. Aunt Martha. *Prize Winning Designs.*

Ca. Dec. 1931. *Indiana Farmers Guide. Old Fashioned Pieced and Applique Quilts.*

Ca. 1931-1932. McKim Studios. *A Penny Apiece for Quilt Patterns.* Catalog of quilt kits.

Ca. 1931-1935. "Mickey" quilt patches. John C. Michael Co., Chicago, IL. At least five catalogs were published.

Ca. 1932. *Colonial Needlecraft Heirloom Quilts For Applique, For Patchwork* Needle art Guild, Grand Rapids, MI.

1932. *Grandmother Clark's Quilting Designs*; Book No. 22. *Grandmother Clark's Early American Patchwork Quilts*; Book No. 23. *Grandmother Clark's Patchwork Quilts*; Book No. 19 (selected designs from Books 20 and 23 plus one new design).

1932. *The Patchwork Book* [new edition]. *Woman's World.*

Ca. 1932. *Quilt Patterns.* Union Specialty Works.

1932. Carlie Sexton. *How to Make A Quilt.*

Ca. July 1932. Aunt Martha. *Favorites—Old and New.*

1932-1933. *Grandma Dexter's Applique and Patchwork Quilt Designs*, Book 36. *Grandma Dexter Applique and Patchwork Designs*, Book 36A. *Grandma Dexter New Applique and Patchwork Designs*, Book 36B.

1933. *Catalog of Quilts and Quilting: Cut, Ready-to-Sew Quilt Tops.* Ladies Art Co., St. Louis, MO.

1933. *The Mountain Mist Series of Patterns for Quilts.* Booklet No. 10.

1933. *Quilting Is in Fashion Again.* J & P Coats, Spool Cotton Co., NY. Leaflet #575.

Ca. 1933. *Rural New Yorker. Old Fashioned Quilts.* Numerous editions; some may have other titles.

1933. H. Ver Mehren. *Colonial Quilts.* Available by November 1932. Home Art Studios, Des Moines, IA. Patterns usually ordered from a Paulina St, address, Chicago, IL.

Ca. 1933. H. Ver Mehren. *Needleart Vogue, Style Book D.* Home Art Studios, Des Moines, IA.

Ca. 1933. *Virginia Snow Quilting Designs.* Book No. 41.

Ca. Jan. 1933. *Quilts.* Book 2. *Farmer's Wife.*

Ca. March 1933. Mae G. Wilford. *Quilt Patterns.*

Ca. Oct. 1933. Aunt Martha. *The Quilt Fair Comes to You.*

1934. Alice Beyer. *Quilting.* South Park Commissioners, Chicago, IL.

Ca. 1934. Nancy Cabot. *Book of Quilts.*

1934. Scioto Imhoff Danner, El Dorado, KS. *Mrs. Danner's Quilts. Mrs. Danner's Second Quilt Book.*

1934. Elizabeth King. *Quilting.* New York: Leisure League of America.

Ca. 1934. *McCall Quilt Book.*

1934. Ouida Pearse. *Quilting.* London & New York: Sir Isaac Pitman & Sons.

1934. *Sears Century of Progress in Quilt Making.*

Ca. 1934. *Hope Winslow's Quilt Book.* Same as Home Art Studios' *Colonial Quilts.*

Ca. Jan. 1934. Orinne Johnson and Eleanor Lewis. *Quilts; The Farmer's Wife Book of New Designs and Patterns.*

Ca. 1934-1935. *Nancy Cabot's Second Book of Quilts.*

Ca. 1934-1935. *Grandmother's Quilt Patterns.* Books 1 through 50, each with 7 patterns.

Ca. 1934-1935. *Patchwork Quilts; How to Make Them.* Needlecraft Supply Co., Chicago, IL.

1934-1939. *Farm Journal.* Four catalogs including *The Farm Journal Quilt Patterns; Old and New.*

Ca. 1935. Thelma G. Heath. *How to Make A Really Different Quilt.*

Ca. 1935. McKim Studios. *Adventures in Needlecraft.* General needlework catalog.

1935. *The Mountain Mist Blue Book of Famous Quilt Designs.*

Ca. 1935. *Needlecraft Embroidery and Fancywork Book of Materials. Needlecraft Magazine.* General needlework catalog. Numerous other catalogs and leaflets published, 1920s-1938.

August 1935. Carrie A. Hall and Rose G. Kretsinger. *The Romance of the Patchwork Quilt in America.*

1936. Mary A. McElwain. *Romance of the Village Quilts.*

1937. Phoebe Edwards. *The Mountain Mist Blue Book of Quilts for 1938.*

Ca. Jan. 1937. *Quilts.* Book 4. *Farmer's Wife.*

1939. Florence Peto. *Historic Quilts.*

Magazines listed without dates indicate that quilt-related articles were published throughout the period. When articles appeared less than the full period, the range is indicated. When a magazine's quilt articles are scattered, the individual years (without months) are listed.

Magazines 1900-1909

American Agriculturist.
American Woman, 1902-1909.
Comfort, 1903-1909.
Country Life, 1909.
Craftsman, 1908.
Delineator, 1906.
Farm and Home.
Farmers Mail and Breeze, 1906-1909.
Fireside Visitor, 1900-1907.
Good Stories.
Happy Hours.
Harper's Bazar [sic], 1905.
Harper's Weekly, 1909.
Hearth and Home.
Hearthstone, 1906-1907.
Home Magazine, 1901-1902.
Home Queen, ca. 1907.
House and Garden, 1909.
House Beautiful, 1907.
Household.
Housekeeper, 1900, 1908.
Housewife, 1907.
Ladies' Home Journal, 1900, 1902, 1905, 1907-1909.
Ladies' Magazine, 1908.
Mail and Breeze, 1904.
Modern Priscilla, 1907.
New England Homestead.
New Idea Woman's Magazine, 1905.
Orange Judd Farmer.
People's Popular Monthly, 1907.
Sunshine for Youth, 1906-1907.
Weekly Inter-Ocean and Farmer, 1906-1909.
Woman's World, 1906-1907.

Magazines 1910-1919

American Agriculturist.
American Woman, 1910-1914.
Comfort.
Country Life, 1910.
Delineator, 1914.
Designer, 1910.
Farm and Fireside, 1911-1914.
Farm and Home.
Farmer's Wife, 1912-1913.
Farmers Mail and Breeze.
Good Stories, 1910.
Happy Hours, 1910-1912.
Hearth and Home.
Home Progress, 1912.
House Beautiful, 1919.
Household Magazine.
Household Journal, ca. 1914.
Ladies' Home Journal, 1911-1913, 1918.
McCall's Magazine, 1913, 1915-1916, 1919.
Missouri Valley Farmer, 1913.
Modern Priscilla, 1912, 1915-1919.
Needlecraft Magazine, 1918.
New England Homestead.
Normal Instructor and Primary Plans, 1917.
Ohio Farmer, 1911.
Orange Judd Farmer.
Outlook, 1914.
People's Popular Monthly, 1914-1915.
Pictorial Review, 1911, 1913.
Plain and Fancy Needlework, 1917.
Southern Agriculturist, 1919.
Southern Woman's Magazine, 1915.
Valley Farmer, ca. 1910.
Weekly Inter-Ocean and Farmer, 1910-1912.
Woman's Century, ca. 1910.
Woman's Home Companion, 1911, 1915-1916.
Woman's World, 1919.

Magazines 1920-1929

American Home, 1929.
American Needlewoman, 1926-1927.
Antiquarian, 1928.
Antiques, 1922-1929.
Better Homes and Gardens, 1927-1929.
Capper's Farmer, 1927-1929.
Comfort.
Country Gentleman, 1925-1929.
Country Life, 1923.
Dakota Farmer, 1926-1927.
Farm and Fireside, 1922-1929.
Farm Journal, 1921-1929.
Farmer's Wife.
Garden and Home Builder, 1926-1927.
Good Housekeeping. Anne Orr, 1921-1929.
Handicrafter, 1929.
Harper's Monthly, 1923.
Hearth and Home, 1922-1929.
House Beautiful, 1924, 1926.
Household Magazine.
Household Guest, ca. 1926.
Household Journal, early 1920s.
Indiana Farmers Guide, late 1920s. Carlie Sexton illustrations.
Kansas Farmer, 1924-1929.
Kansas Homestead, 1922.
Ladies' Home Journal, 1920, 1922.

McCall's Magazine, 1925-1929.

Modern Homemaking, 1927.

Modern Priscilla.

Nebraska Farmer, 1929.

Needle-Art, 1925.

Needlecraft Magazine.

Ohio Farmer, 1929.

Oklahoma Farmer-Stockman, 1920-1922, 1927-1929.

Old Time New England, 1927.

People's Popular Monthly.

Playground, 1927.

Progressive Farmer, 1927, 1929.

School-Arts Magazine, 1927.

Southern Agriculturist, 1928.

Successful Farming, 1923, 1927-1929.

Today's Housewife, 1926.

Wallace's Farmer, 1925-1929.

Woman's Home Companion, ca. 1928.

Woman's World.

Magazines 1930-1939

American Collector, 1938.

American Home, 1934, 1937-1938.

American Speech, 1933.

Antiquarian, 1930.

Antiques.

Arts and Decoration, 1930-1931, 1934.

Aunt Martha's Work Basket, begins Sept. 1935, issue number C900.

Better Homes and Gardens, 1930-1937.

Capper's Farmer, 1931.

Country Gentleman.

Country Home, 1931-1933, 1936.

Design, 1933-1935, 1938.

Farm Journal.

Farmer's Wife, 1931-1938.

Good Housekeeping. Anne Orr.

Good Stories, 1933.

Hearth and Home, 1930-1933.

Hobbies, 1932.

House and Garden, 1934.

Household Magazine.

Indiana Farmers Guide. Carlie Sexton illustrations.

Kansas Farmer, 1930, 1938.

Ladies' Home Journal, 1933, 1938.

McCall Needlework.

McCall's Magazine.

Missouri Ruralist, 1931-1933.

Modern Priscilla, 1930.

Nebraska Farmer, 1930-1931.

Needlecraft Magazine.

Newsweek. "Quilts from Hawaii," Dec. 5, 1938.

Oklahoma Farmer-Stockman, 1930-1933.

Pictorial Review, 1930, 1934.

Practical Home Economics, 1930, 1932, 1938.

Progressive Farmer, 1930, 1934-1935, 1939.

Rural New Yorker, 1930-1937. Carlie Sexton illustrations.

St. Nicholas, 1937.

School-Arts Magazine, 1930, 1937.

Successful Farming, 1930-1931, 1934-1935.

Textile Colorist, 1932.

Woman's Day, 1937-1939.

Woman's Farm Journal, 1930.

Woman's Home Companion, 1934.

Woman's World, 1930-1934.

The Newspaper category only enumerates newspapers that created their own quilt-related features.

Newspapers 1900-1909

None are known.

Newspapers 1910-1919

Capper's Weekly, Topeka, KS. Ca. 1910-1915.

Omaha (NB) *Daily News*. "Many Beautiful Patchwork Quilts in Omaha," Nov. 10, 1912.

St. Louis (MO) *Republic*. "St. Louis Society Women are Making Quilts," Dec. 28, 1913.

Wichita (KS) *Weekly Eagle*. 1913-1914. Possibly a syndicated feature through Western Newspaper Union.

Capper's Weekly, Topeka, KS. From Feb. 12, 1927, attributed to Louise Fowler Roote.

Kansas City Star, 1928-1929 (mostly McKim patterns). Includes one Eveline Foland series, "Santa's Parade," 1929.

Weekly Kansas City Star, 1928-1929 (mostly McKim patterns).

Newspapers 1930-1939

Denver Post. One series, "Indian Princess," 1930.

Capper's Weekly, Topeka, KS. 1930-1934, attributed to Louise Fowler Roote, interspersed with syndicated pattern features and ads.

Seattle Post-Intelligencer. Prudence Penny. Six series by Maxine Buren, 1930-1935, including "Sampler Quilt," 1930; "Applique Quilt," 1931; "Patchwork Zoo," 1933; "Wild Flower Quilt," 1935.

Kansas City Star, 1930-1938. Includes two Eveline Foland series: "Memory Bouquet," 1930; "Horn of Plenty," 1932.

Weekly Kansas City Star, 1930-1952. *Weekly Star Farmer*, 1952-1961.

News-Telegram, Portland, OR. Three series by Mary Erckenbrack in the 1930s: "Noah's Ark," "Golden West," and "Old Glory."

Cleveland (OH) *Plain Dealer*. Four series by Margaret Techy: "Complete Fruit Quilt," 1931; "Old English Quilt," 1933-1934; "Medieval Quilt," 1934-1935; "Ohio Flower," 1935-1936.

Oregonian, Portland, OR. One series: "Modernistic Flower," by C. Mullen, 1933.

Chicago Tribune. Nancy Cabot. Jan. 22, 1933—July 31, 1938.

Christian Science Monitor. Weekly column by Pearl Strachan, Fall 1935.

Omaha (NB) *World-Herald*. Two series by Nadine Bradley: unnamed, 1937; "State Birds and Flowers," 1938; and "Covered Wagon States" series, 1939-1940, attributed to Harry Rasmussen.

Christian Science Monitor. "Design for Shreds and Tatters," Nov. 24, 1937.

The Syndicated Features category enumerates quilt columns distributed nationally in newspapers and magazines.

Syndicated Features 1900-1909

None are known.

Syndicated Features 1910-1919

Ruby Short. 1916-1917.

Ruby Short McKim. 1917-1919.

Syndicated Features 1920-1929

Ruby Short McKim. 1920-1928.

Helen Kaufman. Chicago, IL. Ca. 1927 or 1928—1929.

Nancy Page, aka Jane Page. Publishers Syndicate, Chicago, IL. Three-column feature by Florence LaGanke. Ca. 1927 or 1928—1929.

McKim Studios. Independence, MO. 1928-1929.

Fannie S. Tobey. Distinctive Newspaper Features, Hamilton, OH. Ca. 1929 or 1930.

Syndicated Features 1930-1939

McKim Studios, Independence, MO. 1930-1937.

Helen Kaufman. Chicago, IL. 1930-1933.

Nancy Page, aka Jane Page. Publishers Syndicate, Chicago, IL. Three-column feature by Florence LaGanke. 1930—1937 or 1938.

Fannie S. Tobey. Distinctive Newspaper Features, Hamilton, OH. Ca. 1929 or 1930—1933 or 1934.

Walker Patterns. Mary Evangeline Walker; by Lydia LeBaron Walker. 1930s.

Aunt Martha (Clara S. Tillotson). Kansas City, MO. 1931-1939.

"Quilting Bees Return As Fashion Finds New Beauty in Old Patches," Associated Press in *Omaha* (NB) *World-Herald*, Feb. 22, 1931.

Jane Alan. John F. Dille Co., aka National Newspaper Service, Chicago, IL. Ca. 1931 or 1932—1935 or 1936.

"Happy Childhood Quilt" series by Aileen Bullard, through Cox Features, 1932.

Clotilde. Chicago Tribune-New York News Syndicate, Chicago & New York City. 1932.

Home Art Studios. Des Moines, IA. 1932-1935. Bylines are uncommon but include Colonial Quilts, Bettina, Nancy Lee, Aunt Dinah, and Hope Winslow.

Hetty Winthrop. Bell Syndicate, New York City. Ca. 1932-1940.

Nancy Page, aka Jane Page. Publishers Syndicate, Chicago, IL. Daily, one-column household feature by Florence LaGanke that incorporated a weekly Quilt Club, 1932—1943 or 1944.

Nancy Cabot designs, usually unsigned or with another byline in periodicals outside the *Chicago Tribune*. Chicago Tribune-New York News Syndicate, Chicago & New York City. 1933-1939.

Laura Wheeler. Needlecraft Service, Inc./Reader Mail, Inc., through King Features Syndicate. From April 1933.

Alice Brooks. Household Arts, Inc./Reader Mail, Inc., through King Features Syndicate. From Nov. 1933.

Ruth Orr. Famous Features through Bell Syndicate, New York City. Ca. 1936-1939.

Baroness Piantoni. Famous Features through Bell Syndicate, New York City. Ca. 1939-1941.

Feed, Flour, Tobacco, and Other Sacks

Their Use in the 20th Century

Pat Nickols

To some people around the country the mention of feed and flour sacks invokes colorful, vivid memories or family stories of their varied and extensive use in this century, particularly the years 1930-1960. The recycling of bags was not, however, a 20th-century phenomenon, as sack fabric was reused in the 19th century as well — a common practice of thrift and convenience. Feed, flour, salt, sugar, and tobacco sacks, to name a few, provided the material for numerous household items, clothing for every member of the family as well as for quilts and comforters.

To better understand sack history, the following examples of sacks will serve as an overview. Surprisingly a number of quilts showing sack use from the mid-19th century have survived: (1) A mid-1800s Irish Chain quilt made by Margie Gorrecht of York, Pennsylvania is at the Shelburne Museum, Shelburne, Vermont. Her quilt has some white patches that show stencil printing of bag contents; (2) A Cross and Crown quilt, ca. 1850, at the Dearborn, Michigan Historical Museum, Dearborn, Michigan, has flour and sugar sacks as the backing fabric; (3) An "1855" quilt in the Fall River Historical Society, Fall River, Massachusetts, shows a recycled flour bag from "Bristol County Mills Superfine Flour" used as the backing fabric; (4) A Union quilt (Ladies Art Company Pattern #160) was machine-pieced using a double-pink print and a white fabric with feed and flour sacks for backing fabric. It was made by 12-year-old Hanna Peterson of Salina, Kansas in 1885 and is in the author's collection; (5) An unfinished crazy quilt with red and blue lettering of the Bemis Bag Company and Pillsbury Best XXXX flour sacks clearly visible as the foundation fabric to which were sewn colorful delegate ribbons, dated 1896-1898, from Minnesota, Iowa, and Wisconsin, is also in the collection of the author; (6) Last, Ruth McKendry, in *Quilts and Other Bedcoverings in the Canadian Tradition* (60-63), tells of the Merkleys from the Williamsburg area, Dundas County, Ontario, Canada, who made quilts, — 12 for each of their nine girls for their dowries. Only one, Estelle, ever married. When Ella May, the youngest, died at age 98 in 1974, 115 quilts, *all backed with feed, flour and sugar bags*, were found neatly folded in blanket boxes in the attic. These 19th-century examples show that reusing sacks was an accepted practice.

Local grist mills, where grinding of grains for food as well as animal feed was done, saw containers such as barrels or casks, replaced by bushel baskets and cloth sacks. Linen, often home-woven, had been used in the early and mid-19th century grain bags. Increased cotton production brought about by large cotton crops and mechanization made sheeting, the fabric used to make sacks, inexpensive and readily available. Cotton would replace linen as the fabric for feed sacks. A successful chain-stitch sewing machine was developed in 1846 and added improvements for sewing cotton sacks were made by Morley and Johnson. Additional developments to this machine were made in 1849 by Henry Chase, who founded the Chase Bag Co. (1847), and John Batcheller. These industrial developments, both sewing a sack together by machine and closing a filled sack by machine, resulted in replacing hand labor and lowering cost. Consequently Chase, Bemis, and other bag producing companies expanded by establishing their own cotton mills and bleacheries. By 1910 Bemis Bag Co, founded in St. Louis in 1858 by Judson M. Bemis, had 11 bag factories making cotton sacks. Bemis grew to be the largest bag company.

The start of World War I in Europe and the German occupation of Belgium in 1914 was

Border prints were very popular as they were used as ready–made pillow cases or for kitchen curtains, skirts, and as printed patchwork or "cheater cloth" in quiltmaking. This design, based on an applique quilt pattern, is typical of the "specialty prints" used on sacks and meant to appeal to quiltmakers. Collection of the author.

American relief ship bound for Belgium and loaded with sacks of flour to feed the starving people. These gifts of flour came from all over the country and were received with grateful thanks by the Belgian people, who decorated some of the flour sacks and sent many of them back to their American friends as gifts.

A Belgian–embroidered American flour sack of Acme Spring Wheat, was typical of hundreds returned to the States by grateful Belgians. This sack, decorated with ribbons, embroidery, and knotted fringe and signed "Merci Aux Americains" was sent back to the Thornton & Chester Milling Company of Buffalo, New York with appreciation. Courtesy of the Herbert Hoover Presidential Library, West Branch, Iowa.

of great concern in the United States. The plight of the starving Belgian people was recognized by neutral nations, in particular the United States. President Woodrow Wilson, recognizing the need for organized help, had Ambassador Walter Paige in London establish the Commission for Relief, referred to as the CRB, in Belgium on October 22, 1914. Herbert Hoover was its chairman. This private organization was joined by volunteer representatives from England, Spain, Holland, France, Scotland, Canada, New Zealand, and many other countries. This was the first time in history that a private organization fed and helped clothe an entire nation. Feeding nine million people approximately 160 million pounds of flour, wheat, maize, and beans a month, caused a scarcity of grain in the United States resulting in volunteer rationing programs such as "Wheatless Wednesdays."

Flour was sent to Belgium in 49-pound cotton sacks which increased cotton consumption and helped our severely depressed cotton market in the South. It was also hoped the sacks would give Belgian women fabric to use for making simple clothing. Sewing centers were setup throughout Belgium, to employ women and girls and to keep control of the empty bags, which have been used in German munitions manufacture. In 1916 30,000 flour sacks were made into shirts at the Antwerp Music Hall, a converted sewing center. Girls embroidered, stenciled, painted and added lace to sacks. They also made aprons, children's bibs, shoes, hats, and wall banners, for use as well as for sale as souvenirs.

Countless numbers of these decorated bags were sent back to the United States both during and at the end of the war as gifts. Cartons of sacks were sent to the CRB offices in New York in 1915 with notes of appreciation by the grateful Belgian people. Other sacks were sent back to the mill noted on the sack, addressed to an individual, sometimes sent to a state, or even addressed, "to American friends." Extensive displays of these decorated sacks are at the Herbert Hoover Library, West Branch, Iowa, and at the Hoover Institution on War, Revolution and Peace, Stanford University, Stanford, California.

An appeal for help from Elizabeth, Queen of the Belgians, plus an editorial titled,"The Cry For Milk," asking readers to send money to the Belgian Relief Fund for bulk milk purchases to feed the hungry babies, appeared in the February 1915 issue of *The Ladies Home Journal.* The chairman of this effort was Edward Bok, its editor. *The Ladies Home Journal*, a popular ladies' magazine that featured information and instruction on various types of needlework with circulation of about 2 million copies monthly, pictured sack reuse by the Belgians coupled with the actual decorated bags coming back to the United States. This coverage gave American women repeated awareness for sack cloth use at the time we were drawn into World War I.

In the late-1920s, the Household Science Institute in New York published a monthly paper, "Out of the Bag," about the reuse of flour and grain sacks and offered a 32-page booklet *Sewing With Flour Bags.* President Calvin Coolidge, "Silent Cal," well known for his ideas on thrift, received a pair of feed sack pajamas in 1928 from the ladies of the Millard Avenue Presbyterian Church of Chicago, Illinois. They used five flour bags (at a cost of about 50 cents) and pattern #5539 from the booklet. This booklet was subsequently published by The Textile Bag Manufacturers Association, Inc. and then by the National Cotton Council. It was distributed widely by Sears, Roebuck & Company, *Simplicity* dress patterns, 4-H clubs and others, well into the 1960s.

Needlecraft magazine in March and September 1929, and March 1930 had its readers from Alabama, Virginia, and Washington discuss detailed quiltmaking ideas for using flour, sugar, oatmeal, and cornmeal sacks. Earlier, one of *Needlecraft's* readers, Mrs. J. L. Murray, of Bloomington, Illinois, watched the election of Herbert Hoover with interest and decided to make an inaugural gift to Mrs. Hoover of an Irish Chain quilt, and *Needlecraft* of July 1929 notes "A Colonial Quilt Enters the White House." An article in the May 1926 issue of that magazine had given Mrs. Murray the pattern idea after reading that Mrs. Hoover had seen this pattern in an 1854 blue and white quilt which she had duplicated as a wedding gift for her son. Mrs. Murray dyed six flour-bags Yale blue and used a total of 16 flour-bags to make her token of affection and good-will for a president and his wife who were very familiar with sacks from their efforts with the Belgian Relief Commission.

From the Depression years of the 1930s through the war years of the 1940s, cotton sack use was widespread. Later editions of the *Sewing With Cotton Bags* booklets gave a list of "attractive and practical" items to make "from what is apt to be regarded as waste material."

While quilts are not mentioned, page 18 gives directions and illustrated a child's spread. It was suggested that one use 18 six-inch squares of cotton bag material embroidered with suitable nursery figures (which were usually animals) set with 17 alternate squares of checked gingham. A quilted crib cover is pictured on page 25 with complete directions for making this whole cloth quilt. A comment in the booklet noted "No waste to sewing with cotton bags" and it is suggested any small snips left from cutting clothing are better than bran or sawdust for stuffing dolls and animals. Many of the booklets are undated but it appears they were edited and reprinted yearly.

The cover of a 1938 booklet states, *Style — Sewing with Cotton bags*, and devotes a page to:

> Where to secure cotton bags . . . first she can easily make sure her purchases of flour, cornmeal, sugar and salt for example, are packed in cotton bags and by buying larger quantities (the more economical as a rule) she will secure large bags which are so desirable for certain types of garments shown in this book. Smaller bags of foodstuffs are also of fine material and can be used for making the smaller articles described in this book. Every baker uses supplies that come in cotton bags which they are glad to sell for a few cents apiece. These larger size bags cut to excellent advantage.
>
> Ask your friends to save them for you; frequently they are not considered of much use, but you know they are! Your Mail Order House or local Department Store have laundered cotton bags ready for your immediate use, which have the added advantage of being shrunk.

For the inexperienced, page two of the booklet gives instructions, *To Remove Printing*: "The ease with which printing ink may be removed from cotton bags depends on the kind of ink that has been used. Under ordinary circumstances, it is sufficient to cover the inked places with lard or soak them in kerosene overnight. Then wash out in lukewarm water. If only a faint, barely discernible marking may still be seen, it is safe to assume a few washings will remove the remaining traces." Another suggestion is to "wet a bar of laundry soap and rub on the dry bag. Repeat wetting the soap and rubbing on until the bag is covered with a thick layer of soap. Roll the bag up and let it stand for several hours before washing. When the bag is washed and boiled, it will be as white as any muslin." With all of the work involved to remove *all* of the ink it is easy to understand why we see some printing visible on quilts, especially when used for quilt backing.

There were also numerous illustrations of clothing patterns devoted to using sack cloth in the 32-page booklet. These patterns were available for ten cents each through the mail; one paid for them either with money or postage stamps.

Bemis Bag Co., the leading producer of cotton sacks in the years 1940-1970, also promoted sack use through its company newsletter *Bemistory*. Over the years it illustrated extensive reuse of sack fabric. The August 1942 issue of *Bemistory* told of a nationally known feed company that promoted a contest for its customers with prizes for the best articles using their sacks. They were overwhelmed with the entries, over 1,000 articles! At that time over 3 million people were wearing clothing made from bags. The Bemis Dress Parade was a fashion show of street dresses, evening dresses, skirts, blouses, and other clothing — all made from Bemis sacks. By 1950, local, state, and regional Bemis Dress Contest winners were awarded prizes of $25-$100 savings bonds for attractive dresses made from Bemis bags. The National Cotton Council had traveling fashion shows showing a *complete* wardrobe made from feed and flour sacks.

In 1962, George Dean, Bemis sales executive from Kansas City, used a family treasure from his home, a Grandmother's Flower Garden quilt to be replicated on his company's feed sacks. For the novice complete directions were included in the bag for making a quilt using this printed patchwork. No lessons, fabric selection, cutting, or piecing were necessary to make this antique quilt. Everyone could afford to have one using from four to nine Bemis bags.

A picture in the *National Geographic*, December 1947, shows two women in colorful sackcloth dresses, in front of tall stacks of filled feed sacks. The caption notes, "From the Feed store, Now a Fashion Emporium, Comes Sackcloth for Colorful Dresses. Many a poultryman has overstocked mash to please his wife. 'Give me that one in pink,' says she, pointing to a mountain of 100-pound bags. At no extra cost she gets fine-quality, ready-to-sew cotton prints." Similar stories of picking out sacks prints are often told by those who remember using sacks on the farm in the 1930s-1960s, "The pretty print Mama wanted for sister's dress was on the bottom of the pile of feed sacks" or "It took awhile to get the bags moved so we would have four bags of the same flower pattern for our quilt backing." Emma and Sam Hager had a 16-acre "truck patch" outside of Jefferson City, Missouri, where they had a large garden and kept about 200 chickens to feed their family as well as sell their surplus. Rosemary Hager Scheppers, the youngest daughter, remembers in the early 1930s, "Momma would give one of us a washed sack when we went along with Dad to town to get chicken feed. We were to get some more sacks to match that one or something

MAKE THESE ATTRACTIVE AND PRACTICAL THINGS OF

Cotton Bags

Aprons
Smocks
House dresses
Beach coats
Combing jackets
Pajamas
Rompers
Children's aprons
Sunsuits
Middies
Mattress covers
Card table covers
Luncheon sets
Tray cloths
Jelly strainers
Handkerchiefs
Table runners
Garment covers
Laundry bags
Shoe cases
Broom covers
Pot cloths
Dish towels
Dusters
Bedspreads
Pillows
Curtains
Pillow cases
Ironing board covers
Vanity table drapes
Crib covers
Toast pockets
Bibs
Stuffed animals
Dolls
Refrigerator bags
Suitcase sets
Broom covers
Collar and cuff sets
Handbags
Yardstick holders
Book covers
Scrap books
Dress form linings
Hooked rugs
Muffin covers
Bean bags

This handbook on the uses of cotton bags has been prepared by the association as one of its educational projects and is offered to homemakers, sewing instructors, home demonstration agents, club leaders and other interested groups to show what can be done with what is apt to be regarded as a waste material. The patterns listed in this book are particularly adapted for use with flour and other cotton bags. For your convenience, they may be purchased through the Beauty Pattern Co. at 10c or 3 for 25c. In ordering patterns, send the order blank or write to The Beauty Pattern Co., Dept. T.M., 11 Sterling Place, Brooklyn, N. Y.

If additional copies of this booklet are desired you may secure them by sending 10c in stamps or coin to The Textile Bag Manufacturers Association, 100 N. LaSalle St., Chicago, Ill.

The cover and an interior page of the booklet,* Sewing with Flour Bags. *It was an illustrated idea and pattern book which was widely distributed to womens' and 4-H clubs, home extension groups, and others interested in sewing with sack material. Collection of the author.

A boy's shirt which was made from sacks with nautical designs: a lighthouse, sailboats, and anchors. The sack's original seam thread holes were carefully placed so they did not show on the finished garment. Collection of the author.

National Geographic
December 1947.

pretty because you couldn't make anything out of just one sack, you need two or more. She sent us along because Dad didn't want to ask the man to move sacks, especially if what we wanted was near the bottom of the stack." Often women took care of the chickens and the sale of the chicken's eggs might be their "pin money." The women were very familiar with the different colorful sacks their chickens' feed came in.

In the late 1940s the increased use of cheaper paper bags and the declining sales of cotton bags was of great concern to the cotton bag industry. In the spring of 1948 a committee composed of bag manufacturers, bag fabric manufacturers, textile merchants, textile converters, representatives from the raw cotton industry, and a member of the National Cotton Council met to develop a promotional plan to increase sales of cotton bags. They raised $380,000 to fund their marketing effort.

Farm women had used feed and flour bags for years to make dresses, family clothing, and quilts. Now the cotton men wanted to get the city folks' business. Almost half of the states had passed laws forbidding reuse of bags for food products prompted by concerns of sanitation. Bakers could no longer reuse their flour bags but now second-hand dealers were willing to purchase bags from the bakers, process them into tea towels and sell them to retailers who found there was a ready market for them. Seven months later, *Time* magazine of January 1949 reported sales for cotton bags had more than doubled as a result of this successful promotion. There was a new consumer use for cotton bags.

A 1953 booklet, *Pattern Service, for Sewing with Cotton Bags*, addresses the readers with the news,

> that all during the past year we've been collecting different ideas for cotton bag sewing . . . patterns are available in this completely revised booklet. You know it was a really wonderful day when the chickens, the cows and even the pigs got all involved with home sewing. Thanks to progressive packagers who are using attractive and re-usable containers for livestock and poultry feed, you have an excellent source of inexpensive cotton bag fabric for many home sewing purposes. If yours is an average farm family you buy enough feed each month to give you 24 yards of fabric, enough for six new dresses. You're the boss!, be sure that the products you buy come in the bags you want.

If the brand name was printed on the bags, the washable ink would come out in warm soapy water. The bag companies had continued to develop a better ink used in printing brand information that was easier to remove. Finally they developed a band (which went around the sides of the bag) or spot paper labels (which could just be soaked off). This was an attraction for customers of their colorful floral patterns who did not like the laborious laundry methods of past years.

Many attractive dress patterns were illustrated in the 1953 booklet, *Pattern Service, for Sewing With Cotton Bags*, as well as "Something for the boys," a sport shirt, matching boxer shorts for father and son as well as pajamas. Other small items such as aprons, a laundry bag, hand puppet, frog toy, and butterfly pot holder were illustrated with simple directions.

In looking back at two major events: the Belgian War Relief and the 1949 extensive promotional effort by the cotton bag industry, we see the tremendous public awareness they created and the effect each of these events has had on 20th-century reuse of cotton sacks.

Since then quilt publications have been aware of sacks. Starting in 1969 *Quilter's Newsletter* has mentioned the use in quilts of feed and other sacks in over a dozen articles, as has *Ladies's Circle Patchwork*, *Creative Quilting*, and others.

Exhibits, through publicity they generate in print and media, and those attending the events, have also kept awareness of sack use alive. Carole Austin curated an exhibit "From Aid to Art: Decorated Flour sacks from World War I," at the San Francisco Craft and Folk Art Museum in the fall of 1986. It showed examples of sacks decorated by grateful Belgians and sent as gifts to the people of the United States. These sack examples were on loan from The Hoover Institution on War, Revolution and Peace at Stanford University, Stanford, California. There some of the collection is on rotating exhibit. The Smithsonian also arranged a main floor exhibit about cotton sacks in 1990 that proved very popular with the thousands that viewed it. Yvonne and U Khin made and gathered numerous quilts made of sacks as well as other items made from sacks for a large display at their Exhibit Barn in rural Maryland in the spring of 1992.

Correspondence about sacks led Jane Stapel (as editor), Ellen Fayard, and others to form the Feed Sack Club in 1989. It has an annual membership of 200 members.

A well-illustrated book, *Textile Bags — The Feeding and Clothing of America* by Anna Lue Cook, Books Americana, Inc. 1990, shows printed bags as well as those with paper labels. Of added interest are numerous household and clothing items made from sacks which are pictured.

Renewed interest in sacks had led to countrywide trading of sack pieces to make quilts and in the case of Charlene Brewer, Oklahoma quilter and quilt historian, to gathering the largest collection of sack samples. In 1989 the Central Oklahoma Quilt Guild started making sample blocks to illustrate the 1,068 quilt patterns that had been printed in the *Kansas*

City Star newspapers in the 1930s through the 1950s. The guild members used fabrics of the period including many feed, flour, sugar, salt, and other sack fabrics to make these quilt blocks for display. Charlene started compiling sample books (one for the guild and one for herself) of three inch swatches of different examples that now illustrate patterns of over 5,000 sacks.

Over 20 feed sack quilts made by Helen Wade of Georgetown, Texas, were exhibited at The Benz Gallery of Floral Art, Texas A & M University, in the spring of 1992. Helen Wade remembers her school dresses were made of sacks used to hold the feed from the chickens and turkeys they raised and also recalls her mother searching for at least four sacks of the same print for a special dress or backing for a quilt. Since Helen retired from the Post Office in 1980 she has extensively bought and traded sacks to make quilts and is amazed the colors have remained so vivid. Although more prolific than most of today's quilters of sack quilts, Helen is choosing patterns that would have been made during the popular years of sack use, such as Dresden Plate, Butterfly, Grandmother's Flower Garden, Drunkard's Path, and Double Wedding Ring.

To do primary research on sacks this author has gathered over 2,000 examples of different sacks and found:

- over 40 different products packaged in cotton sacks
- varied weights and thread count of sacks
- different weaves of sack cloth
- unusual fabrics such as flocked and chambray
- regional motifs such as southwest Indian, western cowboy, and southern plantation
- novelty prints such as a rodeo cowboy on a bucking horse, a cupid with arrow in a floral heart, garden tools, lips and lipstick, and a telephone
- a large number of bow prints (some with flowers), in different colors, scale of print, and pattern
- the most popular colors are blue, pink, lavender and shades of purple, grey, red and green; few yellow prints were noted
- popular prints are multi-colored florals by far — first on white backgrounds then colored grounds; also one color florals; printed plaids — a great number of which are on point; border prints — many intended for pillow cases, some for use in skirt or dress making; some printed patchwork or "cheater cloth"
- items printed on the sacks to cut out, embroider, and hem include luncheon cloths, napkins, runners, toys, and children's clothing
- logos near left edge of selvage: Empire, and F & F, were found on a few sacks
- numbers, in set of three, near left edge of selvage were found on some sacks

The renewed interest in sack use is coupled with the interest in antiques and the strong interest in "collectibles." This wave of nostalgia has led collectors, museums, and antique dealers to search out the best examples. The quantity of sacks still being found, or already in circulation, has encouraged quilters around the county to create sack quilts using feed, flour, and other sacks — to make these authentic pieces of the past.

Pat Nickols is a member of the American Quilt Study Group which has published three of her papers in their journal, Uncoverings: *"Strip Quilts" (1982), "The Use of Cotton Sacks in Quiltmaking" (1988), and "Mary A. MacElwain Quilter and Quilt Businesswoman" (1991). Her article, "What's at Hand: Using Cotton Sacks in Quilt Making" appeared in the premiere issue of the magazine,* Piecework, *spring 1993.*

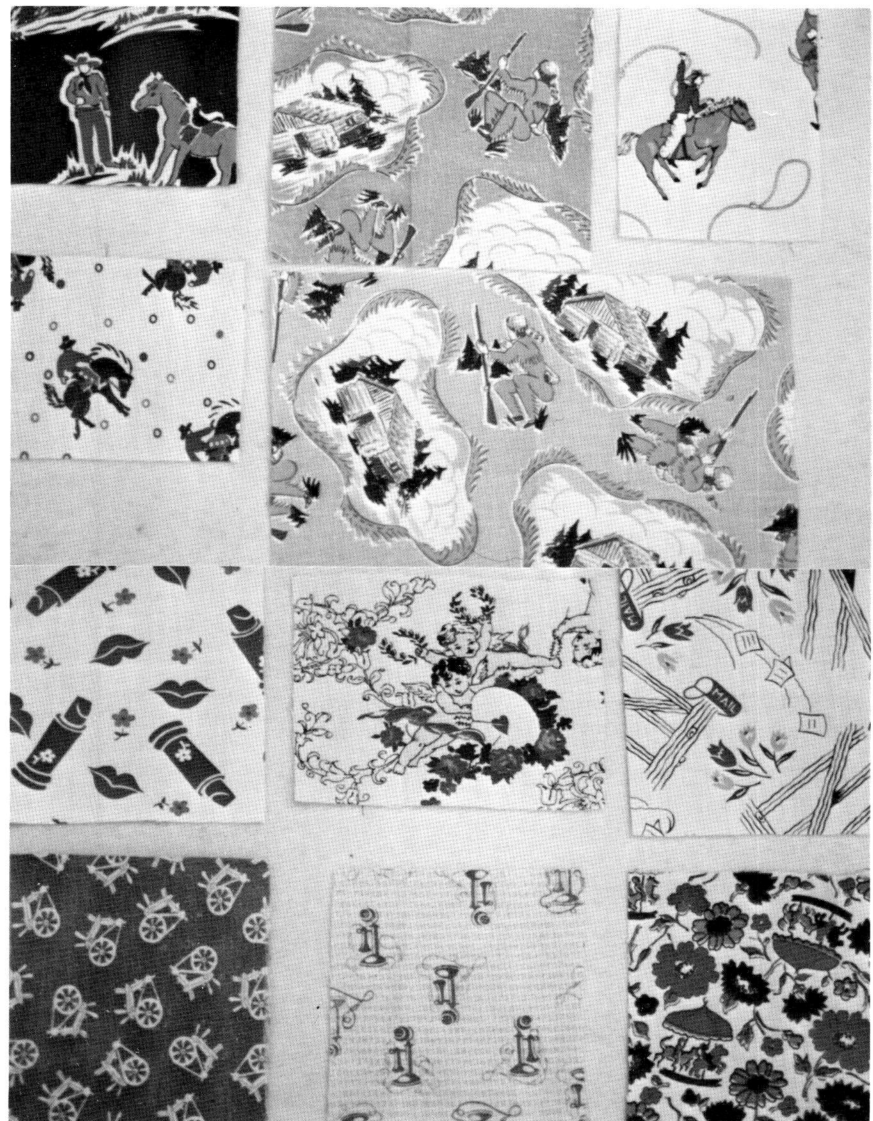

Sack motifs included farm images, cowboy motifs, animals, and novelty prints of merry-go-rounds, mailboxes, telephones, and cherubs. Children's prints, with cowboy prints for boys and dolls as well as children playing house for girls. Novelty prints for older children and countless unusual prints attracted the homemaker when she selected her bags of grain at the feed store. Collection of the author.

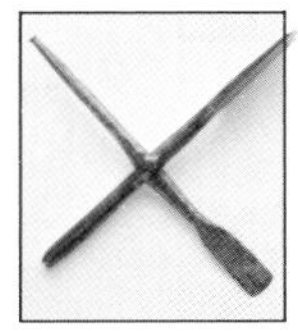

The Hispanic Tradition of Quiltmaking in Taos County, New Mexico

Dorothy R. Zopf

Each horizontal from left to right: Des Montes, New Mexico and Potato Blanket, 60" × 75", made by Beatriz Quintana of Cerro, New Mexico in 1951; Checkerboard quilt, 55" × 74", made by Mary Joyce Fidel of Penasco, New Mexico in 1990 and road to Amalia in Rodarte, New Mexico; an adobe house and Nine Patch, 57" × 81", made by Josepha Rodriquez of Chamisal, New Mexico. Photography of quilts is by Willi Wood of Taos, New Mexico in 1991-1992.

The Hispanic quiltmaking tradition of Taos County in northern New Mexico is a unique combination of frugal necessity and imaginative artistry.

First let me orient you both geographically and historically.

New Mexico is that interminable stretch of highway east and west between Texas and Arizona. On the south it is bordered by Texas and old Mexico. Colorado is to the north. Taos County, an area twice the size of Rhode Island, is situated on that northern border at the base of the Rocky Mountains.

The area was first seen by Europeans in 1540 when Coronado came searching for the seven cities of gold. The earliest settlers arrived in 1598 with a priest who was appointed to establish a mission at Taos Indian Pueblo. Revolts by the Indians postponed permanent settlement until 1693 when the ancestors of many present day Taosenos came to stay bringing with them the language and culture of Spain.[1] Here they have survived 300 years almost forgotten in the rough terrain and isolated villages nearly two miles above sea level. Even today the county averages less than ten people per square mile, the most self-sufficient people I've ever known. Their faith is in each other and in their church.

Traditionally the people are weavers. The high mountain meadows of the Sangre de Cristo mountains were well suited to raising sheep. From the original Spanish stock great flocks of sheep were raised both for mutton and for wool. Every family had access to a loom on which men and women alike wove blankets and serapes for warmth, sayal (woolen yardage) and jerga (strip carpet) for trade.[2]

"Sources of cotton fabric in the earliest (Spanish) times were from India brought by sailing ship to western Mexico, portaged across (the Sierra Madre) to Chihuahua and thence north 600 miles to Santa Fe." No wonder that fine cloth sold for $20.00 to $25.00 per vara (about 33 inches) "and all other dry goods in proportion," a quote from the 1807 report by explorer Zebulon Pike. No wonder patchwork was not practiced in early New Mexico.

After independence from Spain in 1821 the Mexican government opened trade with the United States via the Santa Fe Trail. The most popular trading item from the States was calico. Within a decade the price had dropped from $2.00 to 70 cents per yard. Still, for the rural people accustomed to a barter economy, new fabric was out of reach.[3]

Annexation of the territory by the United States in 1846 made no quick changes. The establishment of a post office in Taos in 1852 with monthly mail delivery was a beginning. Penasco followed in 1879 and Questa in 1883.[4] The real impetus to trade came in 1880 when the railroad entered the state. Store-bought clothing now appears in the old photographs. "Worn but warm" became the household motto. "Hey, this is good to make a blanket out of. Why waste it?"

"The Hispanic women did piecework, as they called it, to make covers for their worn Rio Grande and Navajo woven blankets. These were tacked or tied. My mother did not learn to 'quilt' until the age of 76 (in the 1980s) by taking a course at Northern New Mexico Community College," from the memories of Teresa Archuleta-Sagel, a weaver and student of fiber in northern New Mexico.

It was at the turn of the century that Taos County homemakers began to leave their looms and ease into the stitching of multi-layered bed coverings.[5] Josepha Valerio of Ranchos de Taos received her first sewing machine, a Singer treadle, from her husband-to-be in 1911. In Questa "Mother made these quilts later in life after weaving stopped. (There was) less access to wool. It (the wool) was hard work. Couldn't get any money for

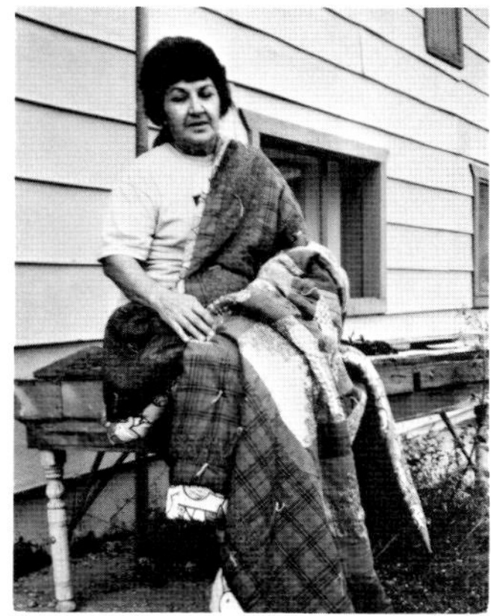

Lucy Trujillo of Amalia, New Mexico.

Fidelia Vigil of Penasco, New Mexico.

Viola Silva of Arroyo Hondo, New Mexico.

Merlinda Cordova of Penasco, New Mexico. Photography by Willi Wood.

them (rugs) to speak of. It was better to turn away to something new." Lila Rodriquez speaking of her mother, Irene Gonzales Rael, whose background, descended from Canadian trapper Anthony Laforette on her mother's side and from an original land grant recipient on her father's side, was typical of the earliest residents. "Our farms were on both sides of the highway. They seemed to go forever."

The layered bed coverings known today as quilts were first called colchas or blankets.[6] There are two styles: the old way and the new way. "We just cut the squares, sort of squares, and sewed in long rows. My mother taught me. We made so many quilts the old way. We used corduroy and heavy material. The same for the back. But now I learn the easy way to make my other quilts. Now I make beautiful quilts I have give away to my grandchildren. Now I use muslin and cotton and have the easy way, the new way, in cutting and sewing," recalled Fidelia Vigil from Peñasco.

Learning to make quilts was, generally, a process of apprenticeship. Recalling her grandmother, Amelia Jaramillo said, "Petrita was a spinner with her two sisters who did the weaving. Her house was always so pretty with aprons and quilts and pillows she taught her daughters to make." For Carolyn Gonzales quiltmaking came with her marriage in 1958, "I enjoyed watching my mother-in-law cutting and sewing squares together. After I learned how, I started making baby quilts, then big quilts for my bed. And I've been making them ever since."

There are exceptions to this tranquil scene. As Lucy Trujillo recalls, "Who taught me? Myself. We were five brothers and four sisters and no mother, so who was going to teach me?"

"I began making quilts in childhood. Myself, my sisters, my aunts and cousins, everyone made quilts when I was young." Mary Joyce Fidel of Penasco was talking about the old days and the old ways of the 1930s. "It was cold here in the winter; still is. We used those quilts under us and over us. To go camping. For my father in the summer when he went with the sheep." Viola Silva of Arroyo Hondo estimated she needed 20 new quilts annually to replace those torn and lost. "Quilts were in the truck, thrown over the backs of horses, to cover the root cellar. We took them to Colorado when we went to dig the potatoes. There was always someone who needed a quilt. They are the best gift."

Hunting for quilts made in the old way, Neoma Martinez said, "I found these at my aunt's house under the mattresses so not so much cold will come up. Between the spring and the mattress."

"When I asked my Mom, 'Why so many quilts?' Mother said, 'Give them away — to your brothers and sisters.' I said, 'No,'" In those three sentences is a complete story. Nothing could be wasted and so materials that could be made into quilts were made up as soon as possible. Every family member was responsible for every other member and the person who made quilts was responsible for quilts for those who contributed other goods or services. When the daughter, Loveida Cisneros, of Cerro said, "No," she committed herself to contributing to the extended family in some other way.

The quiltmaker must fit sewing in with the other myriad tasks of the day. After supper is when Viola Silva has always gone into her bedroom to cut squares and sew, jobs compatible with conversation. "I keep the sewing machine right here near the bed." One drawer of the old Atlas Precision Sewing Machine holds scissors, at least ten pairs to switch around as her hand tires. Her square cutting template is of cloth, several layers stitched together like a potholder.

When the stack of cut squares begins to look really impressive, she reaches for one of her ammunition boxes, her son who is a miner in Wyoming saves them for her, each labeled for color of thread; black is popular. Assembly is checkerboard style in small units, usually nine. However, when a pattern isn't possible the pieces are joined anyway and the result will be a sheet of stuffing. Once she bought a Mountain Mist batt but, for a woman who chopped and sold wood to get the money to buy windows for the house she built, commercial batting is unnecessary.

"I made them (quilts) because I had to." Viola also tends a four acre garden and cans hundreds of jars of vegetables each harvest. Their meat is venison and elk; antlers adorn every building in the yard. She built their adobe house. Thirty-seven years ago (1954) she had come home to Arroyo Hondo to care for her sick mother when her husband was permanently crippled in an accident in Wyoming. Three months later she had bought a truck, learned to drive, and was able to bring him home to New Mexico. "That was August. In seven weeks I built these two rooms, three courses of adobe each day, and plastered right away to save time while the next batch of adobe bricks was drying." Each year thereafter she added another room, seven in all to house a family that eventually numbered 15.

"How did we manage? My husband insisted the first of everything should be given away; the first batch of peas, the first picking of corn. Everything, and it has come back to bless us all."

Sources of fabric for all of the quilts, old and new, are as varied as the quilts themselves. "No new materials, ever." was the flat statement of Neoma Martinez of Valdez, but that is not strictly true. Amelia Jaramillo told, "My father, Alfredo Trujillo (1895-1964), was a school teacher and a judge in Taos too. He was a Gibson Company suit salesman. From his samples my mother, Pilar, made many quilts, but none remain." For her "new" quilt, Maquelita Gonzales carefully saved 609 2 x 4 inch wool suit samples from Saavedra's Store in Questa where each suit company annually displayed a new poster of their newest and best. When Eva Martinez's uncle retired from the Ranchos de Taos General Store the prize gift, his sample books, was given to his niece to make a new wool quilt.

In Questa, Irene Gonzales Rael found another way to acquire new material. "Mother didn't speak English hardly at all but she could make the orders (by telephone) to Monty Ward (Montgomery Ward & Company) and figure the money and all. The material she ordered was 29 cents a yard." The year was 1935.

Another source of "almost new" was flour and tobacco sacking. Emanuelita Esquibel spoke of the fact that her brother drove all the way to the mill in San Luis, Colorado, in the 1920's to have their wheat ground because that flour came back in white sacks that could be used for dish towels and other sewing. Smaller mills expected you to bring your own sacks. Teresa Archuleta-Sagel's great grandmother smoked cigarettes; she rolled her own. When the little tobacco bag was empty it was carefully taken apart, the thread saved and the bag washed and bleached. The "squares" (a Durham tobacco bag measures 3 x 8 inches) were then resewn to make dishtowels. Flour sacks were used in the same way and both of these were sources of fabric for piecework.

"Duke brand tobacco is what they used around here (Cerro). I remember seeing Mom dyeing the material. She used chokecherries and sage. You can tell how she kept using the dye 'til it was real faint." Mayo Archuleta was talking. Both she and Loveida are the daughters of Beatriz Quintana, and as Loveida told it, "Mother was very short. We always had to cut the bottom off any dress that people gave her. That would be new material."

The old material came from coats and jackets, grandma's nightgown, curtains, aprons, the edges from worn bedspreads. drapes, wool shearing couched down with cheesecloth, shirts, blouses, jeans and trousers, polyester knits, corduroy, cotton and wool, flannel, mattress ticking, and rags from the machine shop — anything that could possibly be considered fabric.

"It is a mistake to equate this thrift with poverty; there were few available manufactured goods in New Mexico in the early 20th century. Also, women took pride in the thrift that was part of good housewifery."[7]

Tobacco bags as they are purchased and opened out to be used in a quilt; the yellow drawstring becomes a quilt tie.

There is seldom a distinction between the front and back of these old style covers. They are usually made like a pillow case to be untied and slipped off the fill for washing. "Quilts are washed in the wringer which we still have. The filling is removed first and then put back and sewed up again."

"The filling was old coats — or old clothes, and yardage was bought to cover the old coat pieces (to make a removable pallet)," recalled Neoma. Badly worn old quilts, a sheet blanket or old bedspread, Beacon blankets, old serapes or Navajo rugs, and carded wool — all were used.

From her childhood days in Questa in the 1920s, Lila Rodriquez recalls the preparation of "la pasta" (a filling). "They would get together at night, like relatives, to card and elders told stories and have a merienda (a late

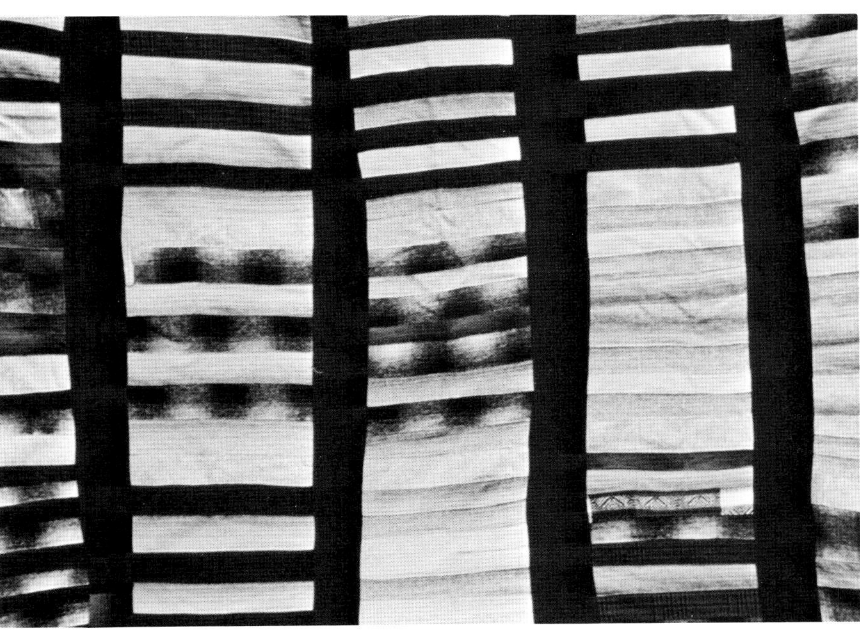

Wool Shirt Strip quilt, 53" × 76", by Beatriz Quintana of Cerro, New Mexico. Photography is by Willi Wood.

snack) around 10:30 of baked apples and other things." The carded wool could be used for spinning or be encased in whole cloth and used for the nicest bedcovers.

An assembled quilt was tied with string saved from warp ends on the loom, from sugar, flour and tobacco sacks, or crochet cotton or embroidery floss. Today acrylic yarn is also used. A quilt not to be disassembled for washing is sewed together by machine, two or three long passes across the entire quilt.

Where durability and warmth were the uppermost considerations, it may seem strange to think of any "old way" quilt as a work of art. The very speed of construction (an "old way" cover could be machine stitched together and tied in a day) would seem to bring a devil-may-care attitude to the organization of scraps. Necessity provided startling color combinations. Compositions are unbalanced. Yet there is no reason to think some makers didn't enjoy the freedom from constraint and the opportunity to experiment. There is spontaneity and joy in these quilts.

The Rural Electrification Administration did not reach Taos County until 1940.[8] In the town of Taos some small groups of people in the 1930s had banded together to share a generator, but the majority of folk depended upon kerosene lamps and a glowing fireplace for light.[9] Treadle sewing machines were prized items given to a bride by her husband-to-be or by a father to the daughter designated as seamstress for the family. "They (the REA) gave a free iron to every household that would sign up." Nonetheless, progress was slow. There were no paved roads in all of Taos County in 1940. The Second World War would change that. 1940 was also the year that Ronald Reagan and Wallace Beery came to New Mexico to make a movie, "The Bad Man."[10] Meanwhile, The Taos County Project, a federal program organized in June 1940, sponsored a visual education effort which brought the first motion pictures to many mountain villages.[11] Television did not reach Amalia until 1978. The mountains that had provided grazing and fuel, refuge and food were also a geographic barrier to progress. Nor did the rural values of harmony, stability, and protection readily welcome change.

"In February 1937 a plan was begun for the 'Rio Grande Problem' . . . The population throughout the area were heavily dependent upon grazing so no sudden stock reductions were contemplated. Such an action, the committee declared, would throw the inhabitants onto public charity, demoralize them, and introduce them to a cash economy and a higher standard of living through relief than they were accustomed to having on their own resources."[12]

Nevertheless, quiltmaking continued. These households were seeing national catalogs of merchandise including quilt suggestions. Relatives who had moved away sent letters with patterns. The home extension agent brought new ideas for every aspect of homemaking including patterned or "new way" quilts. "Maria got this pattern from my mother. They're neighbors. People passed patterns around a lot. They never looked quite alike."

A "new way" quilt is one that uses all materials of a similar weight organized with a specific pattern in mind. It may be patchwork or appliqué.

Merlinda Cordova went back 44 years to remember, "We were building our home and every penny we had went for lumber, etc. So, upon making this quilt (Star and Diamonds) I used only materials I had on hand. My mother had given me a few flour sacks, feed sacks, and also used old blouses. I had an old light blanket for filling. I sewed this quilt on my mother-in-law's sewing machine. While I'd stitch, my mother-in-law would sing gospel songs, and before I knew it, I'd finish one block. I made this quilt for warmth, and utility as well as for decoration. Great joy and moments were cherished while completing this quilt."

Fidelia Vigil recalls, "My mother and me made this quilt (hand appliquéd butterflies) together in 1950. It was my first experience. I don't even know how to sew. But my mother let me (do) sewing and put the filling by myself."

In 1990 Mary Joyce Fidel reported, "My sons cleaned up their closets and had too many jeans that didn't fit. I ended up with three full-sized quilts out of their old jeans. I got the backing at Wal-Mart, plain blue cotton at $1.00 a yard. The type of pattern is 3x5 inch rectangles placed in rows — Hit and Miss sort of but trying to make a pattern of straight rows, attempting to put light/dark pieces to create checkered effect. Many University of New Mexico students wanted my son to sell them his denim quilt that I made for him. He wasn't selling it. My other son has one also.

Streak of Lightning, 53" × 74", by Miquilita Aguilar of Questa, New Mexico. Photography is by Willi Wood.

Their jeans were put to good use and they look at the quilts and find their favorite jeans, spots, snaps, etc. and they love their quilts."

All these quilts are made primarily of scraps. The fillings are as various as can be imagined. The backing is plain or patterned yardage or a sheet on the newer quilts; large scraps on the older ones. The same makers have all continued to construct their hundred plus "old way" quilts. Why do they turn to block patterns? Apparently it is leisure. Note that Mary Joyce's sons are away at the university. Merlinda is speaking of the time before her children were born. In the third quotation Fidelia is telling of a time when she is grown but still at home helping her mother.

About hand quilting: "My grandmother, Petra Padilla, made this quilt. It was the first quilt she made (about 1930). She used old flour sacks — for the quilt back — You can still see the names on some — Penny and Dodge City." Monica didn't know the source of the pattern, maybe from an employer. This Churn Dash is the only fully hand quilted piece I've seen and it is exquisitely done, an indication that it was made before Petra's children were born.

As Carolyn Gonzales says, "I learned how to quilt from our home extension agent in 1988 (after 30 years of quiltmaking). That was the prettiest quilt I have made and the only one I have quilted and I gave it to my sister."

Some "new way" patterns are familiar but as many more are original. Oralia Vigil is a widow living with one of her daughters. "The roses are from a drawing my daughter made for me from the neighbor's seed catalogue." Of the lady with umbrella Oralia says, "Saw the idea on a potholder and decided to make it big. They're all my own plans. The daffodil, I saw a picture on a sewing magazine. The daisy idea was from a friend. Those patches — I saw a picture on a catalogue and worked it out."

In Costilla, Tillie Velasquez said, "In the '50s I ordered transfer patterns from 'Grit,' a national weekly newspaper." These were iron-on transfers of the 48 state flowers. Speaking of another quilt, Tillie said, "This is for me to wrap up in when I don't feel so good." Her children gone, Tillie has extra time now. The colors are her favorite greens. Living in a valley deep in snow for six months of the year green must be an especially appealing color.

We laughed about these northern towns. The more snow the brighter the colors. With quilts laid out on all the tables for our meeting in Questa it was like standing in the middle of an artist's palette. We were surrounded by red roses, blue butterflies, and crazy daisies. When the fabric is available these quilters concentrate on bright colors and strong contrasts. For instance, the appliquéd figures are attached with a contrasting shade of bold blanket stitch, or a dark quilt is tied with white, pink or yellow string — or all three. If environment does influence craftspeople, then the white snow needs to be remembered against the dark presence of the mountains.

Ways of quiltmaking, old or new, vary with time and interest. Blending the pieces together in ingenious ways to create a harmonious whole is independent of method. Gratitude for the abundance of life is illustrated in these coverings conceived in a waste-not, want-not world.

In conclusion Mary Joyce Fidel wrote, "It was our honor to help you with your projects on quilts and the ladies enjoyed sharing some of their work."

End Notes

1Vaughan, John H., A.M., *History and Government of New Mexico.* State College of New Mexico Press, 1925, 30, 46.

2Fisher, Nora, *Spanish Textile Tradition of New Mexico and Colorado.* Museum of New Mexico Press, 1979, 6.

3Vaughan, op. cit., 92, 102-105.

4Pearce, T.M., *New Mexico Place Names, A Geographical Dictionary.* University of New Mexico Press, 1965, 119, 128, 162.

5Fisher, op. cit., 7.

6Romero, Gabriel, *Coolcha Embroidery, an Item of Necessity is Now Called Art.* Romero/Taos Publishing Company, December 1991.

7Pickens, Nora, *New Mexico Country Quilts,* Museum of International Folk Art, 1987.

8Blair, Billie, *Taos' Golden Years.* The Taos News, 1984, 11.

9Taggett, Sherry Clayton and Schwarz, Ted, *Paintbrushes and Pistols; how the Taos Artists Sold the West.* John Muir, Publisher, 1990.

10Williams, Jerry L., *New Mexico in Maps, Second Edition.* University of New Mexico Press, 1986, 136, 350.

11Forrest, Suzanne, *The Preservation of the Village.* University of New Mexico Press, 1989, 40.

12Ibid., 149.

All other quotations are from the author's files of handwritten stories about their quilts prepared by the makers in advance of survey day, quotations recorded during the survey or follow-up telephone calls to clarify and augment the survey sheets.

Dorothy Zopf is a native of New Jersey, who lived most of her life in Ohio where she was a public school art teacher from 1949-1980. Dorothy moved to Arroyo Seco, New Mexico in 1981 and has been involved in innovative approaches to traditional quiltmaking there. This has led her in several directions. In addition to doing her own original quilt designs, she and her husband developed a software program called Patchworks. *Her research on Spanish-American quiltmakers has been extended to Mora County, supported by a Laura Bettens Research grant from the American Quilt Study Group.*

Myth and Reality in Craft Tradition

Were Blacksmiths Really Muscle-bound? Were Basketmakers Gypsies? Were Thirteen Quilts in the Dowry Chest?

Jeannette Lasansky

An eagle quilt from Penn's Creek, Snyder County is representative of several dozen documented in Northumberland/Snyder/Union/Centre counties. They were made from 1876-the 1930s. Contrast the quilt's overall arrangement — including a central medallion — to a mass manufactured, woven multicolored wool coverlet from the 1870s. Courtesy of the collections of Shirley and Robert Kuster and the Shelburne Museum (#10-78, 1952-599).

Interpretation and presentation — these problems challenge us as we go about our work at sites, in exhibition planning and execution, at festivals, and when pulling research together for publication.

The interpretation and presentation of old and new material on historical crafts of Pennsylvania have been the goal of the Oral Traditions Project since close to its inception in the early 1970s. At first we were gatherers, doing field research that concentrated on oral and visual evidence almost exclusively. Within three years we made our first attempts to interpret and present some of our findings to the public in the form of multi-media shows, exhibitions, and workshops. Interpretation, re-interpretation, and the best means of presentation became points of debate for us as they have for others.

We have explored our mission in 15 in-depth studies or monographs on pottery, basketry, forged iron, plain tinware, weaving, holiday traditions, buggymaking, quiltmaking, and the evolution of dowry with its wide range of goods (tools, furniture, ceramics, forged iron and plain tin objects, textiles, animals, and seeds).[1]

Each time it has been incumbent upon us to be aware of, and to shed (as much as possible) our mid-to-late 20th-century mindset — to discard, in short, our cultural baggage. This is necessary in order to be receptive to what the evidence tells us whether the evidence exists as manuscript records such as diaries, letters, account books, estate inventories, census records, and tax assessments; as oral traditions; or as artifacts and material culture. Information is derived not from one but from varying sources with single bits of evidence compared to other sources and evaluated. It is necessary to step outside our present times and attitudes in order to understand the people for whom objects were made, the people who were the craftspersons, and the objects themselves — their crafting and multiple functions. Our 20th-century perceptions and attitudes are formed by disparate influences: exhibitions dating back to the Civil War's Sanitary Fairs and the Centennial; so called "period" rooms in museums; fair and festival presentations with their requisite spinning and weaving, candlemaking, and quiltmaking demonstrations; magazines such as *Early American Life*, *Country Living*, and *Americana;* home furnishings by Ethan Allen, Pennsylvania House, and the giants of mass marketing like Sears, Roebuck.

Our 20th-century perceptions are heightened and sometimes indelibly impressed at sites. Who among us can forget our first encounter as a child with the maze at the Governor's Palace in Colonial Williamsburg or the overwhelming smell of the ubiquitous boxwood in those carefully manicured gardens — now exposed as early 20th-century fantasies of landscape architect Arthur Shurcliff? Who can forget the opulence exhibited by Henry Francis du Pont in the rooms of Winterthur or the audacity of display and juxtaposition of objects by Henry Chapman Mercer at the Bucks County Historical Society? Which of these sights, smells, or other experiences do we choose to add to our 20th-century baggage? And what of their validity?

Recent scholarship has shown that there can be a vast difference between what has been published (and often republished repeatedly) versus what has come from fresh and wide-ranging fieldwork. What has been collected and how it was exhibited also has often led to other distortions. In reading Elizabeth Stillinger's *The Antiquers* (New York: Alfred A. Knopf, 1980) we are exposed to the joys, the biases, the fun and the direction of nearly a century of collecting by the greater and lesser giants such as Cummings Davis, George Francis Dow, Edwin Atlee Barber, Wallace

Nutting, Duke Vincent Lockwood, Electra Webb, and Henry Ford. We could add other names to this list — people who made a local or regional impact through their collecting interest, people whose taste and knowledge did and do affect our sites, collections and exhibitions, their interpretation and educational objectives.

Let us examine some myths and realities that the Oral Traditions Project is examining and reinterpreting here in Pennsylvania. What is discussed here might have application to other areas of the country, albeit with regional shadings but sometimes with major modifications. There is no better place to start in examining myth and reality in craft tradition than with the village blacksmith, his work and workplace. His was a world of which some informants can still remember the actual sight, smells and sounds of the 1920s and 1930s smithy. The blacksmith was accessible in that his shop was entered by young and old alike, male and female, as they brought in their objects for fixing and repair, their horses to be shod, or requested a new item whether that be a hinge or a bolt. He — and it was a male profession — was a jack-of-all-trades, respected for his versatility. By heating and pounding metal, he made not only the tools for others, but his own as well — he was the toolmaker's toolmaker. As early as 1683, Joseph Moxon wrote in his *Mechanick Exercises: On the Doctrine of Handywork* (London: Daniel Midwinter and Theodore Leigh):

> Some perhaps would have thought it more proper to have introduced these Exercises with a Curious and less Vulgar Art than that of Smithing; but I am not of their Opinion; for Smithing is in all parts, as curious a Hand Craft; as any is . . . and they all have dependence upon the Smith's Trade and not the Smith upon them.

This versatility, this accessibility, led to the romance associated with the smith and his shop — a romance heightened by Henry Wadsworth Longfellow.

Did the blacksmith exist as Longfellow depicted him, "strong" and "brawny arms," the Thor of rural communities? "Yes," in peoples' minds then and now. As seen in period photographs, he was often slight. His mind, eyes, and hands were trained to take the best advantage of a good fuel and fire as well as the malleable qualities of his wrought iron. He was often assisted by an apprentice in the 18th and early 19th centuries. Later, when apprenticeships were scarce, the blacksmith was assisted by labor-saving devices such as trip hammers, a second or dead man (to hold iron stock); later, by geared-down tools. The laborious manual bowdrill, for instance, was replaced by a geared and self-feeding drill while the first of many patented nailmaking machines was introduced starting in the 1780s.

In studying blacksmithing, the skills and attitudes of contemporary craftsmen have proved not to be reliable when understanding the earlier man's work. In fact, 20th-century attitudes are contradicted by the evidence as revealed in the records left by 18th- and 19th-century blacksmiths — evidence from nearly 125 account books (1742-1935), from the 19th-century manufacturers' schedules, from decades of tax assessments, and from their wares — and the material goods themselves. While contemporary blacksmiths are quick to point out the difference between what they make and what farriers make, separating forged fine work from horse shoeing — some going so far as to suppose that horse shoeing was added late to the blacksmith's repertoire in order to save the trade and ward off extinction — this is not what the historical record illustrates as typical.

The manuscript record shows overwhelmingly that, with the exception of some specialization in urban centers, horse shoeing was not a distinct trade but rather comprised one-quarter to one-half of the work done in a typical 19th-century Pennsylvania smithy. Horse shoeing was until recently considered a substantial if not the most profitable, reasonable, and expected activity for a blacksmith followed by the ironing of wagons, wheelwrighting, harness work, repair, sharpening, dressing, upsetting and the steeling of iron articles, and finally by the making of new articles, often a doubletree or harrow, but rarely household articles or architectural hardware. I'll cite the work of two exceptional Berks County blacksmiths as examples.

Besides Samuel Yellin,[2] the name most often mentioned as the master Pennsylvania blacksmith has been Johann Peder Derr or Peter Derr (1793-1868), a resident of New Shaefferstown, Jackson Township, Berks County. Though he made a great number of sophisticated fat lamps and household utensils that have been collected and exhibited — skimmers, ladles, tasters, dough scrapers (often made in a combination of brass or copper and iron and frequently signed and dated (1832-1861)) — he also made common tools like screwdrivers, pruning knives, and household pliers. Since he was assessed as either a blacksmith or mechanic by the Berks County tax assessor, it is quite probable that he made more common than fancy goods.

Another Berks County family also associated with particularly fine work is that of Sebastian. The father, William, along with two of his sons worked in the town of Host, Tulpehocken Township, not far from Peter Derr. Similarly, they made utilitarian iron pieces such as axes, hatchets, screwdrivers, chisels, fire tongs, and branding irons. Like Derr, they forged finely crafted brass and iron pieces:

dough scrapers, betty lamps, open-work spatulas, and piewheels, many of which are signed and dated (1844-1886). In 1850, when the census taker came, the Sebastians reported that nearly half of their business, however, consisted of horse shoeing and the ironing of wagon tires. By 1869, just before the father died, their business had doubled with all three men forging $1,200 worth of ware from two tons of wrought iron and 250 pounds of steel.[3] In 1887, when the estate of the oldest brother, Benjamin, was dispersed, the articles seen in the greatest number (in what appeared to be one of the most complete itemizations of a county smith's shop to date) were horseshoes — 228 pairs valued at $25. Next were 65 files at $6.50, 23 tongs, a lot of fire tools at $2, and 13 chisels at $1.50.

All the account books examined show that from the beginning in 1742, horse shoeing was, with few exceptions, a major part of each blacksmith's work day. Men like Christian Frederick Koch of Harrisburg, Dauphin County (active there from 1887-1910), whose reputations were based in large part on their skills in shoeing oxen, mules, and difficult horses, were rarely called "farriers" but rather "blacksmiths." The term farrier was used primarily in some urban business directories and newspapers, and upon rare occasion in census lists or tax assessment records. One county that listed specialty smiths was Lancaster — few were farriers. The first was Martin Kindig in 1818, followed by Ralph Jackson in 1833, and then by Jonas Eby and John Miller, Sr. in 1847.

At the turn of the century, horse shoeing was one of the few sub-specialties within the craft, along with wheelwrighting, that was left for the late smith to do. Others had been eliminated by mass production including nailsmithing, cutlery, and edge toolmaking. However, even the shoeing of horses had changed, for the blacksmith had long ceased to make his own horseshoes but relied on factory-made shoes, caulks, and clips.[4]

Another idea promoted when talking with contemporary smiths, concerns whitesmiths. Twentieth-century blacksmiths feel that the filing on many pieces had to have been done by a specialist — the whitesmith because filing is a time consuming task, one which contemporary workers do reluctantly. Although 19th-century specialty smiths were found in Pennsylvania (stove-, gun-, iron nailing-, lock-, spoon- or ladlesmiths, ship-, anchor-, chain-, nail-, sickle-, and hingesmiths as well as edge tool makers, cutlers, and wheelwrights), the extensive amount of file work done on even the most mundane pieces could never have been executed by the relatively few recorded whitesmiths.

Even the precise definition of what a whitesmith was has been debated. They are found primarily in urban settings where specialization was possible. Their newspaper advertisements show that they made wares like toothdrawers, bridle bits, coach and gig mountings as well as other items that required more than the usual filing, grinding, and polishing. Unfortunately, we have not been able to compare the account books of a whitesmith to those we have found of the general smith. The account books, in any case, be they blacksmiths or other craftspersons like potters, do not note extra filing embellishments such as inlaid work, or presentation prices. The artisans only note objects by name, or in the case of blacksmiths, sometimes by weight. The account books tell us a lot, but details of craftmaking that are important to us now were obviously not so to them — not worth noting.

The terminology used in naming the specialty smiths can be confusing and misleading. The conclusion reached after reading and contrasting account books kept by brothers Jacob Markly, who called himself a "gunsmith" (in Northumberland County) and Benjamin Markly, whom Jacob called a "blacksmith" (in New Hanover Township, Philadelphia County) was that Jacob considered himself a gunsmith. He could, if asked, bore gun barrels, make pistols and rifles, and work in various metals, but the bulk of his work was typical of a country smith (doubletrees, fishing gig, axes, a grid iron, rivets, and much repair work).[5] He was able to case harden, brase, and work with a variety of metals as did other general smiths who had the ability and temperament for a greater range of work, but who never called themselves by a specialty name. Minor specializations seemed to evolve from a combination of a man's ability and temperament in addition to a community's very specific needs like those of a nearby boatyard, railroad, or stone

W. Cerfin's painted sheet iron sign called him a "blacksmith and horseshoer." Courtesy of the Landis Valley Museum.

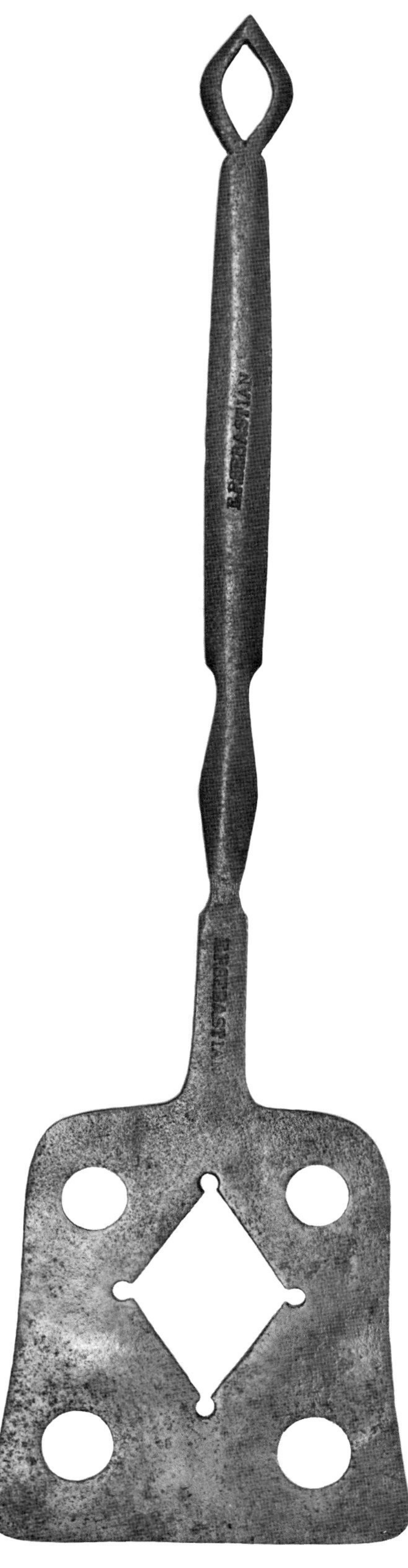

An open-work cake turner or spatula, 20"l., was stamped E.P. SEBASTIAN by the blacksmith, Edward Sebastian of Host, Tulpehocken Township in the mid-19th-century. Courtesy of the Chrysler Museum, Norfolk, Virginia.

quarry. The only accounts that reflect a specialty smith working solely as such were those of the nailsmiths in Chester County.

Another craft attitude of contemporary blacksmiths — to impress their names or initials on pieces — was done infrequently by earlier makers. We do believe that names made by a single struck stamp to be those of the maker in contrast to those made of individually struck letters. Eighty-eight struck stamps have been documented by specific blacksmiths in Pennsylvania while 127 have not yet been attributed. Most of the names that do appear on historical pieces are those of the edge tool makers, which as a group, marked more forged work for some reason than any other smith.

Many of the names or initials on the basic set of household utensils — the skimmer, ladle, flesh fork, spatula, and taster — are those of the recipient who would usually have been a woman accumulating goods for her dowry. One case was Johanna "Hanna" Ditzler who, as she was taught marked all her household linen in counted cross-stitch "HS" after she married William Smith in Northumberland County in the fall of 1831. Her iron kitchen tools have been found and are inlaid in brass "HS 1832." The dowry account books (*aussteier*) kept by the Pennsylvania Germans show this to be a traditionally female grouping of goods along with the bed, the bedding, and a cow. Who made these utensils is not known. They certainly do not appear in significant number in any of the extant account books. Also, not many specialty spoon- or ladlesmiths have been located so far. George Spangler, Simon Struser, and Gottlieb Specht working in Union County from 1832-1843, Jacob Schmidt in Montgomery County from 1805-1832, William Hartzle in Lebanon County in 1850, and Abraham Turner and John Farlowe in Lancaster County in 1832-1843 are among those ladlesmiths who have been identified through tax records.

The Weaver and the Quiltmaker

In historic textiles, weaving is believed by many to have been part of the woman's sphere. While spinning, some dyeing, and tape loom weavings were women's tasks, the weaving of blankets, coverlets, and table coverings on large looms was done primarily by male "professionals" among Pennsylvania Germans. A very complete survey of the tax assessments, estate inventories, census records, and wills was done by Sandra Rambo Walker (*Country Cloth to Coverlets/Textile Traditions in 19th Century Pennsylvania,* Lewisburg, PA: The Oral Traditions Project, 1981) in an eight county region in central Pennsylvania that comprised Scots-Irish, English, and Pennsylvania-German groups. It gives testimony to the dominance of male weaving in this area and corroborates the research on Pennsylvania textiles by others like Alan G. Keyser and Patricia Herr.[6] Quiltmaking on the other hand, was in the woman's sphere. It is a skill with more than its share of myths perhaps in part because it has long been embraced by popular appeal as has blacksmithing. Today in Pennsylvania, Amish quilts are being promoted at the expense of the work of their English or "gay" neighbors. This is a disservice to a large body of excellent contemporary work. Similarly there is a historical bias for a myth surrounding Pennsylvania-German quiltmaking traditions of the 19th century. The elevation of Pennsylvania-German quilts and their pre-eminence has been at the expense of the work of their Anglo neighbors, people who in fact, brought quiltmaking to the Commonwealth.

In fact, the Pennsylvania Germans came late to using the bed quilt as a common bedding type; rather they used feather ticks and later woven coverlets, slowly embracing the Anglo quilt tradition. Historical estate inventories for both groups (see Lasansky's *In the Heart of Pennsylvania,* Lewisburg, Pa: Oral Traditions Project, 1985,10, 22, 65, and 76) clearly illustrates this.

Mary Stites "1804" quilt, which was seen in the recent Goschenhoppen quilt exhibition and described in *Lest I Shall Be Forgotten/Anecdotes and Traditions of Quilts* by Nancy and Donald Roan (East Greenville: Goschenhoppen Historians, 1993, 24) is the earliest extant example of Pennsylvania-German quilting although references to quilts were made in their wills and inventories as early as 1788.[7]

In contrast, the first Amish reference to a quilt in an estate inventory in Pennsylvania was in 1836; their first extant quilt is marked "1849" (both Mifflin County). In fact, Amish material culture adopts "mainstream" Pennsylvania-Germanic decorative arts traditions slowly — consistently about 30 to 50 years later. This is true in their bedding as well. After the 1836 inventory reference, mention of quilts was sporadic until the 1880s.[8] Rather, coverlets, blankets and chaff bags were used predominantly. Most old Amish quilts were in fact made in the 20th century. Their pattern choices were also "old fashioned." On the other hand, Mennonite quilts do not differ in material or pattern choice from quilts of their non-sectarian Pennsylvania-German neighbors like the Lutheran and Reformed.[9]

Another myth is that women accumulated 12 or 13 quilts prior to their marriage. That was first published in Ruth Finley's *Old Patchwork Quilts and The Women Who Made Them* (Philadelphia: J.B. Lippincott and Co.) in 1929.[10] In fact quiltmakers like Mary

Stabnau of Newville, Cumberland County and Harriet Knorr of Berwick, Columbia County, give oral testimony — as did countless others — of quite the opposite: Mary had seven prepared while Harriet had a few more — her perennial favorites as well as a Nine-Patch "put together like rick rack," a basket, two crazy comforts, and a log cabin. In contrast, her sister, who did not like to sew, had only one quilt in her dowry chest. No older quiltmaker has given testimony that even closely corroborates that which is republished with great regularity: 12 or 13 dowry quilts.

Our work and that of Eve Granick's show both Amish men *and* women bringing quilts as their marriage portion or "good start" — anywhere from one to four apiece. Their total together more closely approximates the earliest published reference to dowry quilts — T. S. Arthur's article in *Godey's Lady's Book* in 1849. Arthur said, when relating practices of 20 years earlier, that a half dozen were set aside as dowry.

Neither do many old time quilters acknowledge the accuracy of another myth— that of the deliberate mistake — "only God makes a perfect quilt." Rather they relate being glad to have had even half a dozen quilts in their hope chest and of never needing to make a deliberate mistake. Nor have either of these particularly well-entrenched myths been confirmed in any 19th-century manuscripts. In fact, after looking at hundreds of letters and diaries, we have found few references to quiltmaking at all.

The late Joel Sater in his wonderfully iconoclastic study, *The Patchwork Quilt* (Ephrata, PA: Science Press, 1981), was among the first to raise the issue of how much — or little — may have been quilted at quilting bees. The group quilting bee was first presented to a large audience by an article called "Arthur's Quilting Party" that appeared in *Godey's Lady's Book* in 1849. The quilting bee became the theme of poems and prose in the following decades as well as subject matter for paintings such as those by Grandma Moses.

After talking with family members, with older traditional quiltmakers, and examining nearly 4,000 quilts in central Pennsylvania the consensus emerges that although there were group quiltings in family homes among neighbors and friends, most quilts were made by a solitary woman or a couple of women, who had similar needlework standards and expectations. Those quilts quilted communally were often done in churches as fundraisers.

The details of the bees' events are many, colorful, and fun. Indeed stories of going to such bees,[11] at a church, a community hall, or a neighbor's home, are not untrue but they were not, we feel, the place where most of Pennsylvania's quilts were finished. Quilting, however, continues to be most often presented to the public as a group activity whether in a museum setting or at a festival.

In *Quilted Together: Women, Quilts, & Community*[12] folklorist, Geraldine Johnson, who has done extensive work with contemporary quilters in the Blue Ridge area, notes the group orientation in present-day Delaware County, New York, differs greatly from what she had seen earlier. She writes, "Delaware County women seem to be recreating the process as they believe it took place in the past. . . . By choosing a quilting group as the basis for their social activity, they are participating in a craft that helps to link them to a regional past both real and imagined."

Not only were most of our quilts in Pennsylvania done by solitary quilters (the uniformity of stitches per inch in part attesting to this), they were — when family history allowed us such insight — usually done prior to marriage by women aged 16-22 often aided by their mothers or few selected friends. Or, the quilts were done by older women — well after children were grown. Rarely does oral testimony, evidence in diaries or letters, or from the quilt's history, show women quilting throughout their lives. The exception would be unmarried women or professional seamstresses. Quilts made or given prior to raising a family were used for a decade or two. Young mothers depended on their mother, aunt, or grandmothers to maintain the supply of bedding. This was a chore they in turn would do when they were in that age group.

Another question centers on the ripping out of inferior work in group quiltings. Some maintain that if one was to submit one's top to the vagaries of group work poorer stitches were not ripped out but rather remained intact (for the object of group quilting was "to get the job done"). Others acknowledged having ripped out the toenail catchers and requilted when necessary. Still other groups had their poorer quilters thread the needles, set the table, or play the piano.

In these last five instances of published myth, informants speaking of the early 20th century give testimony that appears corroborated by historical quilts. However an instance of conflict arose when discussing the importance of needlework versus that of color. Today's younger quilters (craftspersons) speak primarily of color and design in both their own quilts and in judging and comparing historical examples. Needlework is viewed as of secondary importance and indeed it has become so, due perhaps, to technological changes in the batting as well as in attitude.

Older informants, on the other hand, are generally not very comfortable when talking about the use of color. Needlework for them was and should be pre-eminent: the closeness

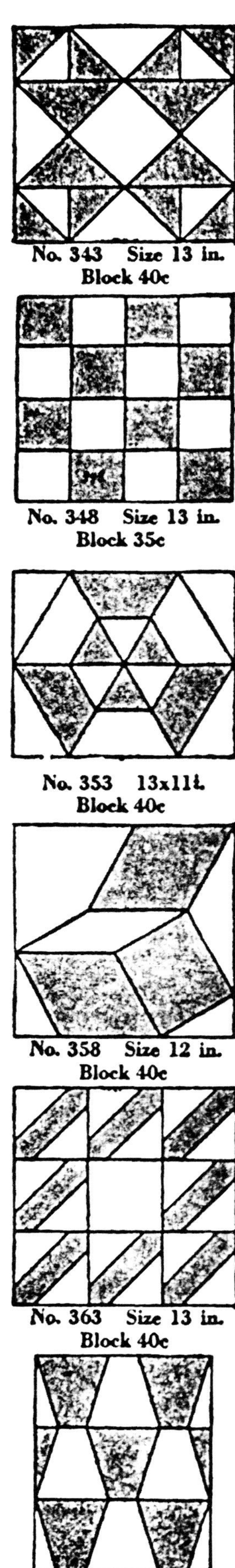

of rows, the evenness of stitches, the stitches per inch, and the diversity of needlework designs. Although color was important, it was the imagination and skill with the needle that was the ultimate criterion in judging a quilt's quality. As the late Sara Heiser Reigle noted, "The Heisers could really use color, *but* the Jodons were masters of the needle." So I contend that although color was important, it was the imagination and skill with the needle (in piecing as well) that was the ultimate criterion in judging a quilt's quality amongst early quilters. These attitudes would have also differed to some extent from those of judges (often males) at late-19th- and early 20th-century fairs where numbers — as in number of pieces— became a new criterion for those swayed by the absolutes of statistics.

On central Pennsylvania's older, darker quilts, where the needlework is less apparent initially, each pieced area, nevertheless was usually quilted in a different pattern — i.e., main pieced block, fill-in block, sashes, and border(s) and the stitches were seven to eight per inch. Needlework on appliqué and blue-and-white quilts made after 1840, is often elaborate and since it is very visible on the white background, stitches usually increase to nine to thirteen per inch. Playfulness in repeating or taking off from appliqué imagery and shapes is readily apparent. Often images are double-row quilted on these white backgrounds. Other images are stuffed between quilted rows. Quilts made prior to the 1840s do not exhibit this abundance of needlework design however, because of the scarcity of thread that was just beginning to be manufactured commercially.[13]

Also, if contemporary quiltmakers were listened to solely, then one would conclude that following color, design, and needlework, a pattern's name was a most important factor. Quiltmakers and quilt owners have become obsessed with pattern names. Quilt historian, Barbara Brackman, tirelessly tracing such names, has documented over 6,000 (and growing) names for almost 4,000 patterns and has compiled an encyclopedia of them as well as written a thoughtful article on their origin and meaning, "What's in a Name? Quilt Patterns from 1830 to the Present."[14] Though quilt names merit further studies their importance to historical quilts should be put in perspective.

What was happening on an orally transmitted level can only be supposed. At the time, print and manuscript references to quilts were generic until commercial interests like the Ladies Art Company of St. Louis, Missouri, mass-marketers of quilting needs, were established starting in the 1880s. Earlier, nostalgic stories and poems that had appeared in the few national magazines like *Godey's*, *Peterson's*, and *Demorest's*, as well as columns by their needlework editors, had referred to illustrated quilts simply as "geometric" or "Grandma's." But in the late-19th century, readers, then influenced by commerce, began exchanging information amongst themselves in rural tabloids such as *The Rural New Yorker*, *Farm and Fireside*, *The National Stockman*, and *Hearth and Home*. Pattern names became codified in the first books on quilts like Marie Webster's *Quilts: Their Story and How to Make Them* published in 1915[15] and Ruth Finley's *Old Patchwork Quilts and the Women Who Made Them* published in 1929.[16] New, slick magazines of the time like *Needlecraft*, *Modern Priscilla*, and *The Ladies Home Journal* continued the trend — of naming patterns — which remains unabated. The question most often asked by those coming to quilt documentation days with family quilts is "What is it called?" They are astounded when those of us documenting defer and want to know instead what — if anything — the quilt was called by the quiltmaker or previous owners even if the answer is simply "Aunt Lydia's."

Some patterns now have myths of their own. An appliquéd eagle pattern became a favorite in a concentrated region within central Pennsylvania. Often thought by present owners to be unique, it was a pattern so popular here that along with a large single Bethlehem Star, it was frequently made again in the 1920s as a copy of "Grandmother's." In the Heiser family of Union County, Matilda Heiser Spiegelmeyer of Buffalo Crossroads made one for each of her grandchildren based on an early example made by her mother, Catherine Alsbach Heiser (married ca. 1840). Of the three dozen or more Eagle quilts seen, a majority had dates from the 1880s sewn on them or showed provenance from that period. The earliest documented example was a crib quilt made by Susanne Beahm Meyer of Coburn, Centre County, for her daughter, Mella Mae, who was born in June 1876.

The pronounced similarity of overall design and construction detailing (four Eagles each headed in from the quilts' corners, wings and feet spread out, with something in their beaks, the eagles often placed facing a series of serrated concentric circles in the quilts' center, the eagle's torso formed a shield) all speak to a single design source. Some, like Robert Bishop, the late director of the American Museum of Folk Art, wrote that a kit was at the root of these Eagles, in his *New Discoveries in American Quilts* (New York, Dutton, 1975) but upon inquiry no kit was ever found. A complete run of periodicals of the second half of the 19th century by the Oral Traditions Project did not yield a printed design source either as had been thought it might. Perhaps, as textile historian Virginia Gunn suggested to us, we need to find a design source of more local origin such as a food wrapper or bag or, perhaps, woven coverlets of the period — the 1870s.

The major myth about 19th- and 20th-century quiltmaking is about its role as a scrap medium. The degree to which this is myth or reality will vary a great deal from region to region within the country. In Pennsylvania, even when there is a great deal of scrap material in a pieced quilt it was usually supplemented by large expanses of specially purchased fabric — for the back, border(s) and for the fill-in blocks. A note attached to one such quilt illustrates this point. One was made by Mary Magdalena Guss (b. 1829 in Mifflintown, Juniata County, d. 1921 Reedsville, Mifflin County): ". . . patches began when she and brother Will watched cows together, when she was a very small girl from bits she gathered that other sisters discarded. Red, larger patches of material her grandmother bought for her a dress." While the bulk of fabrics in the Guss quilt were dress scraps from the 1820s and 1830s, large expanses of blue and white as well as the backing fabric were purchased near the time of the quilt's completion which was in the late 1830s.

Appliqué quilts of the 19th century were made in Pennsylvania *exclusively* of purchased fabric, particularly, those red/green appliqués which were described in the following way by quilt expert Ruth Finley in 1929: "Only a soul in desperate need of a nervous outlet could have conceived and executed . . . the 'Full Blown Tulip' a quilt of Pennsylvania Dutch origin. It is a perfect accomplishment from a needlework standpoint yet hideous. The 'tulip' block is composed of eight arrow-shaped patches of brilliant purplish red, the eight petal sized patches inserted between the red arrow are a sickly lemon yellow. The center of each tulip is made of the material used for setting the blocks together — homespun of the most terrifying shade of brownish green, beyond question the accident of a private dye pot. . . . The whole is surrounded by a second border . . . of dazzling bright orange. The green-red-lemon-orange combination is enough to set a blind man's teeth on edge (38)."

In contrast to Pennsylvania quilts, most of those historical quilts (1880s-1930s) that I surveyed in New Mexico in 1985 for the Museum of International Folk Art, Santa Fe, New Mexico, were truly scrap quilts. Even today some of the older quilters like Mable Head of Farmington work within that tradition — a tradition of using every inch of fabric — of taking apart tobacco-, sugar-, flour-, or feed sacks and of recycling good parts of used clothing. The scrap tradition there included the rewinding of the sacks' thread, also the gleaning of cotton bits from the sides of the cotton gin or recycling the innards of the mattress to make the small squares which when laid next to each other would make the quilts' batting.

The advantage in New Mexico for the contemporary researcher is the ability to experience "frontier" through the remaining material culture and through a selected group of informants, while in Pennsylvania, neither is at hand. The quilt back in the East was not a true scrap quilt from the time there are extant examples left; for by 1840, frugal, rural Pennsylvania farm wife was able to indulge herself with a wide range of available purchasable fabric, and she generally had the means to do so. That is now the case in New Mexico as well. Many of those quilts produced in the 20th-century's second quilt revival attest to this change — in availability, affluence, and hence, attitude. A few New Mexican quiltmakers still cling to the earliest mindset.

Yet another myth is disputed by a combination of oral and material evidence. It has been said that early and large quilts became small in the second half of the 19th century because beds got smaller. Indeed the earliest quilts documented in central Pennsylvania often were 106 to 90 inches square as late as mid-century, while they range from 78" x 82" to 51" x 60" in the last quarter of the century. The overall shape over the entire time period was usually square or somewhat longer than wide. It was not until the 1920s that we registered quilts as large as a century earlier or drastically different in shape — like those made for twin beds.

The reason for the general shrinkage in quilt size from 1860-1920 is, I feel, not due to smaller bed frames but rather where the quilt is placed on the bed vis-a-vis the other bedding. In questioning older quiltmakers in the Southwest we thought to ask how they made up their beds. We discovered that quilts at the turn of the century were not the topmost covering but rather store-bought counterpanes were. Quilts, layered one upon another in cold weather were meant to go from the foot of the bed to just under one's neck. (We have sometimes seen quilts here as well as there with protective muslin strip basted over the top edge — where it would have rested by the sleepers' heads — sometimes called "beard guards.") This is in contrast to the late-18th and early 19th century when quilts were the topmost bed coverings that might have been removed at night or turned down. Beds also were higher then and the quilts covered all the layers on the bed as well as hung down to hide from sight other furniture such as a trundle bed.

Prevalent use and the dictates of fashion probably had more to with the quilts' size than

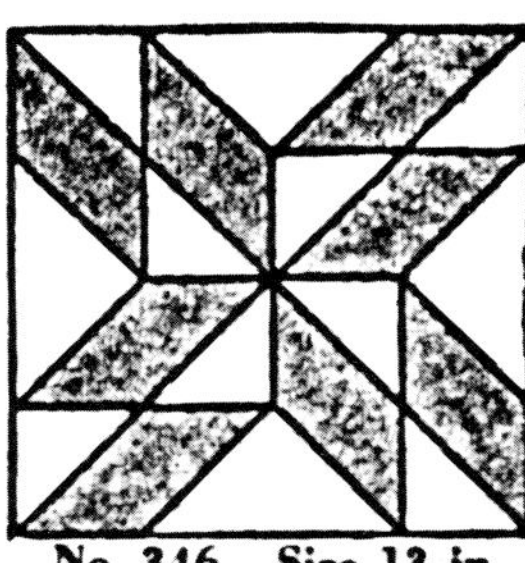
No. 346 Size 13 in.
Block 40c

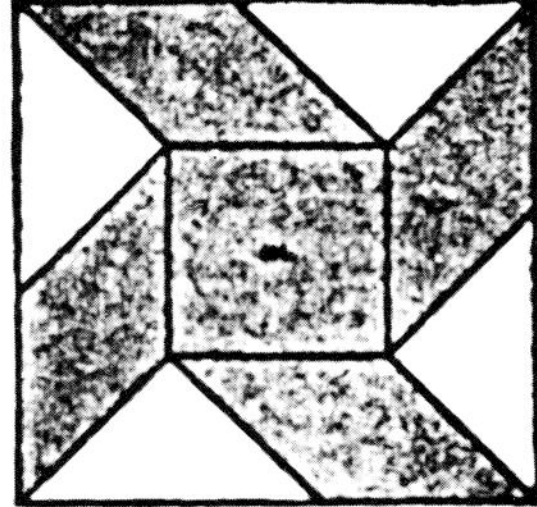
No. 351 Size 9 in.
Block 35c

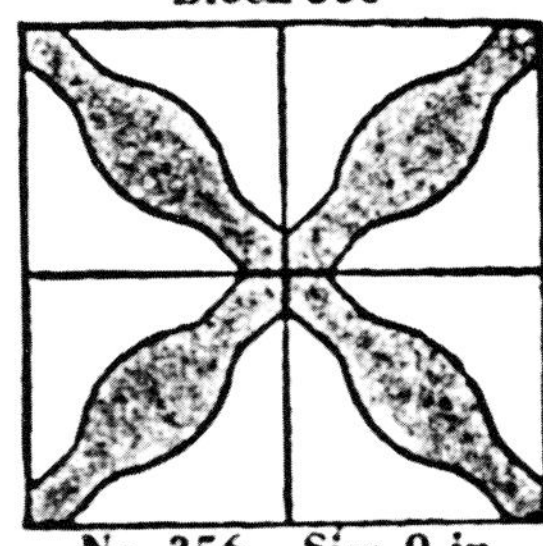
No. 356 Size 9 in.
Block 40c

No. 361 18x19i.
Block 85c

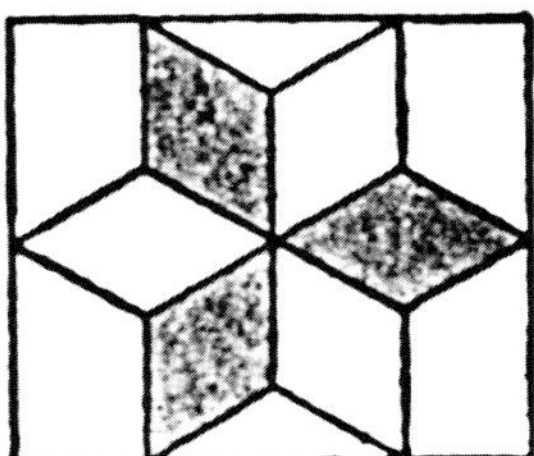
No. 366 Size 9x7i.
Block 35c

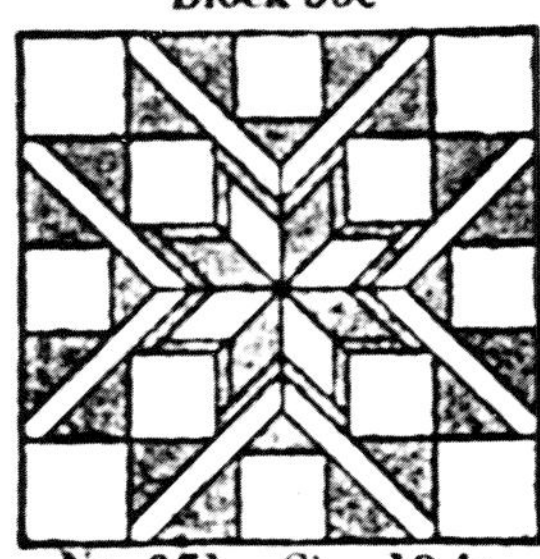
No. 371 Size 18 in.
Block $1.25

did the size or shape of the bed until relatively recently. The Amish informants of Eve Granick's have remarked on the change in quilt size as being a major one within their own conservative sect: the young people want fancier patterns and very large quilts, not the two-yard-square-size of the previous generation. They too have "new" fashion.

Answers to our questions are sometimes problematic and rarely absolute. One major question about quiltmaking is still especially puzzling — "Who were the quilters in the past and what percentage of the female population quilted at any given time?" Clues might be expected to be found in women's diaries. Results are now available from two research efforts that focused on diaries through the 1860s.

George Einsig's Gypsy family from York is seen here camped at McKees in southern Blair County in the spring of 1924. A descendant of his, Lewis Einsig of New Oxford, Adams County currently makes willow baskets in a wide variety of forms. Courtesy of the Pennsylvania Historical and Museum Commission.

The diaries reflected all the activities of the writers in some detail. If they were quilting or going to quiltings it would have been indicated along with the moldings of "437 tallow candles [in one day]" or the baking of "23 mince pies."

Lynn Bonfield in her paper "New England Quilters as Revealed in Diaries Prior to the Sewing Machine"[17] said that in the 38 published and unpublished diaries she read *half* of the women mentioned quilting at least once. Of the 152 entries she located, nearly half were for *one* maiden lady and ten more were for another leaving only 66 quilting entries for the remaining 17 women, many of whom only mentioned it once (these women who were not making enough for their own or families use though more than half did make a quilt).

In 87 unpublished diaries examined by our project in the Chester County Historical Society (we too excluded travel diaries or school girl journals but did include those of young men since they went to quiltings) we found only five diaries or 5.2% mentioned quilting *at all*: Mary Ann Charleton 16 times, Sarah Wilson four times, William Ambler three times, Mary Hopkins two times, and Mary Parker once. Mary Ann Charleton wrote on November 1, 1847 "Clear warm this afternoon went to a quilting and sewing party at Stephen Townsend's. Spent the afternoon, very pleasant. They had a kissing party in the evening" while Sarah Wilson mentioned binding a quilt as well as quilting a skirt, and Mary Hopkins said on March 29, 1857 "Yesterday we put a quilt in the frames and had some neighbors assist us."

In both of these projects the diarists were from groups that historically have made and owned quilted bed coverings: New England Protestants and Pennsylvania Quakers, yet neither diary project showed quilts being made in sufficient numbers. More questions remain than are answered from this source.

The Basketmaker

Last, we turn our attention to a craft traditionally practiced by farmers on a seasonal basis, more recently by families on the periphery of society in Pennsylvania or in the craft revival movement elsewhere — basketmaking. Until recently, little romantic myth was associated with basketmaking, since people who were full-time basketmakers were also either old and feeble like John Tule of Balls Mills or disabled like Asher Cox of Alvira (both of Lycoming County).

In specific instances in Pennsylvania — Union and Berks counties, for example — we can point to whole families who were considered "marginal" by "the main stream." They lived in the backwoods, never holding down a full time farm or factory job and did odd jobs only when they needed to work and they were not infrequently part-time basketmakers.[18]

Little capital was needed to start up — just a few hand tools and access to material. People still talk about Jim Diehl stringing together his wares on his leather belt, slinging them over his back and going from house to house selling his round-oak clothes, bushel, and market baskets sometimes as far as 20 miles from his home near Forest Hill. His baskets were quality items and appreciated by his customers. Today they are vigorously sought after.

In searching through the tax assessments for basketmakers as we have for potters and other craftspersons, we found few working full time.[19] We found fewer still in business directories, the census, or the manufacturers' schedules. The written record confirmed oral accounts — most basketmaking, in this area at least, was practiced seasonally in winter, by those farmers, miners, sawyers, and carpenters who have been trained within their communities, usually family members, and were adept at it. They appear to have made the bulk of what they and their neighbors needed.

Henry Plum in describing a typical winter scene in his *History of Hancock Township and the Wyoming Valley* wrote:

> Until bedtime all were employed; the woman carding wool or spinning tow or flax or some other occupation. The men and boys would be shelling corn or making splint baskets or chairs, twisting tobacco to press into a plug or making rakes or flails or some other useful thing.

While Esther Snook described the rye-coil basketmaking of her father, a miner in Rebuck, Northumberland County, this way: "Why, it was just the natural thing to do in the wintertime." Another informant writing to the editor of *The American Agriculturist* in 1867 said:

> I observed your call for information as to how willow baskets were made. Having often, when a boy, seen my father's plowmen making baskets for farm people during long winter evenings, I will endeavor to tell you.

Of course, baskets were also imported but they appear to have been limited in form and material to willow types

In the early to mid-20th century, some baskets in our area were also made by Gypsies. Hence our question, "Were basketmakers really Gypsies?" Yes, some were but few when compared to the farmers doing it seasonally.

Gypsies like the Einsigs would regularly come through an area, camp by a local stream or the Susquehanna River and gather willow shoots, making a supply of baskets and plant stands and selling them locally. Willow, however, is not nearly as durable as the oak used predominantly here in Pennsylvania. Consequently, their baskets were sometimes thought to be inferior. Contributing to that perception was the fact that they were not made by a trusty neighbor or friend — indeed, Gypsies are still feared and suspected of much mischief. The fact that there was a regularity to the Einsigs' visits in part allayed those fears and gave more credibility to their product. Today, Lewis Reinhardt and his sons, descendants of the Einsigs, are still practicing the craft and are peripatetic only in the sense of their going to fairs to sell (since they live permanently in the New Oxford area).

Basketmaking has been put down as a simple task by many. Was this a result of some of our own experiences of making a small basket in school (ca. 4th grade) for a Mother's Day gift — of reed and a pre-drilled base? A standard put-down in the 1960s was to remark, "He goes to ________ College and is majoring in underwater basket weaving." The inference was that basketmaking was a simple task for the simple-minded. This is a myth because the gathering of materials can be tricky particularly in selecting the correct oak tree that will yield good splints. The preparation of the materials is hard work, tedious in some cases, but it is no more or less monotonous than are other traditional crafts such as weaving or pottery.

What we have learned and what has been reinforced in the study of Pennsylvania's basket traditions, is how strong is the conservative nature of traditional crafts. In an era when "new and different" is touted as better, we are again reminded that the opposite may be true.

Contemporary traditional basketmakers who were relatively unaffected by fairs, magazines, or consumer request, repeatedly reminded me of their cultural communities' self-imposed constraints as customers, hence the rigidity of their attitude as makers. In seeing how a rim was bound or how a handle was attached by another traditional basketmaker, they would gently, but firmly, advise me that the rim handle would not last as long because it was not made correctly (i.e. not the way they had been taught by their father, uncle or neighbor).

Experimentation has been minimal for most traditional artisans. An observation made in 1822 about farmers, but applicable, I feel, to traditional craftspeople says: "The farmer believes nothing he hears, but requires to see and feel before he gives credit to what he has been told, and then rarely acts immediately upon his belief."[20]

Having heard their admonitions so often (regardless of the actual merits of the basket) one can easily imagine what Jim Diehl, who made oak baskets of drawn, round rods, must have thought as he watched his son-in-law Norman Sanders who made baskets of pounded ash splint — both their baskets of similar functions, but using very different methods, and yielding different forms. As even more dramatic illustration of strict adherence to tradition is the case of the Pennsylvania-German round-oak basket.

Both German and English settlers coming to Pennsylvania had both accustomed to using and making numerous forms of basket willow (*Salix purpurea* or *Salix viminalis*). It was an old established European tradition and willow was the major basket material. Since baskets have traditionally been made of local materials, a problem arose because cultivated basket willow was not native to America. Basketmakers either abandoned the use of the material and its basket forms (as indeed most of the English practitioners did) while others attempted, as advised by *The Cultivator* in 1835, to bring plants here and cultivate them, retaining both basket material and method intact. In Pennsylvania, only a few basketmakers, like the Zongs and David Moad of Juniata County or a group in the Oley Valley of Berks County, were know to have done this.

Basketmakers could also adapt other materials to yield the long familiar form — the rod. Some used pollarded large black willow trees

Willow trees could be pollarded in the spring, yielding osiers which this farm couple are preparing for market by trimming and then removing the skin by pulling through a pronged steel tool as shown in the American Agriculturalist *of 1872.*

Round-rod white oak rod baskets made by Irwin Shively (1868-1955) a Pennsylvania-German from Laurel Park, Union County. Large handled-clothes basket 25½"l., single-handled utility basket 8¾"l, and round work-basket, 10¼" dia. The basic tools of the round-rod oak basketmaker are the graduated wrought iron die and pair of pliers. The oak rod lengths were drawn through the die with the pliers, rounding the rounds. Collection of John W. Shively.

as was advocated in *The Agriculturalist* of 1872. The pollarded trees would produce new growth that approximated the long-familiar cultivated willow osier or withe. The Einsigs and others like Jerome Gemberling of Liverpool, Perry County, and Thomas Hajostek of Salona, Clinton County, apparently did this.

Some of the German basketmakers chose none of the above, but rather, decided to replicate the willow osier by adapting the material that was abundant and new to them here — the white oak tree. Round rods were made by first cutting down young trees (usually 10 inches in diameter and without branches for the first 8-10 feet). The trees were cut in half, then quartered and worked up into roughly ¼ inch square splints and as long as possible. These rods were then pulled through a series of dies in a homemade hand forged device and painstakingly worked round and smooth and to the desired diameter. The rods were then woven into the forms long sought after and traditionally made back home. The resulting baskets were even more practical than before. White oak was much more durable than its predecessor, willow, had ever been. This was indeed a basket for a lifetime. It is found only in areas of Pennsylvania-German settlement — in Ohio, the Carolinas, Virginia, and Missouri for example.[21] However, not all Pennsylvania Germans made round-oak baskets. Some, like their English neighbors, abandoned willow and its basket forms entirely, but many made this amazing transition to the new material.

For a long time the round-oak basket was not identified nor its tradition and evolution understood. However, round oak can easily be identified by the cut end of the splint or rod as can basket willow.

Both were often replaced by reed starting here in the last half of the 19th century. Reed was used in much Victorian furniture and in today's wickerwork outdoor furniture. In many peoples' minds all baskets made in rod form became labeled "Victorian wickerwork" as well, and their origin and tradition became misunderstood in the process. On the positive side, baskets in traditional forms — hundreds of years old and carefully learned in the guild system — were joined by new Victorian forms including urns, flower and plant stands, wood chip holders, etc. Basket repertoire in general expanded. On the negative side much of what was made had a more limited life because of the nature of aging reed. All rod baskets suffered in terms of esteem.

This prejudice continues but not among the informed and enlightened. In the selection of one half dozen baskets for the Pennsylvania-German Tercentenary Show, researched by Winterthur and the Philadelphia Museum of Fine Arts, the staff was urged to be so bold as to limit their selections to some typical rye coil forms and a few made of rounded white oak. The curator in charge of "miscellany" was not comfortable with the shapes in which the round oak was woven for many came close to those of "Victorian wickerwork." Reluctantly one was chosen, only to be rejected later by a consultant who claimed these baskets were made by Gypsies. The show was mounted and traveled across the country with examples made of rye-coil and flat oak splint. Missing was the one basket type that best illustrated the conservative nature of traditional crafts and of many Pennsylvania Germans. Perpetuated by its absence was the myth, not the reality of the Pennsylvania-German attitude and experience of basketmaking.

Conclusion

Were blacksmiths really muscle-bound and were basketmakers Gypsies? As we all go about our field work on traditional folk crafts and in our interpretation and presentation, we will answer many questions and raise even more. We will understand more and less at the same time. We have a better understanding of the rural Pennsylvania blacksmith now than when we started, but we still do not know who made all the skimmers, ladles, tasters, and flesh forks needed in great numbers in the home well past the mid-19th century. We have a better understanding of the role of scraps and of attitude toward needlework on the part of the Pennsylvania homemaker, but we do not know what she really thought about the English patterns advocated by the 19th-century ladies' magazines, or the importance of pattern names to her. We do understand what basket types Gypsies really made.

We have learned and are sure that it is important to be true to the evidence and not to fool ourselves or the public by perpetuating myths unless our task is the presentation of tall tales. Just as Colonial Williamsburg was bold in closing the Governor's Palace and reinterpreting it based on Governor Botetourt's 1770 inventory, the placement of crafts and craftmaking at sites should be guided not by popular sentiment, a 20th-century mentality, or old evidence, but rather, by what all the evidence is telling us. We should try to address a myriad of issues as we evaluate the evidence — the importance of the role of the individual versus that of the group, the influences of technological change, the role gender plays, the position of evolution versus abrupt change, and more. So too, our exhibits of craft traditions should feature pertinent, revealing, and accurate examples, whether they are about Pennsylvania-German basket traditions or what blacksmiths really made — horseshoes, bolts, and cotter pins.

End Notes

[1]*Made of Mud/Stoneware Potteries in Central Pennsylvania 1831-1929* (1977); *Willow, Oak and Rye/Basket Traditions in Pennsylvania* (1978); *Central Pennsylvania Redware Pottery 1780-1904* (1979); *To Draw, Upset and Weld/The Work of the Pennsylvania Rural Blacksmith 1742-1935* (1980); *County Cloth to Coverlets/Textile Traditions in 19th Century Pennsylvania*, (1981); *To Cut, Piece and Solder/The Work of the Rural Pennsylvania Tinsmith 1778-1908* (1982); *Holidays Victorian Women Celebrate in Pennsylvania*, 1983; *Buggy Town/An Era in American Transportation*, (1984); *In the Heart of Pennsylvania/19th and 20th Century Quiltmaking Traditions* (1985); *In the Heart of Pennsylvania/Symposium Papers*, (1986); *Pieced By Mother/Over 100 Years of Quiltmaking Traditions* (1987); *Pieced By Mother/Symposium Papers* (1988); *A Good Start/The Aussteier or Dowry* (1990); *Bits and Pieces/Textile Traditions* (1991); *Collecting Guide Holiday Paper Honeycomb: Cards, Garlands, Centerpieces and other Fantasies of the 20th Century* (1993).

[2]Samuel Yellin was a famous Philadelphia blacksmith who worked there from 1906-1940. He was born in Galacia, Poland (1885) and was known for his elaborate ironwork for gates and doors including those of the National Cathedral in Washington, DC.

[3]At the time it was taking four blacksmiths about two months and well over 400 pounds of iron to fashion all of the iron parts for a Conestoga wagon; in 1785 Abraham Grisch of Donegal Township, Lancaster, County, charged £19.16.8 to steel a wagon with feed trough and box with 498 pounds while in 1825 Henry Eckroyd of Halls Station, Lycoming County, charged $65 for his materials for his time and materials to iron a new wagon with 400 pounds.

[4]Henry Burden patented the first horseshoe-making machine in 1835. Eventually, it made one shoe per second and was refined with subsequent patents in 1843, 1857, and 1862.

[5]Jacob Markly's account book shows him shoeing only one horse from 1780-1803.

[6]Alan G. Keyser and Ellen J. Gehert. *The Homespun Textile Traditions of the Pennsylvania Germans* (Harrisburg, PA: Pennsylvania Historical Museum Commission, 1976); Patricia Herr. "Jacquard Coverlets" and "Handwoven Masterpieces" in *Early American Life*, 1982 and the exhibition, "Lancaster County Jacquard Coverlets," Heritage Center of Lancaster County, 1978.

[7]Alan G. Keyser's work on early Pennsylvania-German bedding, made available to a broad audience and republished recently in *Pieced By Mother/Symposium Papers* (Lewisburg, PA: Oral Traditions Project, 1988), should dispel any doubt about what was *not* their bedding preference.

[8]One each in 1847, 1849, 2 or 3 in 1850s

[9]Nancy Roan "What is a Mennonite Quilt?" in *Mennonite Historians of Eastern Pennsylvania Newsletter* 19:6, 5-7.

[10]"The dower chest of the old-time bride was supposed to contain at least a 'baker's dozen' of quilts. Twelve of these were fashioned with a view to everyday use: the thirteenth was a 'bride's quilt,' a pièce de résistance so elaborate of design in both pattern and quilting that it was, for all intents and purposes, a counterpane. The bride's quilt was planned and executed after a girl was definitely engaged."

[11]*Lest I Shall Be Forgotten*, 37-39.

[12]Delhi, New York: Delaware County Historical Society, 1989, 55-56.

[13]See Rachel Maines' "Paradigms of Scarcity and Abundance/The Quilt as an Artifact of the Industrial Revolution," *In the Heart of Pennsylvania/ Symposium Papers* (Lewisburg, PA: Oral Traditions Project, 1986) 84-89.

[14]*Pieced by Mother Symposium Papers* (Lewisburg, PA: Oral Traditions Project) 1988

[15]New York: Doubleday, Page, and Company.

[16]Philadelphia: J. B. Lippincott & Co.

[17]*Uncoverings 1987* (American Quilt Study Group: San Rafael, California, 1988).

[18]Martha Wetherbee and Nathan Taylor explore the New York State basketmaking trade in the book *The Legend of the Bushwacker Basket* (Sanborton, NH: Martha Wetherbee, 1986). These baskets, often attributed to the Shakers, were made near Hudson, New York, in the Taghkanic region.

[19]Some full-time makers were those working in the crossroads community of Basket in the Oley Valley of Berks County. These basketmakers were affiliated with Milton Lorah's shop. It had been established after the Civil War by Reuben Reifsnyder, then continued by Lorah who had as many as five employees growing, preparing, and weaving willow. John Kline and Ollie Strausser were the last basketmakers who worked there. Freddie and Annie Bieber of Fredericksville, Berks County, Asher Cox of Alvira, Lycoming County, and George Yarger of Wabash, Union County, were taxed as "basketmakers."

[20]Fletcher, Stevenson. *Pennsylvania Agriculture and Community Life 1640-1840* (Harrisburg, PA Pennsylvania Historical and Museum Commission, 1950).

[21]See Rachel Nash Laws and Cynthia W. Taylor *Appalachian White Oak Basketmaking Handing down the Basket* (Knoxville: University of Tennessee Press, 1991) for the most thorough examination of this basket type. See also Rosemary Joyce *A Bearer of Tradition/Dwight Stump, Basketmaker* Athens, Georgia: University of Georgia Press, 1989 and Jeannette Lasansky " White Oak Round Rod Basketry," in the *Magazine Antiques*, April 1984, 886-895.

Jeannette Lasansky has produced a series of 15 monographs on Pennsylvania craft traditions which have received awards from the American Association for State and Local History, the Historical Foundation of Pennsylvania, the Pennsylvania Federation of Historical Societies, the American Institute of Graphic Arts, and Communication Arts. She has curated numerous exhibitions and lectured at the Smithsonian, Winterthur, the Philadelphia Museum of Art, and the Museum of American Folk Art. She has also organized four national textile symposia. Jeannette organized a large fieldwork project on contemporary traditional quiltmaking for the Museum of International Folk Art and has been a consultant for the Delaware, Lancaster, and Northumberland county quilt documentations as well as for state efforts in Minnesota, Ohio, Oregon, and West Virginia. She has also published extensively in the Magazine Antiques, *in the European magazines* Volkskunst *and* An Ethnographic Journal: Folk Life, *and served on panels of the Pennsylvania Council on the Arts, the Smithsonian as well as chaired the Pennsylvania Folklife Advisory Committee.*

Index